SCARED
STRAIGHT!

and

the Panacea

Phenomenon

Gwyn L. Nestle

SCARED STRAIGHT!

and
the Panacea
Phenomenon

James O. Finckenauer
Rutgers University

Prentice-Hall, Inc., Englewood Cliffs, New Jersey 07632

Library of Congress Cataloging in Publication Data

Finckenauer, James O.
    Scared Straight! and the panacea phenomenon.

    Includes bibliographical references and
index.
    1. Scared Straight! 2. Juvenile delinquency
—New Jersey—Prevention—Case studies.
3. State Prison, Rahway, N.J. I. Title.
HV9105.N5F53   364.4'8'09749   81-12089
ISBN: 0-13-791558-6   AACR2

Prentice-Hall Series in Criminal Justice
James D. Stinchcomb, Series Editor

Editorial production/supervision and interior design:
Natalie Krivanek
Cover design: *Tony Ferrara Studio*
Manufacturing buyer: *Ed O'Dougherty*

Printed in the United States of America

10 9 8 7 6 5 4 3 2 1

ISBN: 0-13-791558-6

Prentice-Hall International, Inc., *London*
Prentice-Hall of Australia Pty. Limited, *Sydney*
Prentice-Hall of Canada, Ltd., *Toronto*
Prentice-Hall of India Private Limited, *New Delhi*
Prentice-Hall of Japan, Inc., *Tokyo*
Prentice-Hall of Southeast Asia Pte. Ltd., *Singapore*
Whitehall Books Limited, *Wellington, New Zealand*

To my mother and father.

Contents

PART IV   THE AFTERMATH

9
The National Response   173

10
The Juvenile Awareness Project and Scared Straight Revisited   194

11
Future Implications: Does Anything "Work"?   220

Foreword

Over the years the pendulum has swung in wide and nervous arcs in a frenetic search for solutions to the problems of delinquency. Let a community feel a rush of violence and the cry goes up to return to the woodshed at home, to the strap in the school and to all sorts of so-called decisive and dramatic solutions in the community. Why is it that delinquency, far from a simple phenomenon—and anyone who has tried to solve the conundrum is acutely aware of its frustrating complexity—elicits simplistic solutions? Why do we fall for the strange and ingenuous assumptions that all we have to do is to scare children into the quality of life that we know is best for them? Where has fear proven itself competent to unlock the door that will enable us to escape the consequences of a communal neglect of our children? Those of us who have spent a lifetime in the courts, schools, backlanes of big cities and in the homes of children struggling with their problems have fantasized about discovering quick solutions. But no valid and lasting panacea has been found. I strongly support Professor Finckenauer in his concern about instant solutions to such complicated human misconduct. We are dealing with a much more intricate matter than drawing a straight line between two points. The fact that the principle of individual differences exists and that young people not only have their own lives to live but also respond to society in their own frequently unpredictable ways gives the lie to universal remedies and cure-all prescriptions. Common sense and professional knowledge tell us that the slower road is the safer road. Fear is a hazardous antidote. How can we assume that the processing of children through a jail, taking lessons along the corridors from those that society has isolated for substantial reasons, can do more than add to the inner instability that needs careful and skilled attention? The remedy of "Scared Straight!" is too simple, too dangerous and too fraught with fear.

In 1959 Eileen Younghusband wrote in *The Dilemma of the Juvenile Court*[1]

It is comparatively easy, straightforward, precise, and measurable to punish offenses—an eye for an eye and a tooth for a tooth—whereas to understand and treat persons presupposes that we do in fact know how to diagnose and treat them and that we have the necessary facilities available. This is not a valid assumption.

Younghusband's observation of twenty-two years ago is just as applicable today. Victor Hugo put it succinctly when he said of society that it "stands in the dock with every criminal." Or to put it another way—in Sybille Bedford's *The Faces of Justice*—every nation's concept of justice to the individual is at the heart of its civilization." [2]

Now a new panacea has pushed its way to the surface claiming to do by fear and shock what example, teaching, social casework and a host of community efforts have, in some measure, failed to do. Let us stop right here to think about what we have been doing right and what we have been doing wrong. Has the time come to change the direction of our efforts? Let us start at the beginning. The wise community alerts itself to early signs of trouble and examines with great care the hidden meanings beneath behavior. The Gluecks of Harvard spent their lives searching for answers. They observed that "the onset of persistent misbehavior tendencies among our delinquents was at the early age of seven or younger." To recognize this fact is in no way to ignore the seriousness of later criminal conduct. It simply says that social policy needs to focus on the fact that crime prevention should begin in early childhood. It is here that bulwarks against later tragedy need to be constructed.

Peter Ustinov, in his preface to *Justice and Troubled Children Around the World*[3] says:

---

[1] Eileen Younghusband, "The Dilemma of the Juvenile Court." *Social Service Review.* March 1959. U.S. Department of Health, Education and Welfare.

[2] Sybille Bedford, *The Faces of Justice.* Collins, London, 1961.

[3] V. Lorne Steward, ed., *Justice and Troubled Children Around the World.* Vol. 2. New York University Press, 1981.

Delinquency, like virtue, has many faces and many sources of inspiration. Like all exceptions to the workaday rules of existence, it is a question indivisible from the individual, and its diagnosis and cure require individual attention. Doctors do not dispense the same remedy for every disorder; equally, the expert in juvenile delinquency or the psychiatrist are reduced to denying any labour saving facilities, and facing every case with the attention, the intensity, the humanity, and the intelligence which it deserves. All this takes a time, an energy, and a devotion not always compatible with the pace and superficiality of an epoch in which efficiency tends to be the province of machines and truth is relegated to computers.

As we study the causes of delinquency and the history of corrections we observe that no definitive answers have been discovered that meet universal acceptance. Each country pursues its own methods of prevention and cure and this is as it should be. Some prefer to delay the decision to classify miscreant children as lawbreakers by applying a procedure better understood as social justice. This is interpreted by some as guaranteeing children biological, psychological, and social fulfillment. In other places there is a ready and continuing reliance on juridical justice, proceeding as early as the accepted age of criminal responsibility will allow. In between these two approaches are many variations and combinations all attempting to solve the riddle of the child who errs. All are confounded by the fact that a child is essentially a "nonadult" presenting a special challenge and a need for consummate wisdom in nurture and guidance.

Professor Finckenauer has written an important and controversial book. It needed to be written. Common sense and much contact with children in trouble makes us leery of instant solutions, scary cures, universal remedies, and the avoidance of carefully documented research and experience.

V. Lorne Stewart

—Senior Judge (Retired)

—Consultant on Juvenile
Justice to the United Nations
in New York (1977-79)

Preface

In Part I of this case study I introduce the notion of a panacea phenomenon. A phenomenon which has seemed to characterize our efforts to prevent and control juvenile delinquency over at least the past two decades. One of the causes *and* effects of our failures and frustrations in dealing with juvenile crime seems to be our continuing search for a cure-all. This search has been conducted not only by the general public, but by politicians, lawmakers, juvenile justice officials and social scientists as well.

I review diverse efforts in the "war on juvenile crime," ranging from Mobilization for Youth, to diversionary efforts, to community-based programs, to youth service bureaus, and others. This review explores what seems to be a pattern of failure in which programs pose as cure-alls; they fail to live up to frequently unrealistic expectations; frustration sets in; and, the search for the next panacea begins anew.

Here I also describe and discuss the concept of criminal deterrence as it pertains to juvenile offenders. The use of fear as a deterrent is explored—drawing upon the history of drug education, antismoking campaigns and venereal disease education. Youth aversion programs of the "scared straight" genre, but preceding it in time, are also reviewed. This particular deterrence/aversion approach to preventing delinquency has a considerable history, but most of it is not well-known.

The evolution of the Lifers' Juvenile Awareness Project at New Jersey's Rahway State Prison is described in Part II. This description includes the origins of the inmates' formation of the Lifers' Group in 1976. Beginning in 1977, the JAP began to attract media attention, including an article in *Readers Digest*. This article brought the project to the attention of Arnold Shapiro of Golden West Broadcasting, who ultimately made the film *Scared Straight!* I include here a personal interview with an ex-Lifer who conceived and implemented the program. Who was involved? Why did they become involved? What about the officials who supported the project? What were the original goals and objectives of the project? What role did the New Jersey Department of Corrections play? Was the project permitted because it was good for kids or because it was good for the inmates?

The making of the film is explored separately. What motivated the film makers? Was it social "do-gooding," financial gain, public education, or what? The film's national impact since November 1978 is related to the public receptivity seemingly engendered by the panacea phenomenon.

I describe and discuss my evaluation of JAP and its results in Part III. Problems with and roadblocks from the funding agency, the corrections department, the courts, the advisory group and others are detailed. My approach here is to try to convey a sense of the difficulties and the obstacles which must be overcome in attempting a program evaluation of this kind.

Criticisms of my research are fully disclosed, and new and additional data analyses are presented to respond to these criticisms. Considerable confusion and ignorance exists about just how the study was done and why it was done that way. My purpose here is to inform the uninformed and the misinformed, and to try to clear up the confusion.

New self-report data from the participating juveniles are presented (this was not available before). The perceptions of the juveniles themselves are also disclosed for the first time. This interview information sheds new light on just what these juveniles think about being scared straight.

Finally, in a section which I call the aftermath, I cover the period of April 1979 through the present. Here I detail the outpouring of response which equals or exceeds that accorded any previous juvenile delinquincy study in recent American history. The nature and effects of the massive response on me, on the Lifers' Group, on the sponsors, on the Department of Corrections, and on others are described. Of particular interest here is the role of the media, of the National Center on Institutions and Alternatives and of the U.S. Congressional investigation.

This final part pulls together all the available research to date on the Juvenile Awareness Project in order to test the reliability of the results from my own research. Also, research on other similar programs is becoming available all the time, and this too is brought together for the first time.

Most important, the implications from this case study are delineated, and I try to answer the ultimate question, "So what?" There are certainly implications for the media, for juvenile justice and other officials, for researchers, for students and others. My goal is to tie "Scared Straight!" and its progeny into the notion of a panacea phenomenon.

I would be remiss in not acknowledging that the research and this resulting book could not have been successfully completed by me alone. There were many helping hands and minds—but special thanks are due to Janet Storti, Audrelee Dallam, and Eugene McGrath, graduate students at the School of Criminal Justice. I must also thank those at Prentice-Hall who encouraged, supported, and worked to make the book possible. Finally, and most especially, my wife Midge, and my colleague and student Bernadette Fiore, who worked long, hard, and uncomplainingly for over two years to make all this a reality. I appreciate their efforts.

Introduction

In early 1979, during "sweeps" week of T.V. stations across the country, "Scared Straight"—a film "documentary" on the "Juvenile Awareness" program at Rahway Prison, New Jersey—was shown. It depicted "hardened cons" and "lifers" yelling and screaming at "hardcore" delinquent teenagers—threatening them with assault and rape— telling them what would be likely to happen to them, if and when, they came to prison. The use of four letter words and prison profanity was probably unprecedented on T.V., particularly during "family hour." The ratings were extremely high and the film itself won an Academy Award. Not only that, but the program claimed a 90 to 95% "success" rate in scaring kids out of their delinquency. Fourteen-thousand New Jersey teenagers had been bussed to Rahway to be "scared straight." Few observers thought to ask why juvenile crime was not plummeting in New Jersey now that the majority of its "hardcore" delinquents was scared into the straight world.

Professor James Finckenauer was among those few. He had an unusual vantage point in that he was not only able to conduct controlled research procedures on the claims for the "Juvenile Awareness" program, but he was privy to much of the daily anecdotal happenings which reached soap opera proportions both within the program and in the making of the film, "Scared Straight." This combination has led to an intriguing book, which gives a flavor of the times—how we view our youth, our approaches to crime and punishment, and our need to cling to ideology, reason, and fact when dealing with an issue as sensitive as juvenile delinquency. The "Scared Straight" phenomenon provides classic case history for those who would understand why we seem to make so little progress in dealing with problems like delinquency—and why our so-called correctional programs, for the most part, miss the mark. In reading Professor Finckenauer's work, one wonders whether we could tolerate effective programs for long; it seems that we not only can tolerate, but we must trumpet and shore up ineffective and destructive programs. It is a paradox that those programs most likely to compound the problem are those programs which provide ideological reassurance.

Contemporary dictionaries refer to "panacea" simply as a "cure-all." Older unabridged versions, however, note that "panacea" refers to a mythical, hoped-for herb which has the power to cure all ailments and maladies. No more apt term than "panacea" could have been found to characterize the claims surrounding the "Scared Straight" phenomenon. One might be excused the fleeting thought that the publicists for this approach might themselves have been given to puffing away on an herb of another sort, engendering delusions of grandeur.

This "delinquency prevention" program, with its 90 to 95% cure rate of "hard core" delinquents, pointed the way to ineffable social well-being and universal happiness. The yellow brick road led straight to Rahway Prison, of all places, where the wizardry is hatched amid the shouts, threats, and stories of rape and pillage. In this unlikely land of Oz, the pilgrims find their "answers" where the rest of us have always believed it would be found—in those same threats. Why else do we use the prison so deftly and easily in this country? But for those who feel guilty in fact, "Scared Straight" offered confession and penance leading ultimately to a "confirmation" of sorts, whereby inmates are turned into protagonists for their own maltreatment, and that familiar machine for crime production, the prison, is transformed into a delinquency prevention program.

The claims of success for the "Scared Straight"-type programs were always highly questionable, though hardly ever questioned. The figures were among the most elusive in memory. Some, like Professor Finckenauer, tried to chase them down. It was clear, following the hysterical national embrace of "Scared Straight" in late 1979, that those who would question its claims would be a distinct minority. They would meet a couple of curious and contradictory, if unseemly, reactions. Liberals, a group long ago having thrown in the towel on decent care for truly "bad kids," saw the questioning of "Scared Straight" as an attack upon the well-meaning efforts of "cons" trying to redeem themselves through youth work. That was probably predictable. The response of conservatives, however, went more to the heart of the issue. Questioning "Scared Straight" undermined a whole ideology of crime, punishment, and deterrence. In denigrating the claims of "Scared Straight," one was implicitly calling into question a tradition which has constantly sought revalidation of the existing system of prisons, jails, and reform schools. The false claims of "Scared Straight" bestowed value on the inhumanity of the average adult prison in treating and preventing juvenile delinquency.

Having been head of a couple of major state juvenile correctional systems, and having been, from time to time, aggressively involved in controversy surrounding substantive reform of that system, I learned long ago to be wary of certain kinds of support for "new" programs. The supporters of "Scared Straight"-type programs are a case in point. Ideology was crucial to that support. Not ideology as a particular belief or political orientation, but ideology as a stance whereby one carefully picks and chooses "facts" as a means of avoiding reality of truth.

"Scared Straight" took state legislators and certain congressmen by storm. The praises of the program were sung in state legislatures across the land (probably to the tune of "Somewhere over the Rainbow"). Senator Bumpers of Arkansas commented in Senate Budget Hearings on federal youth programs that "Scared Straight" programs should replace the majority of the funded delinquency prevention and treatment programs in the nation. Representative "Ike" Andrews of North Carolina, after hearing evidence that the "Scared Straight"-type programs do more harm than good, suggested that the program is a good one, on which critics and supporters "agree." President Reagan, in his previous life as a radio commentator, saw the "Scared Straight" program as an answer to juvenile crime. Police, prosecutors, and legislators, known for "law and order" approaches to juvenile crime, stood in line to praise "Scared Straight." The protagonists of longer mandatory sentences, greater use of prison, death penalty, and generally "tougher" handling of offenders were outspoken in support of the program.

When I looked back to the states in which I had sought support to humanize state reform schools, establish more effective, less destructive "alternative" programs, etc., I found those politicians who had previously opposed every decent reform now standing tall to propose this program. The "lock 'em up and throw away the key" crowd had been transformed into juvenile justice reformers. And they had been able to do it without altering anything, be it their attitude, or the state budget.

Curiously, as is common in such matters, certain facts which scream out to the impartial observers were ignored. For instance, if the average young inmate brought into prison is immediately subject to assault and rape, why does the prison continue to operate that way? Others might ask, if the prison *has to* operate that way, why do we have it? How can the warden of a prison sit through a meeting of inmates of his facility, hear them talk of the daily pillage and mayhem as the rule, not the exception, and not feel compelled to take responsibility for allowing the situation to exist? Of course, if such prisons are really "treatment and prevention" programs for delinquent youth, one need only wring one's hands or now and then throw them up in frustration while accepting one's cross—the abiding obscenity which one supervises and operates.

"Scared Straight" gave both liberals and conservatives an "out." Those who wished to believe in the perfectibility of man could look to the efforts of the "cons." Those who believed in the essential evil of man could accept the redeemability of the fallen—the "cons," . . . . while at a deeper level maintain their quiet belief in man's maliciousness as seen in the routine events in prison. In this odd scenario, inmates redeem themselves by acting out for others—stereotypes of caged animals, mostly black, lying in wait to assault the rest of us.

We have always felt that we could scare people straight. In some cases we undoubtedly can, though a life lived in fear of the retribution narrated in this documentary, is likely a brittle one. Those not prone to get "into trouble" by virtue of their status, upbringing, connections, etc., often feel they are deterred by the threats directed at those who are more likely to end up in the criminal justice system. The fears of those, primarily middle-class citizens, who are unlikely to end up in jail or prison, are much deeper than any threatening con could produce. "Scared Straight" gave credence and validity to these deeper, essentially unspoken, fears.

For the youngster who is more likely to land in reform school, jail, or prison, threats and violence hold little import. If anything, they stimulate other reactive violence among youngsters all too familiar with abuse, beatings, assaults, misuse, etc. They inevitably visit this back upon whomever stands in the role of their abusers. This sort of fear hums like a giant wasp, vibrating the bones, making the fearful ticklishly inviting.

It is no accident that the showing on national T.V. of "Scared Straight" preceded the era of "That's Incredible" and "Real People." The leering voyeurism, now and then draped with saccharine intimations of social concern, gives most people a jolt of sorts. Indeed, one "Scared Straight"-type program (equally non-productive) in Michigan, was called the "JOLT" program. Such social concern demands no long term commitments, asks for no changes in thinking or prejudices, and guarantees solutions while reconfirming ideology and stereotypes. It is the familiar rearranging of chairs on the deck—the semblance of change where none has occurred.

Now, with the prisons in most states in abominable conditions, with suits over the inhumane and unconscionable peppering the land, the true dimensions of the "Scared Straight" phenomenon are becoming clear. As one goes down the roster of jails and prisons, one sees it has become a rule of thumb that the more inhumane and obscene the prison, the more likely it is to have a "Scared Straight"-type delinquency prevention program. From Angola, Louisiana to Jackson, Michigan, the more brutal and indecent the daily living, the more common the publicity around the "success" of institutional programs for deterring delinquent youth from their errant ways. Norman Mailer has recently described one prison as a "vision of hell." He is right, of course. But in our need to embrace devils, possessed children, and other Beelzebubs, we have blessed these hells and become, ourselves, fathers of lies. Professor Finckenauer has done us a service by insisting we avert our eyes from current obsessions and look again at the less seductive solutions to our problems of crime and delinquency—solutions which inevitably demand something of ourselves as well.

Jerome G. Miller
President, National Center on
Institutions and Alternatives
Washington, D.C.

SCARED STRAIGHT!

and

the Panacea

Phenomenon

part one

Introduction

chapter one

The Panacea Phenomenon in Delinquency Prevention

Juvenile delinquency is one of the most complex and intractable social problems facing America today. Because it is complex, and because there are multiple paths by which any kid can become delinquent, it follows logically that there can be no easy or simple solutions to it. But that doesn't seem to keep us from trying.

A current model for solving the juvenile crime problem is to scare delinquents or suspected delinquents straight. "Scared Straight" has become the nationally-known label for the Juvenile Awareness Project at New Jersey's Rahway State Prison and for other programs like it which have sprung up across the country in the past few years. This label derives from the title of an Oscar award-winning documentary film about the project; a project run by a group of prison inmates called the Lifers' Group.

In the time since the first showing of this film, there has been a clamor to create, mandate, and legislate similar programs in everything from local jails to state prisons. This new approach has been touted as the way to stop juvenile delinquency once and for all. Why?

Its appeal seems to stem in part from a receptivity caused by the fear of juvenile crime, especially a fear of the violent youthful hoodlums who are presumed to be present in much larger numbers than is actually the case. It comes too from a sense of frustration resulting from the ex-

pensive antidelinquency failures of the past. The Lifers' Juvenile Awareness Project has the intriguing combination of kids, cops, and cons
working together in a joint endeavor. These three ingredients are readily
available to every community. The programs cost little or nothing—an
almost unbelievably attractive feature in a time of shrinking resources.
Best of all, the Lifers' "success rate" has been claimed to be close to 90
percent. It is this unbeatable combination which seems to be responsible
for the "Scared Straight" bandwagon or panacea.

Before the bandwagon gets out of control and becomes a ride to
nowhere, it is not only appropriate, but vitally necessary to present a
sober assessment of this project and others like it. Does this approach
work? Is it really possible to simply scare kids straight?

The argument I will develop in this chapter is a slightly altered
version of a statement once made about correctional history by
sociologist Daniel Glaser.[1] My hypothesis is this: *The highway of delinquency prevention history is paved with punctured panaceas.* If the
utility of this argument can be established, it will serve as a sort of
conceptual theme underlying this case history of so-called scared
straight programs.

The presence of a panacea phenomenon seems to have
characterized many of our efforts to prevent and control juvenile delinquency over the years. This view is echoed by James Parham, a
Washington official with the Department of Health and Human
Services.

> The public is looking for an inexpensive panacea. . . . These
> periodic panaceas for delinquents come along every 2–3 years in
> my experience. The harm they do is they divert the attention of the
> public from any long term comprehensive program of helping
> youth, working to strengthen school systems, communities, job op-
> portunities, housing and recreational programs.[2]

David Rothenberg, who runs the Fortune Society, says it even
more simply: "We always seem to seek simple solutions for complex
situations." One of the simultaneous causes *and* effects of our failures
and frustrations in dealing with juvenile crime may be the refueling of a
continuing search for the cure-all. This search has been conducted,
encouraged, or exploited not only by the general public and politicians
and law makers, but also by juvenile justice officials and social scientists
as well.

[1]Daniel Glaser, "Achieving Better Questions: A Half Century's Progress in
Correctional Research," *Federal Probation* (September 1975), pp. 3–9.

[2] U.S., Congress, House, Subcommittee on Human Resources of the Committee on
Education and Labor, *Hearings, Oversight on Scared Straight*, 96th Cong., 1st Sess., June
4, 1979, p. 305.

This phenomenon seems to have spawned a particular pattern in our battle with juvenile crime. First, a certain approach is posed as a cure-all or becomes viewed and promoted as a cure-all—as an intervention which will have universal efficacy and thus be appropriate for nearly all kids. It may be promoted and sold as *the* all-encompassing solution to the delinquency problem. Each promoter/salesman believes, or at least behaves as if, his idea is effective in saving children and "hypes" it accordingly. Unfortunately, the approach, no matter what it is, almost always fails to deliver; fails to live up to the frequently unrealistic or unsound expectations raised by the sales pitch. As this failure slowly becomes apparent, frustration usually sets in; but then the search for the next panacea or "answer" begins anew. One danger of this pattern is that the resulting disappointment and pessimism sometimes leads to a conclusion that delinquents are too dangerous or too intractable to be helped, and therefore more repressive measures including severe punishment are required. This cycle of futility is illustrated in Figure 1-1.

In order to explore and test for the existence of this phenomenon, there are a number of pieces of a complex puzzle which we must examine. We must review the history of delinquency prevention efforts with an eye to what has been tried, with what justification and rationale, and with what results. We must also look at the aftermath of those results. For this purpose, I will adopt a broad definition of delinquency prevention as any "societal action to deter, correct or preclude potentially harmful conditions or behavior."[3]

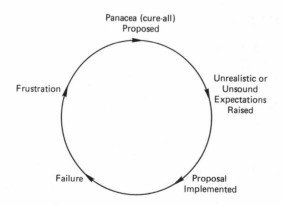

The Panacea Phenomenon

---

[3] National Advisory Commission on Criminal Justice Standards and Goals, *Juvenile Justice and Delinquency Prevention* (Washington, D.C.: U.S. Government Printing Office, 1976), p. 23.

Have we received fair warning to be suspicious of and stay away from supposedly rapid, glamorous, or simplistic cures? If so, then why do we and they continue to persist? Most important, what can we learn from the experience of this phenomenon which might be of future value? But first, a brief history.

A SHORT HISTORY OF DELINQUENCY PREVENTION

The history of attempts to prevent juvenile delinquency is uneven and unpromising. The dismal results have been attributed to underfunding of programs, to lack of coordination with juvenile justice operations, to poor program designs, and to lack of community support, among other things. But they have also been attributed to unrealistic demands or expectations.[4] This latter point is at the heart of my panacea theory.

There have been a number of reviews and critiques of studies of juvenile delinquency prevention programs published in recent years. These critiques outline what has been done, with whom, and with what results. They provide a wealth of information which may help us solve some of the puzzle.

One of the more controversial of these reviews was the early work of Robert Martinson and his colleagues, Douglas Lipton and Judith Wilks. These researchers analyzed 231 studies of correctional treatment—including juvenile corrections—reported between 1945 and 1967. Martinson published a summary of this research in 1974.[5] His then dramatic conclusion was: "With few and isolated exceptions, the rehabilitative efforts that have been reported so far have had no appreciable effect on recidivism." This conclusion hit the world of correctional treatment like a bombshell because it was widely interpreted as saying that "nothing works" to prevent repeated criminal behavior.

We should keep in mind that Martinson's studies included both adult and juvenile treatment. However, if we look specifically at the juvenile programs discussed by Martinson, we find the following examples of his conclusions:

- *Education and vocational training* " . . . many of these studies of young males are extremely hard to interpret because of flaws in research design. But it can safely be said that they provide us with no clear evidence that education or skill development programs have been successful."

[4] Ibid., p. 27.

[5] Robert Martinson, "What Works?—Questions and Answers About Prison Reform," *The Public Interest* (Spring 1974), pp. 22–50.

- *The effects of individual counseling* " . . . when one examines the programs of this type that have been tried, it's hard to find any more grounds for enthusiasm . . ."
- *Group counseling* " . . . one must say that the burden of the evidence is not encouraging."

Martinson was very critical of the work which had been done in this field over the two decades he studied. He was also pessimistic about the possibility of future successes. I should point out that Martinson drew back from his overall conclusion some five years later. He said, in 1979, that contrary to his previous position, *"some* [emphasis mine] treatment programs do have an appreciable effect on recidivism."[6] This later work will be discussed in my final chapter.

Martinson's initial work was severely criticized by supporters of correctional treatment. Among his critics was one Ted Palmer, a noted researcher with the California Youth Authority. Palmer said about Martinson's work: "Martinson emphasized the indisputable fact that no sure way of reducing recidivism has been found in connection with any of the treatment categories under consideration."[7] Special note should be made of Palmer's words, "no sure way." According to Palmer, "His [Martinson's] systematic review enabled him to establish beyond any doubt, that not one of these rather general approaches had 'produced' positive results on every, or nearly every, occasion in which it had been implemented and researched. . . ." "One by one, each method had failed to satisfy this exacting standard of success; no one 'serum' had even approached being universally applicable," said Palmer.[8]

In other words, Martinson failed to find the cure-all or sure way to prevent future criminal activity by offenders as a whole which Palmer contends he apparently was seeking. This criticism of Martinson and other researchers was echoed more recently by Michael Gottfredson. Gottfredson, who was with the School of Criminal Justice in Albany, N.Y., points out that seeking universals is a widely known treatment destruction technique. In seeking what he calls universals, an evaluator (like Martinson) simply shows that although a treatment method has been found to work with some offenders, it is not effective with others; or, that it has not been tried with all offenders.[9] However, in either event, it simply hasn't cured all of them; ergo, it isn't a panacea.

[6] Robert Martinson, "Symposium on Sentencing, Part II," *Hofstra Law Review,* 7 (1979), p. 244.

[7] Ted Palmer, "Martinson Revisited," abstract in, *Crime and Delinquency* (April 1976), pp. 178–79.

[8] Ted Palmer, "Martinson Revisited," *Journal of Research in Crime and Delinquency* (July 1975), pp. 138–39.

[9] Michael Gottfredson, "Treatment Destruction Techniques," *Journal of Research in Crime and Delinquency,* 16 (January 1979), pp. 48–49.

This point seems to be little more than a slightly different way of looking at the panacea phenomenon, to which social scientists are apparently not immune. The difference is that the unrealistic demands or expectations are raised at the end of a program by its evaluators, or by evaluators once-removed, rather than at the beginning by its promoters. The end result however is usually the same failure and frustration.

In the mid-1970s, Michael C. Dixon and William E. Wright pulled together the specific literature on juvenile delinquency prevention programs for the National Science Foundation. One of their general conclusions based upon their work was that, "There is a relative paucity of research or evaluative information available in the field of juvenile delinquency prevention."[10] Despite a considerable expenditure of funds, for example $11.5 billion by the federal government alone for juvenile delinquency and related youth development programs in fiscal 1970, most programs are not evaluated. This means that we cannot know whether some things work or not.

Dixon and Wright collected 350 articles, pamphlets and reports for their reviews. From these, they found only 95 which contained empirical data derived from scientific study of project efforts. These 95 studies, they said, ". . . confirm that an extremely small percentage of delinquency and youth development efforts are ever evaluated, even minimally."[11] Further, according to Dixon and Wright, ". . . when adequate evaluation is performed, few studies show significant results."[12] Concluding that there is little in the way of programs which work in the area of delinquency prevention, Dixon and Wright emphasized that ". . . several of these program areas have consistently failed to demonstrate that they reduce or prevent delinquency."[13] These areas include: individual and group counseling, social casework, detached or street-gang workers, and recreational programs. Despite their consistent failures, these approaches continue to have their vocal advocates and salesmen. This implies that there are some who are unaware of the evidence against their pet approach, or who choose to fly into the face of it for some reason.

Dixon and Wright alluded to the panacea phenomenon in pointing out that delinquency consists of a variety of behaviors; therefore, a treatment program that may be beneficial to some types of young offenders may actually be detrimental to other types. No one approach should be expected to work with all kids. "No method of delinquency

[10] Michael C. Dixon and William E. Wright, *Juvenile Delinquency Prevention Programs: Report of the Findings of an Evaluation of the Literature* (National Science Foundation, October 1974), p. 2.

[11] Ibid., p. 34.

[12] Ibid., p. 35.

[13] Ibid., p. 36.

prevention or treatment is foolproof," they said.[14] "There is no answer or set of answers to delinquency prevention."[15] In short, they could see no panaceas, either now or in the forseeable future.

Three other researchers, Richard J. Lundman, Paul T. McFarlane, and Frank Scarpitti, also assessed delinquency prevention projects reported in the professional literature.[16] Some of their twenty-five projects had also been reviewed by Dixon and Wright. Their assessment was that: ". . . it appears unlikely that any of these projects prevented delinquent behavior."[17] They too concluded that little or nothing of what they looked at seemed to work. The authors pointed out that one of the possible explanations for the failures they found was the inaccurate or incomplete theories to support the prevention efforts. The projects, for the most part, were not well founded upon integrated theories which had been constructed from what is known about juvenile delinquency. Theory was either weak or absent. Those who developed prevention projects did so without establishing any clear links between what was causing the delinquency and how they were trying to prevent it. This is not uncommon, as will be seen shortly.

The same Lundman and Scarpitti also collaborated on a later study again concerned with delinquency prevention. There they added fifteen continuing projects to the twenty-five previous efforts mentioned above. They concluded that: "A review of forty past or continuing attempts at the prevention of juvenile delinquency leads to the nearly inescapable conclusion that none of these projects has successfully prevented delinquency."[18] The authors went so far as to advise that, "researchers should expect future projects to be unsuccessful," because such an expectation would be more realistic, given the poor history of past attempts at delinquency prevention.

Finally, David F. Greenberg extended Martinson's approach by surveying evaluations of corrections through 1975.[19] He excluded community delinquency prevention programs, but did include a number of juvenile programs in which juveniles entered by means of some contact with the juvenile justice system. The range of methods reviewed included such things as early diversion, intensive probation, probation

[14] Ibid., p. 81.

[15] Ibid., p. 82.

[16] Richard J. Lundman, Paul T. McFarlane, and Frank R. Scarpitti, "Delinquency Prevention: A Description and Assessment of Projects Reported in the Professional Literature," *Crime and Delinquency,* 22 (July 1976).

[17] Ibid., 307

[18] Richard J. Lundman and Frank R. Scarpitti, "Delinquency Prevention: Recommendations for Future Projects," *Crime and Delinquency,* 24 (April 1978), p. 207.

[19] David F. Greenberg, "The Correctional Effects of Corrections: A Survey of Evaluations," *Corrections and Punishment* (California: Sage Publications, 1977), pp. 111–48.

with nonresidential programs, academic and vocational education, individual and group therapy, halfway houses, foster homes, etc.

One of Greenberg's program types, in which I have more than a casual interest, is behavior modification methods. These methods illustrate a particular psychological approach to changing behavior which has occasionally included the use of fear and aversive techniques. This aspect accounts for their particular relevance here, and they will be discussed in considerable detail in the next chapter. But just as an example, one such program critiqued by Greenberg operated at the Nevada Youth Training Center. A so-called "token economy" was used to reward desired social behavior and educational advancement among delinquent boys whose average age was fourteen. These tokens were used to purchase certain privileges and were considered in parole release decisions. According to Greenberg, "Although the treatment did result in a modest gain in educational achievement, it did not change the recidivism rate."[20] This failure to find an effect upon future delinquent behavior is fairly typical of behavior modification programs. By now it should be clear that it is unfortunately typical of other prevention efforts as well.

Greenberg's overall conclusion from his survey was that ". . . many correctional dispositions are failing to reduce recidivism. . . . The blanket assertion that 'nothing works' is an exaggeration, but not by very much." Finally, in his most damning, but relevant comment, he said: "Where the theoretical assumptions of programs are made explicit, they tend to border on the preposterous. More often they are never made explicit and we should be little surprised if hit-or-miss efforts fail."[21]

WHY DO PROGRAMS GO WRONG?

"Preposterous" theoretical assumptions is David Greenberg's way of saying that the programs he reviewed had unrealistic or unsound expectations. There are several explanations for how unfounded expectations can come about; but one of them is certainly faulty theory—which is what Greenberg seems to mean by his phrase preposterous theoretical assumptions. It is also what Lundman and his colleagues referred to as imprecise or contradictory theorizing.

I want to emphasize that the notion of theory is not something which should be limited to "fuzzy-headed" academics. Every effort to prevent juvenile delinquency is premised on there being some con-

---

[20] Ibid., p. 130
[21] Ibid., pp. 140–41.

nection between what is done for purposes of prevention on the one hand, and the delinquent behavior itself on the other. That which is done is known to researcher/evaluators as an independent factor or variable; the delinquent behavior is known as the dependent factor. Independent factors such as academic achievement, self-esteem, attitudes, or job skills can be manipulated by a program or a researcher in order to try to effect (usually reduce) the dependent factor (delinquency). Manipulation of the factors cited might entail increasing academic achievement, increasing self-esteem, changing negative attitudes, or improving job skills. Thus, there is some theoretical assumption that the independent factor being manipulated causes or is at least associated with juvenile delinquency. If this assumption is not or cannot be made, then we can ask the program promoter, why are you doing what you are doing? What do you hope to accomplish?

These causal assumptions are not always or even usually made explicit by persons trying to develop and implement delinquency prevention programs. They don't tell us why they think what they are doing or propose to do is expected to work. Glaser criticizes this approach by saying: "Causal theory can logically be tested only by theory-relevant programs applied to theoretically appropriate types of populations.[22] In other words, the program must have some theoretical grounding; and, there must be some evidence or argument as to why it is expected to be helpful for the kids to be subjected to it. It quickly becomes apparent to anyone who reviews the delinquency prevention literature that if there is any such theorizing, it is at best implicit. In other cases there is no apparent theoretical underpinning at all. Programs are conducted for no better reason than because someone thought they seemed like a good thing to do at the time. Dixon and Wright concluded that there were two general approaches to juvenile delinquency prevention: (1) systematic exploration of treatment alternatives from a theoretical perspective; and (2) trial and error to see what works.

Faulty theorizing which leads to unfounded expectations can occur in any one of three ways:

1. *The theory underlying the prevention effort is made explicit, but is simply wrong.* For example, Lundman and Scarpitti describe a delinquency prevention project proposed by Georgetown University psychologist, Juan B. Cortes.[23] Cortes said a program should be organized in Washington, D.C.'s "wickedest" precinct, aimed at identifying families who have children under the age of seven. "Potentially delin-

[22] Daniel Glaser, "Concern with Theory in Correctional Evaluation Research, *Crime and Delinquency,* 23 (April 1977), p. 175.

[23] Lundman and Scarpitti, "Delinquency Prevention," pp. 213–214.

quent" families would be determined from among these. For those with parents who would and could cooperate, techniques for "tactfully and helpfully informing and training the parents . . . in the necessary modifications of their child-rearing practices and in their relationships with each other" were suggested. "Both cooperative and uncooperative families should be helped," Cortes concluded. Sounds good! However, because of the known high error rate in predicting potentially delinquent families and children, Lundman and Scarpitti conclude, ". . . it is certain that such a project would be unsuccessful." Cortes' proposal was based upon the faulty assumption that delinquency prediction can be done sufficiently well to use it as the basis for the mass intervention he was advocating.

2. *The theory is vague and/or only implicit.* This is simply a different version of the first fault. Here some rather general, but ill-defined links may exist between the type of prevention effort proposed, the types of juveniles to whom it is to be applied, and the effects which are anticipated. This means, there is even more room to go astray. Also, it is difficult if not impossible to determine just what happens and why it happens in such programs.

3. *No theoretical or causal assumptions support the effort.* This seems to be the most common characteristic found in delinquency prevention programs. Burns and Stern, in a report to the 1967 President's Crime Commission, pointed out that:

> While there is a paucity of supportive evidence for the effectiveness of programs which have been implemented, there is no shortage of those who claim to have the solution. . . .
>
> But the conventional wisdom also perpetuates mythology and exaggerated confidence in simple approaches: exhortation and moralizing; censorship of television and literature; recreation to keep youth off the streets; harsh sanctions to set examples for others; counseling the family.[24]

Programs are often started on an ad hoc basis, or are founded upon so-called theories which are naive or already proven wrong. Absence of grounding in theory leads to simple solutions being posed for complex problems—and juvenile delinquency is a complex problem, if nothing else. These same simple solutions lend themselves to being readily sold as panaceas. This is because they are easy to understand and perhaps make good common sense. For example, the recreation idea mentioned

---

[24] President's Commission on Law Enforcement and Administration of Justice, *Task Force Report: Juvenile Delinquency and Youth Crime* (Washington, D.C.: U.S. Government Printing Office, 1967).

by Burns and Stern is one of the more popular prescriptions for preventing delinquency. It is frequently put forth as the cure-all for the problem of delinquency. All we have to do, its promoters say, is get kids off the street and give them something to do. You and I can probably agree that recreation for kids is good, but it obviously isn't going to solve the delinquency problem all by itself.

Another possible explanation for unsound or unrealistic expectations being raised for a particular approach to delinquency prevention seems much more sinister to me. Earlier I reported that Lundman and Scarpitti suggested that researchers should expect future delinquency prevention projects to be unsuccessful. Although they had good reasons for making this recommendation, the reality is that most prevention efforts are not research projects, but are action projects that usually do not get evaluated. All prevention efforts require some amount of funding and resources such as staff, a building or storefront, etc. There is a great deal of competition for these scarce resources, particularly in urban areas where the juvenile crime problem is most serious. It doesn't seem realistic to me to expect planners and program developers to advertise their proposed projects as potential failures and yet expect to secure funding support.

On the other hand, it does not appear unreasonable to expect officials and agencies not to promise something they know they cannot deliver. Delivering has not been easy in this area, but "too many programs set their goals too high and promise too much in order to obtain federal [or other] funding. In effect, each program promises to be the panacea for youth crime, which has sometimes led groups to disastrous competition for federal [or other] dollars."[25] Various community agencies exploit the public concern because they find it easier to obtain support for youth programs if they claim to be delinquency prevention endeavors. In these instances a panacea may be fabricated by a deliberate, intentional, and knowing oversell. The motivation may be funding, or it may be something else. Overly ambitious expectations for narrowly focused programs whether innocent or not, seem sure to result in failure.

On the issue of evaluation, I do not think it is asking too much to expect programs to be evaluated, the results of program evaluations to be reported, and to be reported honestly in order that others may judge for themselves the value of any particular approach. The reporting of results that are not derived from careful evaluation, or the selective and biased reporting of only certain results is not only misleading, but

[25] Clemens Bartollas and Stuart J. Miller, *The Juvenile Offender: Control, Correction, and Treatment* (Boston: Holbrook Press, 1978), p. 423.

patently dishonest. All of these acts have occurred in the past, and all of them have been contributing factors to the panacea phenomenon. They have led people to believe that magic solutions have been found. They have raised false hopes only to have them dashed at a later point.

A FEW CASE STUDIES

In order to better explore the historical presence of a panacea phenomenon, we can closely examine some case examples of delinquency prevention efforts for evidence of its existence. I have chosen these particular cases because they are well known (they are in fact among the best known projects in the history of juvenile delinquency); they were massive in size, scope, duration, and funding; and, they have had major and lasting effects upon the field of juvenile delinquency. In addition, they have been selected because they represent both programs that were directed toward changing the feelings, attitudes, and eventually the behavior of individual delinquents; and programs that were directed at changing the nature of the environment in order to control delinquency.

As we look at each of these programs, we should have a number of questions in mind: Were there causal, theory-based assumptions underlying the program? Were these assumptions made clear? What were the goals and objectives of the program? Was it believed to be appropriate for all kids (universal efficacy)? Was it seen as an all encompassing or general solution? Was it evaluated? Was it successful? What were the results of the program? Is there any evidence that the program was deliberately and intentionally oversold at any point? What has been its aftermath?

The Cambridge-Somerville Youth Study

One of the best known pieces of action research ever undertaken in the field of juvenile delinquency prevention was established in Cambridge and Somerville, Massachusetts in 1935 by Dr. Richard C. Cabot. The two main objectives of the Youth Study were: (1) to prevent delinquency by employing friendly counselors who would deal with a selected group of boys (no girls) over a long period of time (up to 10 years); and (2) to measure the effectiveness of this effort by comparing a treatment group with a matched control group which would receive no help or guidance from the study.

Two groups of 325 boys each were formed from approximately 2,000 referrals. The two groups were carefully matched and included equal numbers of "problem boys," so judged by their teachers, and "predelinquents," so judged by a team of experts. The treatment program used many of the practices common to social welfare work: family guidance, medical assistance, coordination of community services, academic help, entertainment, etc.

The study had a stated hypothesis, that delinquent and potentially delinquent boys could be diverted from criminal careers if they were given continued friendship by adults who were interested in them and who could help them to obtain needed community services. However, the only basis for this hypothesis seems to have been Dr. Cabot's opinion, actually more of a hunch, based upon his own experience.

The absence of any underlying causal theory that would provide a foundation for the study was lamented by Dr. Helen Witmer who was responsible for its evaluation. She said:

He (Cabot) seemed to be assuming that the disorder in question was like a medical disorder, in that it transcended the differences in the subjects in which it appeared, and that the treatment method to be employed was also sufficiently uniform that variation in its application from case to case could be disregarded. . . . To give a great variety of services to a great variety of boys, each practitioner doing what he thinks best without reference to any commonly held body of theory, seems . . . no more a scientific experiment than a medical one would be in which different kinds of medicine were given to patients suffering from different kinds of disorders by doctors who held different theories as to the causes of the illnesses.[26]

The project was deemed to be appropriate for all boys, which is evident in the fact that none were excluded because they were not considered amenable to the treatment. In addition, "an intensive effort was made to discover *all* of the so-called bad boys or potential criminals in Cambridge and Somerville," as subjects for the study.[27]

I can discern no evidence of deliberate overselling or of ulterior motives behind the study. The confidence and cooperation of school authorities was needed, and the program was presented somewhat ambitiously as "a scientific effort to determine the causes of crime and the

[26] Edwin Powers and Helen Witmer, *An Experiment in the Prevention of Delinquency: The Cambridge-Somerville Youth Study* (New York: Columbia University Press, 1951), p. 343.

[27] Ibid., p. 6.

treatment of juvenile delinquency," in order to obtain that cooperation. But, Dr. Cabot was essentially a "do-gooder," and he had no problem with funding because of a $500,000 grant from the Ella Lyman Cabot Foundation which he created as a charitable corporation. This was a considerable amount of money in 1935; today it would be a multi-million dollar budget.

Psychological tests, school adjustment checks, and a review of court records while the program was still in progress failed to show any significant differences between the treatment and control groups. Three years after the project ended (1948) a second assessment determined that the treatment group had committed as many and just as serious offenses as had the control group. The counselors' services did not significantly reduce the incidence of delinquency nor otherwise improve the boys' poor social functioning.

Some of Dr. Witmer's conclusions are pertinent to my panacea hypothesis. She said, ". . . the study attempt(ed) to serve many boys whose needs were beyond the capacity of this program to meet."[28] It had unrealistic expectations in other words. Dr. Witmer stated: "What the investigation does show . . . is not that work of the study type is useless but that its usefulness is limited, and that no such generous, ambitious, but professionally rather naive program can diminish to any con- siderable extent that persistent problem juvenile delinquency."[29] Finally, but most important is this: ". . . the chief lesson of this exper- iment is that there is no one answer, no one form of service by which all manner of boys can be helped to deal with the difficulties that stand in the way of their healthy incorporation of social norms, which is the es- sence of good social adjustment."[30] This statement speaks for itself.

The aftermath? In 1956, Joan and William McCord traced into adulthood 253 of the treatment boys and 253 of their matched mates in the control group. Their conclusion: ". . . using the standard of 'official' criminal behavior, we must conclude that the Cambridge-Somerville Youth Study was largely a failure. Some individuals undoubtedly benefited from the program; but the group, as a whole, did not."[31]

Cambridge-Somerville was seen as a cure-all in the eyes of Dr. Cabot, and perhaps his colleagues, when it started. In this sense, therefore, it seems to support the panacea hypothesis. However, it was

[28] Ibid., p. 575.

[29] Ibid., p. 577.

[30] Ibid., p. 583.

[31] Joan and William McCord, "A Follow-up Report on the Cambridge-Somerville Youth Study," *The Annals of the American Academy of Political and Social Science: Prevention of Juvenile Delinquency*, 322 (March 1959), 96.

carefully documented and evaluated, and the disappointing results were made fully known. It was at least an honest effort all the way.

Mobilization For Youth

Over twenty years later, Mobilization For Youth, Inc. (MFY) was founded in New York City. It began as a "nonprofit membership corporation composed of representatives of agencies and institutions on the Lower East Side . . . and persons recommended by the New York School of Social Work at Columbia University." MFY undertook a four and one-half year planning process that culminated on December 9, 1961 in a 617 page "Proposal for the Prevention and Control of Delinquency by Expanding Opportunities." Six months later MFY was given a three year, $12.5 million grant by the Ford Foundation, New York City, and the federal government. When the actual program was launched on May 31, 1962, President John F. Kennedy called it, "the best in the country at this time, and the furthest along."[32] Not a bad promotion!

The actual program involved five areas: work training, education, group work and community organization, services to individuals and families, and training and personnel. It was directed at the poorest 20 percent of the more than 100,000 people who lived below 14th Street on the East River. This area did not have an especially high rate of juvenile delinquency—in fact the rate had been consistently lower than that of Manhattan as a whole. However, the Henry Street Settlement around which MFY developed happened to be located there, and so this massive social experiment was located there.

MFY operated on the premise that delinquency had to be approached in the context of social frustration and alienation—its emphasis was upon changing the environment rather than the individual. It assumed that social conflict is necessary to alleviate the causes of delinquency. Consistent with the preoccupation of the President's Committee on Juvenile Delinquency and Youth Crime (one of the federal agencies supporting the program) with prevention rather than treatment, there were very few projects that dealt directly with delinquent children. MFY was to be a "model for developing a policy of comprehensive community action research projects, aimed at the complex social causes of delinquency."[33]

[32] Daniel P. Moynihan, *Maximum Feasible Misunderstanding: Community Action in the War on Poverty* (New York: The Free Press, 1969), pp. 38–59.

[33] Peter Marris and Martin Rein, *Dilemmas of Social Reform: Poverty and Community Action in the United States* (New York: Atherton Press, 1969), p. 131.

MFY was exceptionally well grounded in theory. That theory was the so-called "opportunity" theory developed in the book *Delinquency and Opportunity* by Richard A. Cloward and Lloyd E. Ohlin, published in 1960. The prospectus of the MFY proposal reflected the influence of the assumption that delinquent behavior arose in the opportunity structure:

> . . . it is our belief that much delinquent behavior is engendered because opportunities for conformity are limited. Delinquency therefore represents not a lack of motivation to conform but quite the opposite: the desire to meet social expectations itself becomes the source of delinquent behavior if the possibility of doing so is limited or nonexistent.
>
> The importance of these assumptions in framing the large-scale program which is proposed here cannot be overemphasized. The essence of our approach to prevention, rehabilitation, and social control in the field of juvenile delinquency may be stated as follows: in order to reduce the incidence of delinquent behavior or to rehabilitate persons who are already enmeshed in delinquent patterns, we must provide the social and psychological resources that make conformity possible.

Cloward and Ohlin interpreted the causes of delinquency exclusively in terms of inequality in economic and educational opportunity. "Whatever the difficulties of this approach as a comprehensive theory of delinquency, it justified delinquency programs in seeking [a] broad scope of intervention. . . ."[34]

One of the difficulties with the theory was that it could not and did not explain all delinquency, and was thus not "comprehensive" in that sense. There is more to delinquency than absence of opportunity, even among juveniles who suffer from that absence. It followed therefore that the program built upon the theory could not be truly comprehensive. In fact, as Peter Marris and Martin Rein pointed out, there was no clear definition or understanding of what comprehensive meant.[35] In this way, MFY had unrealistic and unsound expectations. In addition, it shifted its goals from opening the neighborhood opportunity structure to challenging it as a power structure resistant to helping the poor. It moved away from its carefully planned, although overly ambitious, social experiment, and became a community action agency.

Between 1962 and 1968, MFY received and spent more than 30 million dollars. Was this approach successful? First, I think we can safely conclude that the opportunity theory remains just that—a theory.

[34] Ibid., pp. 19–20.
[35] Ibid., p. 142.

"Even if the ultimate criteria—the reduction of poverty and juvenile crime—were in principle measurable, the intermediate criteria were either unquantifiable or doubtfully relevant."[36] Thus, Marris and Rein challenge the basic premise and results of MFY and other similar projects. Further, they conclude: "After five years of effort, the reforms had not evolved any reliable solutions to the intractable problems with which they struggled."[37] Harold Weissman points out that MFY did have considerable impact on the Lower East Side, ". . . helped more people, influenced more professional thinking, and effected more social changes than any other social agency in our time."[38] However, we must ask the bottom line question of whether MFY reduced delinquency rates. Weissman's data show that delinquency rates in the MFY service area were only slightly higher than those in the surrounding areas in 1962, when the program began. After four years and millions of dollars, they were slightly lower. But this change was too slight to permit the conclusion that MFY was effective and successful as a juvenile delinquency prevention effort.

MFY did have considerable influence upon both the War on Poverty program—particularly the community action component; and, upon the work of the 1967 President's Commission on Law Enforcement and Administration of Justice. This commission recognized the difficulties of implementing large scale programs, on the order of MFY, because of the relatively long causal chain linking them with delinquency. They concluded that no quick and sizable reductions in delinquency could or should be expected from such efforts.

Mobilization was oversold at the outset, and it failed to meet expectations as a juvenile delinquency prevention effort. It was only partially evaluated in terms of its effects upon delinquent behavior. MFY was an embittering and disenchanting experience for some, but it had a chastening effect upon many social reformers. I should point out that MFY still exists on the Lower East Side today, but it does so as a traditional social service agency.

The Community Treatment Project

During this same time, but some three thousand miles away, the California Youth Authority was conducting the first part of a large scale experiment called the Community Treatment Project (CTP). CTP's major goal was to determine if certain kinds of juvenile offenders could

[36] Ibid., p. 193.

[37] Ibid., p. 222.

[38] Harold H. Weissman, ed., "Epilogue," *Justice and the Law in the Mobilization for Youth Experience,* (New York: Association Press, 1969), p. 192.

be successfully kept in the community, as opposed to being institutionalized, if they were given intensive supervision and treatment
in small-sized parole caseloads. The project was carried out in
Sacramento and Stockton, beginning in 1961, and from 1965 on in San
Francisco.

Two theoretical assumptions supported the CTP approach to
treatment and control of delinquents: (1) delinquents are not all alike,
and (2) delinquents can be subdivided into types which have clear
implications for the kinds of treatment required.[39] The particular
typology used in CTP was called the "Interpersonal Maturity Level
Classification: Juvenile" or I-level for short. Thus, the designers of CTP
not only recognized the dangers of attempting to treat all offenders as if
they were alike, but made specific attempts through classification for
purposes of treatment, to avoid these dangers.

CTP was founded upon certain theoretical assumptions and these
assumptions were made explicit. Its goals and objectives were also made
explicit. The Project was not assumed at the outset to be appropriate for
all juvenile offenders. Instead, the approach taken was to find out for
just what kinds of delinquents, what kinds of treatments might be effective. In the words of Marguerite Q. Warren, one of the collaborators on
CTP, the crucial question was: "What kinds of treatment programs, in
what kinds of settings, are most effective with what kinds of juvenile
delinquents?"[40]

The CTP experiment was also designed with an experimental
group and a control group. The experimental kids were placed in CTP,
and the controls were sent to the traditional Youth Authority program
which consisted of confinement in a youth institution for some months,
followed by release to normal parole supervision. The CTP program
itself included: "(1) Individual and/or group centered treatment; (2)
group homes, individual foster homes, and other out-of-home placements; (3) an accredited school program which was located within the
CTP 'community center' building, and which included tutoring as well
as arts and crafts; (4) recreational opportunities and socializing experiences (e.g., outings and cultural activities) both within and outside the
community center."[41]

Between 1961 and 1969, a total of 686 experimental kids and 328
control kids were part of the project. The National Institute of Mental
Health picked up $1 million in research costs, and the State of Califor-

[39] Marguerite Q. Warren, "The Community Treatment Project: History and
Prospectus," *Crime and Justice: The Criminal in Confinement* (New York: Basic Books,
1971), p. 302.

[40] Ibid., p. 298.

[41] Ted Palmer, "The Youth Authority's Community Treatment Project," *Federal
Probation*, 38 (1974), 4.

nia expended at least $4 million.[42] Over a thousand kids and more than $5 million for eight years is obviously not a "small potatoes" project.

CTP was also extensively evaluated. In fact, in all its phases it has probably had more evaluations than any delinquency prevention program in history. The initial reports showed that overall, experimental kids returned to crime less often than did the controls. However, some "types" did better in CTP, others did better in the traditional program, while the remainder did about equally well in either approach. Dr. Warren concluded in 1966 that, ". . . the feasibility of substituting intensive community programs for incarceration of many juvenile delinquents has been demonstrated . . ."[43]

Based upon these generally favorable results and some others that were reported later, CTP began to be cited in the mid-1960s by national crime commissions as a model program which substituted community-based treatment for institutional confinement. It was hailed as being more effective in curbing delinquency, more cost-effective and thus economical, and more humane because it depended less upon incarceration. The project received its greatest single promotion on February 6, 1967. In his Special Message to the Congress on Crime in America, President Lyndon B. Johnson said the following:

> Many offenders, the young most of all, stand a far better chance of being rehabilitated in their home communities, than in ordinary confinement. Recently the California Youth Authority concluded a 5-year experiment with various methods of treatment. Convicted juvenile delinquents were assigned on a random basis either to an experimental group where they were returned to their communities for intensive personal and family counseling, or to the regular institutions of correction. The findings to date are dramatically impressive:
>
> —Only 28 percent of the experimental group had their paroles revoked.
>
> —More than half—52 percent—of those confined in regular institutions later had their paroles revoked.
>
> Falling back into crime was almost twice as great for those treated in regular institutions, as for those treated in the community. And it appears that the community treatment program costs far less than institutional confinement.
>
> On the basis of this California experiment and its other studies, the Crime Commission concludes that local institutions related to the community, each housing as few as 50 inmates, and

---

[42] Paul Lerman, *Community Treatment and Social Control: A Critical Analysis of Juvenile Correctional Policy* (Chicago: The University of Chicago Press, 1975), p. 24.

[43] Warren, *Crime and Justice: The Criminal in Confinement*, p. 309.

each supported by a wide range of treatment services, should be developed throughout the country.[44]

So what happened? A Rutgers University social work professor named Paul Lerman undertook a major reevaluation of CTP at the request of NIMH. He published his shocking findings and conclusions in 1975. One finding was that, based upon reported offense rates per 100 youth, ". . . it appears reasonable to conclude that CTP probably did not have an impact on the commission of those offenses deemed to be criminal."[45] Two of his specific conclusions were the following:

The reanalysis of CTP data provides rather clear evidence that CTP did not have any measurable impact on youth behavior, in comparison to a traditional CYA program. Using this standard of comparison, the program was relatively ineffective.[46]

The major findings of this study indicate that major goals of the community treatment strategy were not realized in practice. Community treatment was proposed as an effective alternative to traditional institutionalization and proved to be no more effective. Community treatment was proposed as a noncoercive substitute for state-delivered sanctions, and proved to be associated with increases in state and local social control. And community treatment was supposed to be less expensive, but proved to be associated with cost overruns.[47]

Although some CTP researchers and agents continued to claim success, the results are at least doubtful. One of its supporters, the aforementioned Ted Palmer, admits that the overall effect was not favorable to the experimentals.[48]

The Community Treatment Project offers another example of a program whose implementation did not match its aims. It was supposed to provide a variety of services to juveniles in the community. In fact, Lerman points out that it provided more social control and detention than treatment. The I-level maturity classification was largely ignored in the delivery of treatment. This and other changes in the project were not necessarily taken into account in the interpretation of the findings

[44] Lyndon B. Johnson, 1963–1969, "Special Message to the Congress on Crime in America, February 6, 1967," *Public Papers of the Presidents* (Washington, D.C.: U.S. Government Printing Office), p. 138.

[45] Lerman, *Community Treatment and Social Control,* pp. 63–64.

[46] Ibid., p. 95

[47] Ibid., p. 210.

[48] Ted Palmer and A. H. Herrera, "Community Treatment Project Post-discharge Analysis: An Updating of the 1969 Analysis for Sacramento and Stockton Males." (unpublished paper).

by the original evaluators. It is this last point which seems to account for the misleading of the crime commissions, President Johnson, and others into selling CTP as some kind of magic potion.

Unified Delinquency Intervention Services

As a final example, we come to a more recent and, in several ways, even more controversial illustration of the panacea phenomenon. The setting in this case was the dawn of the decade of the 1970s when it was becoming more and more the popular wisdom that incarcerative and otherwise restrictive methods of handling youthful offenders were inhumane, costly, and generally ineffective. The preferable alternatives were diversion and deinstitutionalization. The National Advisory Commission on Criminal Justice Standards and Goals, among others, advocated minimizing the involvement of young offenders in the juvenile justice system, reintegrating them into the community, and avoiding confinement whenever possible.[49] Community-based corrections had become the vogue, in part because of the influence of the California Treatment Project. The idea of employing a so-called least drastic alternative in the handling of children in trouble had a basic appeal on grounds of compassion, and humane and understanding treatment. This principle is consistent with the historic notion of parens patriae—that the treatment of children be benign, helping, therapeutic, nonpunitive, and nonstigmatizing.

It was within this setting that Cook County, Illinois (Chicago) conceived and implemented a program called Unified Delinquency Intervention Services (UDIS) in 1974. UDIS was intended to serve as an alternative to institutionalization for so-called chronic delinquents. Its average client had more than a dozen arrests—most for serious crimes—and numerous court appearances and temporary detentions. UDIS had a small staff, but annual funding of approximately $2 million per year which was used to purchase contract services.[50] Contract services included counseling, educational and vocational training, advocacy, residential placements in group homes and foster care, wilderness programs, work camps and intensive psychiatric facilities.

Among the goals of UDIS were the provision of services at a cost much less than institutional placement; and, the reduction of recidivism to a rate less than 50 to 60 percent of the rate experienced by youth

[49] National Advisory Commission on Criminal Justice Standards and Goals, *A National Strategy to Reduce Crime* (Washington, D.C.: U.S. Government Printing Office, 1973), pp. 23–25.

[50] Dale Mann, *Intervening with Convicted Serious Juvenile Offenders* (Washington, D.C.: U.S. Government Printing Office, July 1976), p. 3.

released from the Illinois training schools.[51] In 1976, the Rand Corporation referred in glowing terms to the first year results of UDIS in a report prepared for the National Institute for Juvenile Justice and Delinquency Prevention. The Rand report said:

> UDIS appears to have good potential as a model of community-oriented corrections. It has demonstrated that it can offer alternatives to confinement for serious, as well as less serious, juvenile offenders without increasing the risk to the public. This is being achieved . . . at substantially reduced comparative cost. If continued, the achievements of UDIS will be most impressive.[52]

The report also indicated that, ". . . only 15 (7 percent) of the 221 youths who participated in UDIS during its first year had recidivated."[53] Those reported results certainly contributed to the promotion of UDIS and other community corrections programs like it.

In 1976, the American Institutes of Research (AIR) undertook an extensive evaluation of UDIS. The AIR researchers (Charles A. Murray, Doug Thomson, and Cindy B. Israel) evaluated the results of the various UDIS placements, and compared them to results from the traditional placement (incarceration) in juvenile institutions of the Illinois Department of Corrections.

The premise of its evaluators was that UDIS was designed to test "the proposition that deinstitutionalization could be extended to the chronic, seriously delinquent; that it need not be limited to first-time offenders, to misdemeanants, or to status offenders. UDIS was to be an alternative to incarceration."[54] Murray and a later coauthor, Louis A. Cox, Jr., make clear that "the least drastic alternative principle" was the centerpiece of the UDIS approach. It was a clear test which, its advocates claimed, was providing convincing evidence for the superiority of community-based alternatives.

If one accepts the premise that the arguments for deinstitutionalization and minimal intervention had generally resulted in these alternatives taking on the trappings of a panacea, that is, being promoted as good for nearly all kids and, in this case, being advertised

[51] Unified Delinquency Intervention Services (Chicago), Grant Application to Illinois Law Enforcement Commission.

[52] Mann, *Intervening with Convicted Serious Juvenile Offenders*, pp. 40–44.

[53] Ibid., p. 43.

[54] Charles A. Murray and Louis A. Cox, Jr., *Beyond Probation: Juvenile Corrections and the Chronic Delinquent* (Beverly Hills: Sage Publications, 1979), p. 96.

as an answer to the inequities and imperfections of the juvenile justice system, and, if one accepts the premise that UDIS was an embodiment of these notions, then it provides us an excellent case example.

First, we should look closely at the causal assumptions underlying UDIS. As indicated, UDIS provided a variety of services to juvenile offenders. Although the services in general seem like good things to do, for example, dental care and client advocacy, there were not specific rationales given for them, nor were there clear links between the service and the delinquent behavior it was supposed to affect.

The target offenders were not randomly assigned to UDIS and to the Department of Corrections for the evaluation, nor were they randomly assigned among the UDIS placements. However, the UDIS and DOC juveniles were comparable in their backgrounds, including criminal histories, and UDIS was considered to be an appropriate placement for a large majority of serious offenders who would have otherwise been institutionalized. In addition to their extensive arrest records, the UDIS placements had arrests for such crimes as homicide, rape, battery, and armed robbery—offenses which normally bring incarceration. The study itself included 266 delinquents in the UDIS sample and 317 youth sent to DOC.[55]

The results from the AIR evaluation have stirred up considerable controversy about this project and the implications of its results. Using a before-after measure which they call suppression effect, the evaluators found that, contrary to expectations, UDIS did not do as well as DOC in reducing post-release arrests. More specifically, the UDIS community-based placements (the at-home services) did worse than the more intrusive residential placements, and worse than the DOC placements. For example, the suppression effect—the before and after comparison of preintervention and postintervention arrests—was 52 percent for non-residential services, but 68 percent for the DOC institutions. Clearly, these results were far short, in fact the reverse of one of the major goals of UDIS. The researchers concluded: "For this group of delinquents—big-city, chronic, during the mid-1970s—community-based intervention strategies were not as effective as out-of-town programs."[56] The least drastic alternative ". . . failed to suppress arrests as effectively as harsher interventions. . . ."[57]

The implications from these findings certainly challenge the proposition that minimal intervention works with chronic, serious

[55] Ibid., p. 116.
[56] Ibid., p. 124.
[57] Ibid., p. 125.

juvenile offenders, and they "contradict the hypothesis that 'less drastic' approaches are superior."[58] Not only do the data show that more restrictive controls including incarceration were more effective in reducing arrests and enhancing public safety, but that they were not necessarily more costly. Providing more cost-effective services had been another UDIS goal.

The UDIS study is controversial in part because it questions liberal tenets about reforming the juvenile justice system, but also because it challenges the "nothing works" doctrine which was extensively documented earlier in this chapter. The researchers claim that deterrence was the significant factor because each more drastic level of sanctions produced a larger decrease in rearrests. (The subject of deterrence will be discussed extensively in the next chapter.)

Finally, the UDIS research is controversial because several respected researchers have scrutinized the original report and reanalyzed some of the data. They have concluded, "that the major conclusions either are an artifact of the methodology employed or have been exaggerated by that methodology."[59] This particular controversy remains unresolved. These same critics offered some advice to administrators of delinquency programs which, apart from its validity with regard to the UDIS study, is certainly relevant to the idea of a panacea phenomenon. The advice is: "Above all, distrust simple answers to questions that are not simple. Delinquency and delinquency program impacts are complex and complicated phenomenon [sic] which probably cannot be monitored effectively in terms of a single, simple indicator."[60]

WHY DOES THE PANACEA PHENOMENON PERSIST?

Perhaps the best answer to this question lies in what Stratton and Terry nearly twenty years ago called the "isms" fallacy.[61] In particular they referred to the ideas of "doism" and "newism." Doism is the rather naive and overly optimistic belief that it is better to do something than nothing. Motivated by the belief that we've got to do something, we frequently plow ahead with good intentions, but with an almost utter dis-

---

[58] Ibid., p. 135.

[59] Andrew C. Gordon et al., Letter to the Editor, *Criminal Justice Newsletter,* 9, (July 31, 1978), pp. 1-4.

[60] Andrew C. Gordon et al., "How a Regression Artifact Can Make Any Delinquency Intervention Program Look Effective." (unpublished paper).

[61] John R. Stratton and Robert M. Terry, (eds.), *Prevention of Delinquency: Problems and Programs* (New York: The Macmillan Co., 1968).

regard for the possible consequences of our actions, consequences which can be negative or detrimental. We have failed to learn the history of juvenile justice in America, namely that the path to hell is paved with good intentions. A considerable amount of harm has been perpetrated upon children under the guise of doing something which is "good" for them.

Americans seem peculiarly susceptible to the belief that every problem, including every social problem, has a solution. We are also inclined to seek or to accept simple and often simplistic solutions. Politicians frequently appeal to this desire for action by offering simplistic answers. These fall on receptive ears because we are afraid and frustrated by juvenile crime, and because we want to do something, almost anything, about it.

Newism refers to the appeal of approaches or programs because they are new. Stratton and Terry point out that, "This orientation is reinforced by the failure of older programs and the continuing rise of delinquency rates." "This results," they say, "in the bandwagon effect of implementing new programs and policies without carefully assessing their validity or reviewing the history of similar types of programs that preceded them."[62] This is akin to Santyanna's theory that those who fail to remember the past are doomed to repeat its mistakes. In delinquency prevention, we frequently don't even know what our mistakes are.

Faddism, which encompasses elements of both doism and newism, is also a good descriptive term for our battle against juvenile crime. We seem to be taken with fads in this area just as we are in so many others, for example, hairstyles, clothing, dances, etc. Unfortunately, faddism in delinquency prevention is much less benign in its effects. Delinquency prevention fads are generally cheap and simple, as well as quick. They may also come and go rather quickly.

In reviewing delinquency prevention literature, we find numerous warnings against fads and against panaceas. Two such warnings stand out in my mind. The first is the following statement made by James Hackler in his book on prevention: "Drastic and over-simplified cures have failed to work in the past, yet they continue to attract supporters."[63] And Ted Palmer in an article commenting upon Robert Martinson's early research states:

> The history of science teaches that all-encompassing solutions are seldom to be found . . . the search for rapid or glamorous solutions, and for methods that will work with everyone, is sure to

[62] Ibid., pp. 2-3.

[63] James C. Hackler, *The Prevention of Youthful Crime: The Great Stumble Forward* (Againcourt, Ontario: Methuen Publications, 1978), p. 21.

die very hard, if at all . . . it is precisely this type of search, the search for the impossible, which has ended in so much disillusionment thus far.[64]

We should keep in mind what we have learned about panaceas as we narrow and sharpen our focus in the chapters that follow. The next subject—deterrence—is illustrative of an almost childlike faith in punishment and the use of fear of punishment as a way of dealing with criminal behavior.

---

[64] Ted Palmer, "Martinson Revisited," *Journal of Research in Crime and Delinquency*, (July 1975), pp. 150-51.

chapter two

Deterrence and Criminal Behavior

Deterrence of crime and delinquency has always been one of the justifications for the use of punishment and other criminal sanctions in our society. But the idea is not unique to us. Its history can be traced back thousands of years to the times of the Greeks and the Romans. Deterrence is one way our criminal justice system attempts to prevent crime. Professor Johannes Andenaes has pointed out that messages are sent to society by means of the criminal law and its specific applications.[1] Deterrence is premised on a very basic belief that the threat of punishment will keep people from committing crimes, and perhaps from engaging in other kinds of socially undesirable behavior. This is so, the argument goes, because we are generally rational creatures who wish to limit the pain we suffer and to increase the pleasure we experience. The effectiveness of the "threat" is important because it is neither possible nor desirable to actually inflict the punishment on all or even most of us.

When a parent threatens a child with punishment if the child misbehaves, that parent is demonstrating the use of deterrence. The parent is assuming that the child wishes to avoid the threatened punishment and will, therefore, avoid the unwanted behavior. This same

---

[1] Johannes Andenaes, "The General Preventive Effects of Punishment," *The Criminal in the Arms of the Law,* Leon Radzinowicz and Marvin E. Wolfgang (eds.) (New York: Basic Books, Inc., 1971), p. 75.

notion applies to antismoking efforts which confront smokers with the possible consequences of their smoking, or to drug education programs which show young people the bad things that can stem from their use of drugs.

In theory, criminal deterrence works when a potential offender, in deciding whether or not to commit a crime, weighs the chances that he or she might be caught and punished and is, therefore, discouraged from committing the crime. Our knowledge of deterrence is limited. For example, we do not know which factors determine in any particular circumstance whether deterrence will be effective. Nor do we know how to make it effective in all cases. We assume that some of the factors involved in susceptibility to deterrence include the personality of the person to be deterred, his moral and social values, awareness and knowledge of the law, the immediate circumstances surrounding the behavior (presence of peers for example), the potential rewards of the behavior contemplated, the perceived likelihood of being caught and punished, the perceived swiftness and severity of the punishment, etc.

The effectiveness of deterrence seems to depend more on perceived risk than it does on real risk. Perceived risk is that degree of risk actually calculated by the potential offender. What we believe to be true seems more important and influential than what is actually true. Referring to knowledge of the law, which is a part of risk perception, Richard Henshel says:

> . . . every theoretical explanation of how deterrence operates assumes knowledge of the sanctioning conditions on the part of the population at risk if general deterrence is to occur.
>
> . . . we might conclude, if we find low awareness, that a program to heighten awareness could have greater efficacy than alteration of the objective sanctioning conditions themselves.[2]

Thus, if punishment is to have any deterrent effect, potential offenders must know about it. Following this thinking, we might suppose that deterrence could be increased if potential offenders were informed of the likely consequences of their behavior.

There is some evidence that this may be easier said than done, and also that the supposition may be more complicated in some cases. For example, Charles Silberman, in his book *Criminal Violence, Criminal Justice,* points out:

> . . . most criminals, even the disorganized lower-class youths who do not plan their crimes, would rather avoid a prison term if

---

[2] Richard Henshel, "Considerations on the Deterrence and System Capacity Iodels," *Criminology,* 16(1) (1978), 41.

they could. Their lack of planning reflects their general incompetence, an exaggerated (and often liquor- or drug-heightened) faith in their own omnipotence, or a belief in "fate," rather than indifference to punishment.[3]

Incompetence, and beliefs in omnipotence or fate are difficult to overcome or to change by increased awareness. Second, a recent study by Handler and Vitoux, which compared the perceived and actual probability of arrest among junior and senior high school students in three Illinois communities, found that the youngsters grossly overestimated the actual risks of their being arrested. The authors concluded that this was not a result of deterrence arising from the actual effectiveness of the police, but rather was "related to culturally imbued attitudes."[4] The girls in that study had a high expectation of arrest, despite the fact that girls are actually arrested far less frequently than boys. This was attributed to the upbringing girls receive which makes them more compliant and obedient, and possibly more fearful of arrest than boys.

Deterrence includes a number of aspects. One is the difference between what we call general and special deterrence. General deterrence refers to prevention in advance by the use of threats or examples. Millions of older Americans grew up listening to radio programs which dealt with crime subjects and invariably concluded that, "Crime does not pay!" The bad guys were always caught and punished. This could lead to an overestimation of the risks involved and act as a deterrent to generally law-abiding people. This is an example of the culturally imbued attitudes which were referred to above.

This approach has also been used with targets other than crime. World War II G.I.'s headed overseas were shown films depicting the horrible results of promiscuous sexual activity. The 1936 pseudo-documentary film "Reefer Madness" was intended to illustrate the bizarre consequences of the use of marijuana. The following quote from that film's introduction provides an impression of its content:

The motion picture you are about to witness may startle you. It would not have been possible otherwise to sufficiently emphasize the frightful toll of the new drug menace which is destroying the youth of America in alarmingly increasing numbers. Marihuana is that drug—a violent narcotic—an unspeakable scourge—
The Real Public Enemy Number One!

[3] Charles Silberman, *Criminal Violence, Criminal Justice* (New York: Random House, 1978), p. 190.

[4] Ellen Handler and Mary Vitoux, "The Overestimation of the Probability of Arrest: Support for Deterrence Theory?" (Unpublished paper presented at The American Society of Criminology Meetings, November 1978, Dallas, Texas), p. 11.

Its first effect is sudden, violent uncontrollable laughter; then come dangerous hallucinations—space expands—time slows down, almost stands still . . . fixed ideas come next, conjuring up monstrous extravagances—followed by emotional disturbances, the total inability to direct thoughts, the loss of all power to resist physical emotions . . . leading finally to acts of shocking violence . . . ending often in incurable insanity . . . the dread Marihuana may be reaching forth next for your son or daughter . . . or yours . . . or YOURS![5]

Most of us find this laughable today, but the film reflected the belief that thinking people would want to avoid whatever terrible consequences existed once they had been made aware of them. I should note that the success of these films in accomplishing their objectives is questionable.

Special deterrence refers to after-the-fact inhibition of the person punished. If a child has already been punished for a particular behavior, the assumption is that the child will then avoid that behavior in the future. Special deterrence is used frequently with juvenile offenders when judges, police officers, and probation or parole officers lock up youngsters in detention for a few days or longer in order to "teach them a lesson" to "put a little fear in them"; or to get them to "shape up."[6] Silberman says, ". . . extraordinary numbers of juvenile court judges, including some of the most sensitive and thoughtful, have persuaded themselves, as one such judge told me, that 'detention does work therapeutically in most cases.' "[7]

Does special deterrence work with juveniles? Some evidence would suggest that it does not. In 1967, Daniel Claster did a study in which he compared risk perception between incarcerated delinquent boys and nondelinquent boys.[8] Claster studied the accuracy of knowledge these boys had about risk of arrest and conviction for various crimes, likelihood that the boys might commit various criminal acts, and for those who thought they might, estimates of the risks that they would be running. He found no significant differences between the delinquents and nondelinquents in their knowledge of risks. However, he did find that the delinquents who thought they might commit crimes saw less risk of personal arrest and conviction than did the nondelinquents who also thought they might commit crimes. In other words, boys already in

---

[5] Louis Gasnier, *Reefer Madness* (United States Government, 1936).

[6] Silberman, *Criminal Violence, Criminal Justice.* p. 190.

[7] Ibid., p. 323.

[8] Daniel Claster, "Comparison of Risk Perception Between Delinquents and Nondelinquents," *Journal of Criminal Law, Criminology, and Police Science,* 58 (1967), pp. 80–86.

a training school for juvenile offenders were more likely to think that they could get away with committing new crimes. This seems to illustrate a common complaint regarding correctional institutions, namely that they may be little more than "schools for crime."

In 1978, Lotz, Regoli, and Raymond repeated Claster's research.[9] Their overall conclusion was that punishment (training school incarceration) had limited or no deterrent effect upon the juveniles committed to the training school. Their speculations as to why this might be so were that adolescent boys are not as calculating and rational as adults in weighing potential risk; that risk may be disregarded by adolescents because engaging in deviant behavior may be status enhancing; and, that experiencing negative outcomes may reduce the fear of such outcomes in the future. This last point is particularly important because it relates to the idea that we all have a certain amount of fear of the unknown. Once the unknown becomes known, our fear of it often diminishes. Both of these studies indicate that once a youngster has been committed to a training school, and perhaps to other institutions, the fear or anxiety about a subsequent commitment is reduced. As a result, deterrence is reduced.

Much of the research on deterrence, particularly the early research, has been limited to studies of the deterrent effect of the death penalty. More recently, researchers have looked at the relation of other offenses to certainty of punishment; and, some have studied the relation of estimates of certainty or severity of punishment and deterrence. This research has opened another aspect of deterrence—the importance of its swiftness, its surety or certainty, and its severity. The studies do not seem to have accomplished a great deal in terms of providing us with definitive answers about some of the factors raised earlier. Suggestive evidence has been compiled, but is not conclusive. The differences of opinion on deterrence are illustrated in the following views from three well-known contemporary scholars who have written about crime and deterrence:

It seems reasonable to assume that because you punish a person for committing a crime, therefore he will be deterred from repeating it, and other people will be deterred from even trying it. Most people would find no fault with this argument. Indeed, some people might wish to extend it to say that the more severely you punish a person, the more he will be deterred from repeating the act, and also the more other people will be deterred from undertaking it. Statistics have been published in many countries showing

[9] Roy Lotz, Robert M. Regoli, and Phillip Raymond, "Delinquency and Special Deterrence," *Criminology*, 15(4) (1978), 539–46.

that there is very little basis for this hypothesis. . . . You may flog people for certain types of offences, but rather than deter them, it seems to have the opposite effect. Although the punishment is severe, the rate of recidivism is, if anything, greater than it would have been without the flogging. . . . It has proved surprisingly difficult to demonstrate that any form of treatment or punishment has any measurable effect on people.[10]

There is scarcely any evidence to support the proposition that would-be criminals are indifferent to the risks associated with a proposed course of action. . . . The deterrent capacity of criminal penalties is supported by statistical data for large numbers of offenses over long periods of time.[11]

. . . recent research on deterrence suggests that increasing the certainty of punishment has considerably more impact on crime than does increasing severity . . . ours is a system in which certainty of punishment is low and severity high.[12]

After a recent review of studies on the deterrent effect of criminal sanctions, criminologist Linda Anderson concluded, ". . . there is not yet any clear or cohesive support for deterrence. At this point it remains an unverified criminological 'truth.' "[13] Anderson cited a number of deterrence studies involving juvenile subjects which have been carried out over the last ten years or so. All of these studies used questionnaires or interviews to survey juveniles who had not been subjected to criminal sanctions. Most of the studies relied on self-reported behavior as their outcome measure. This means that the subjects themselves were asked to report their own behavior. All of the studies used perceived sanctions based upon the belief that perception of risk of swift, certain, and severe reaction by officials is what acts to deter a contemplated offense. Little potential deterrent effect was found in these particular studies for either perceived severity or perceived swiftness of legal reactions. Some support was found for the deterrent effects of perceived certainty. In other words, the youngsters were not so much concerned with how quickly or harshly they might be punished, but they did show some concern for how certain it would be that they would be punished.

[10] Hans J. Eysenck, *Crime and Personality* (London: Paladin, 1970), p. 151.

[11] James Q. Wilson, *Thinking About Crime* (New York: Vintage Books, 1975), pp. 175–77.

[12] Silberman, *Criminal Violence, Criminal Justice,* p.192.

[13] Linda S. Anderson, "The Deterrent Effect of Criminal Sanctions: Reviewing the Evidence." (Unpublished paper presented at The American Society of Criminology Meetings, November 1978, Dallas, Texas) p. 16.

These results and others suggest that we may all be gamblers at heart. We are interested in knowing what the odds are, and in our chances of beating these odds. Kids know that the odds on their beating the law are pretty good.

An offender must come to the attention of the police, be arrested, be referred to juvenile court, be convicted, and be sentenced to an institution before actually facing the severity of imprisonment. Delinquents, both those we know about and those we don't, are readily aware of the uncertainty of their being caught and punished from their own personal experiences. These youths know that their chances of being caught are small. Those who have been caught are also aware of the severity of sanctions, having been subjected to them. They know that these sanctions are not very severe, and that there is a good chance of getting off lightly even if they are caught.

Kids who have beaten the system and gotten away with it are not likely to be deterred. Others, and particularly those who commit the most violent crimes, are psychologically unlikely or unable to rationally calculate the risk of penalties. For example, they may have little inner control; and, they may act on impulse with little intellectual or moral understanding of what they are doing. Still others may be willing to run what they know are great risks in order to maintain their status in the eyes of their peers. After all, peers are the single most important reference group for adolescents. Finally, it is in part the elements of danger and adventure that make delinquent behavior exciting and attractive in the first place.

A "GET TOUGH" POLICY

Despite the lack of evidence to support the importance of severity, our general disillusionment with the effectiveness of the juvenile justice system and its inability to rehabilitate youthful offenders has led to deterrence being given a more important and upfront role in dealing with juvenile offenders. For example, the Joint Commission of the Juvenile Justice Standards Project of the American Bar Association and Institute of Judicial Administration supported increased use of confinement for longer periods for juvenile felons (those convicted of serious crimes such as murder, rape, or robbery) in order to isolate dangerous youngsters and deter others.[14]

[14] Barbara D. Flicker, *Standards for Juvenile Justice: A Summary and Analysis,* American Bar Association Juvenile Justice Standards Project (Cambridge, Massachusetts: Ballinger, 1977), pp. 22–23.

The most visible change in state revisions of their juvenile codes has been an increasing severity in public policy involving the handling of serious and repeated juvenile offenders. More than a dozen states have amended their laws so that juveniles who commit certain crimes can be prosecuted as adults and sentenced to longer terms, or so that some minimum period of incarceration is made mandatory. New York passed a Juvenile Offender Law in 1978 requiring 13-year-olds charged with murder and 14- and 15-year-olds charged with murder, kidnapping, rape, robbery, manslaughter, arson, and sodomy to be tried in adult courts and faced with adult punishments. This effort to get tough with youths committing violent crimes is intended in part to be both a general and special deterrent.

What accounts for these actions? Certainly our fear of juvenile crime and the sense of futility with what is viewed as a failing system are factors. I tried to show in Chapter I why there may be a sense of futility and how it contributes to the panacea phenomenon. The fear is illustrated and perhaps has been fanned over the past decade by such news media headlines as:

- They think, "I can kill because I'm 14"—New York Times Magazine[15]
- Violent Crimes by Juveniles Rising—*The Washington Post*[16]
- Juvenile Justice in New York is Characterized as "Futility"—*The New York Times*[17]
- The Youth Crime Plague—*Time* magazine[18]

In addition to this fear and sense of frustration, there is a belief in deterrence as an article of faith. Frank Hellum says, ". . . the inclination to accept the basic tenets of deterrence theory is so well grounded in both culture and legal philosophy that even a pebble's worth of proof may be sufficient to release an avalanche."[19] And, maybe a pebble's worth isn't even necessary.

Finally, there is the reality that one of the easiest and simplest steps to be taken against juvenile crime is to increase the harshness of penalties and to make them applicable to a larger number of youngsters. This is, however, another example of a simplistic solution to a complex

[15] Ted Morgan, "They Think 'I Can Kill Because I'm 14,' " *The New York Times Magazine* (July 19, 1975), p. 9.

[16] Martha M. Hamilton, "Violent Crimes by Juveniles Rising," *The Washington Post* (June 1976), p. C1.

[17] Joseph B. Treaster, "Juvenile Justice in New York is Characterized as 'Futility,' " *The New York Times* (April 22, 1976).

[18] Edwin Warner, "The Youth Crime Plague," *Time* (July 11, 1977), pp. 18–28.

[19] Frank Hellum, "Juvenile Justice: The Second Revolution," *Crime and Delinquency*, 25(3) (July 1979), 304.

problem. The result is that the severity of punishment, which I have already tried to show has little or no deterrent effect, is increased; whereas certainty, which may have some deterrence value, is not and cannot be so readily increased. As a result, the juvenile justice system becomes more like the adult system—higher on severity, but still low on certainty. This is so because the odds of being arrested, convicted, and punished are difficult to increase when some of the conditions affecting these odds are beyond the reach of juvenile authorities, and when relatively small improvements in efficiency and effectiveness would require more money and resources than we are willing to provide. Perhaps an even more important explanation is our unwillingness to pay the costs in due process trade-offs that would be necessary to significantly increase the certainty of juvenile punishment. The latter, in my judgment, is fortunate because it suggests we have been willing to go only so far in giving up our individual freedoms to make our crime control capacity more effective. So far, we have found a "police state" approach to be unattractive.

BEHAVIOR MODIFICATION AND AVERSIVE TECHNIQUES

In order to better understand how deterrence, both general and special, may be individualized and internalized by the individuals subjected to it, we must consider such psychological concepts as conditioning, behavior modification, negative reinforcement, punishment and aversive techniques or therapy.

Conditioning is a basic form of social learning. It involves sequences of stimuli and responses in which repeat behavior is either encouraged or discouraged by the use of rewards and punishments. The idea is that behavior that is rewarded tends to recur; that which is punished tends to cease. Rewards or so-called positive reinforcers may include attention, food, money, praise, privileges, etc. Punishments or negative reinforcers could be confinement, corporal punishment, ridicule, threats, etc. Although there is considerable disagreement about how these reinforcers work and with whom and under what circumstances, there does seem to be some agreement that rewards are more effective than punishments in bringing about lasting changes in behavior.

Psychologist H. J. Eysenck says the following about the effects of punishment as a negative reinforcement with offenders:

> These effects always tend to be extremely variable and unpredictable. Punishment may produce the desired end, that is,

the elimination of a certain type of conduct, but on the other hand, it may have exactly the opposite effect, stamping in the undesirable conduct even more strongly than before and making it a stereotyped pattern. Sometimes punishment may have no effect at all, one way or the other, and it is not even possible to say that strong and weak punishments differ in their effects in any predictable way. It is not surprising, therefore, that empirical studies of the effects of punishment on criminals have led to more confusion, so that no positive statements of any kind can be made.[20]

The idea that punishment may have an effect opposite that which is intended is not only intriguing, but may perhaps be unsettling to advocates of deterrence. One of the findings from studies of children who were disciplined by physical punishment is that they tend to be more aggressive than other children, although the punishment was for being overly aggressive.[21] There are at least three possible hypotheses which may explain these findings. First, the frustration-aggression hypothesis contends that since physical punishment is frustrating, and since frustration creates aggression, the effects of punishment are to increase aggression, no matter what the reason for the punishment. Second, the imitation hypothesis proposes that children who experience aggression through physical punishment become aggressive because they are imitating the behavior of their punishers. Third, the reinforcement hypothesis states that children who are physically punished are encouraged to be aggressive toward their peers. Being punished teaches them that punishment is okay.[22] The latter two hypotheses incorporate the idea that children learn more by what adults do than by what they say.

As I indicated previously, ridicule, threats, and other efforts to induce fear may and have been used as negative reinforcers. Verbal threats of punishment, as opposed to actual punishment, seem likely to only suppress rather than eliminate undesirable behavior. For persons who do not associate the threat of punishment with actual punishment, the threat may have little or no meaning. The use of fear may sometimes work with individuals if its timing is closely tied to the behavior to be

---

[20] Eysenck, *Crime and Personality,* p. 156.

[21] R. R. Sears, "The Relation of Early Socialization Experiences to Aggression in Middle Childhood," *Journal of Abnormal Social Psychology,* 63 (1961), 466-92. And, L. D. Eron, T. J. Banta, L. O. Walder, and J. H. Laulicht, "Comparison of Data from Mothers and Fathers on Child-Rearing Practices and their Relation to Child Aggression," *Child Development,* 32 (1961), 457-572.

[22] W. C. Becker, "Consequences of Different Kinds of Parental Discipline," in M. L. Hoffman and L. W. Hoffman (eds.) *Review of Child Development Research* (New York: Russel Sage Foundation, 1964), pp. 169-208.

deterred. However, it becomes less effective as the time span between the scaring and the object behavior increases. Andenaes says: "The time element is important. Threats of punishment in the distant future are not as a rule as important in the process of motivation as are threats of immediate punishment."[23]

Here too there is evidence that the use of fear, like the use of punishment, may sometimes have a boomerang effect. One of the basic principles in the psychology of communication is that high-scare tactics can backfire. If people are given frightening descriptions of the possible consequences if they behave in a certain way, they often are impressed initially, but later push the ugly or unpleasant information out of their minds. There is some evidence that this type of thing occurs in drug education programs. Young people are told of the terrible things that can happen to them from drug use, but there is a tendency for them to dismiss the information as overstated or irrelevant.

Social psychologist Alfred Cohn says that although the effects of fear induction, of scaring, are not fully known nor understood, "it does seem that they are more influential if an alternative path is clearly mapped so that the target knows what must be done in order to avoid the dreadful fate depicted for him."[24] He also says that persons who feel vulnerable to the threat may be so frightened as to feel compelled to deny or otherwise reject it. Or, the subjects may reject the scaring because they feel incapable of complying with what it is they are supposed to do in order to avoid the consequences. Alcoholics, overeaters, or heavy smokers may conclude that they simply cannot give up drinking, eating or smoking. Finally, persons who feel themselves competent to control their own lives and destinies may be less influenced by threats.

Psychologists Bandura and Walters have described a form of social learning called vicarious reinforcement. This suggests that in some circumstances behavior may be influenced by a fear of punishment generated from observing others being punished for various kinds of behavior. This is akin to the notion of general deterrence, namely that we can learn from what happens to others. Bandura and Walters explain vicarious reinforcement as follows:

> It is generally assumed that resistance to deviation results from the association of noxious stimuli with the commission of prohibited responses during the life history of an individual. However, as modeling studies demonstrate, children may acquire inhibitions without committing a prohibited act and without

---

[23] Andenaes, *The Criminal in the Arms of the Law,* p. 103.

[24] Alfred Cohn, "A Social Psychologist Views 'Scared Straight,' " (Hempstead, N.Y.: Hofstra Univ., 1979), p. 2.

themselves receiving any punishment. There is thus considerable evidence that response inhibition and response disinhibition can be vicariously transmitted, particularly if the immediate consequences to the model are apparent or the model is a person who has evidently been competent or successful in life.[25]

Modeling may also backfire however. If people modeling the fear are seen as examples for getting into trouble, but then getting out of it or away with it, they may be examples that the activity or behavior is worth the risk. This could certainly be the case in a society where so much juvenile crime goes unpunished and is rewarding in one way or another.

Behavior modification, which was referred to briefly in the first chapter, is a type of conditioning that involves varying, in a systematic way, behavioral and environmental factors thought to be associated with an individual's behavior. ". . . behavior modification procedures are based on the general principle that people are influenced by the consequences of their behavior."[26] It is claimed by behavior modification advocates and supporters that these procedures are not much different from what we historically and generally have done to try to influence other people's behavior; the procedures are simply more systematic. Whether or not that is true, some of them certainly have raised a storm of controversy, particularly the so-called aversive control techniques.

Aversive techniques use punishments or negative reinforcers such as brief, low-level electric shocks, fines, or what is known as the time-out procedure to alter behavior. In the last method, when a child or other person engages in disruptive or unwanted behavior of some kind, he is removed and temporarily isolated from the remainder of his group.

Positive reinforcers such as tokens exchangeable for food or trips, money, points, and what are known as behavior change units have been used with delinquents to decrease destructive behavior, improve educational training performance, or increase compliance with rules. Many of these methods are generally accepted and commonly used.

Stephanie Stolz and her colleagues prepared a report for the National Institute of Mental Health on behavior modification in 1975. On the subject of aversive techniques, which are those techniques for

[25] From *Social Learning and Personality Development* by Albert Bandura and Richard H. Walters. Copyright © 1963 by Holt, Rinehart and Winston, Inc. Reprinted by permission of Holt, Rinehart and Winston.

[26] Stephanie B. Stolz, Louis A. Wienckowski, and Bertram S. Brown, "Behavior Modification: A Perspective on Critical Issues," *American Psychologist,* 30 (November 1975), 1028.

eliminating certain behaviors and which are the most controversial, these authors said the following:

> Some types of inappropriate behavior, such as addictions and certain sexual behaviors, appear to be maintained because their immediate consequences are naturally reinforcing for the individual. In such cases, aversive control techniques are sometimes used to combat long-term consequences that may be much more detrimental to the individual than the aversive methods themselves. . . . No explanations of how aversive therapy works or why it is effective only under some conditions are generally accepted yet . . . it is important to note, however, that in the absence of rewarded alternatives, a response suppressed by an aversive technique is likely to recur.[27]

The above quotation makes three points: (1) the behavior or the consequences of the behavior to be modified must be worse than the aversive technique used; (2) how aversive techniques work is unknown; and (3) they don't always work or don't always have a long lasting effect. Over the years, behavior modification has been popularized in the media and in literature, but largely in a negative sense. *Brave New World, 1984, The Manchurian Candidate,* the book and film *A Clockwork Orange*—all looked at such things as psychosurgery (the use of brain surgery to permanently and irrevocably alter behavior), chemotherapy (the use of drugs such as Anectine, which produces sensations of drowning or dying, to modify behavior), electric shocks, and brainwashing. These are all aversive techniques in their most dramatic and sometimes horrifying form. Stolz and her coauthors claim that it is incorrect to link these techniques with behavior modification, but that seems to be largely a matter of opinion. These authors do admit that aversive procedures are easy to abuse and have raised serious concerns.

Behavior modification techniques have been and are being used extensively with juvenile offenders. They are generally less aversive than those described above, but some are still sensitive. For example, the Robert F. Kennedy Youth Center in Morgantown, West Virginia, has used behavioral modification therapy since the 1960s. Reinforcement strategies are built into every activity and are designed around a class-level system and a token economy. Wayne Sage in an article in *Human Behavior* entitled, "Crime and the Clockwork Lemon," says that kids who are conforming and who learn to be manipulative do well at the Kennedy Center. Most disturbing, he says, "is the possibility that the

[27] Ibid., p. 1028.

Quay typology may create a self-fulfilling prophecy."[28] The Quay system is a classification scheme which divides delinquent behavior into types that include: inadequate-immature, neurotic-conflicted, unsocialized-aggressive (psychopathic), and socialized (subcultural). Sage alleges that, "the Federal Bureau of Prisons' own study, which it is suppressing, indicates that once a kid is typed according to such behavioral problems and conditioned to believe he will commit certain types of crimes unless he does as the staff says, he is more likely to become that sort of criminal."

Verbal and corporal punishment are used extensively in some programs for delinquents. The Vindicate Society in Newark, New Jersey, employs something called "Amosian" therapy. This is also known as "boxing therapy." Named after its inventor, Ben Amos, it is as its name implies, boxing used as a form of therapeutic intervention with youthful offenders.

A therapeutic community called Elan, in Poland Spring, Maine, also relies on punishment to control discipline problems in that school. This program was the subject of a 1980 television documentary. Elan adopted from the Synanon/Daytop Village drug treatment approaches the notion of a "haircut." This is a form of verbal reprimand by which the kids discipline themselves. There are four levels of haircuts used at Elan: a "blast" (just one person); a "round robin" (a dozen or so people); a "21-gun salute" (about two dozen people); and a "charge" (a general meeting where everyone lines up on the target youngsters). Elan also uses spanking and the "ring" (boxing). The ring is said to be limited to provokers and bullies who have to learn that the community will not tolerate aggression. Although admittedly rough, Elan's directors claim it is carefully monitored to keep it from getting out of hand.

Haircuts, spanking, and boxing are overtly aversive techniques. Both Vindicate and Elan are highly controversial programs having their own detractors and supporters. Whether or not they work is part of the controversy, but they certainly exemplify the use of negative consequences as a means of modifying behavior.

On the less controversial side, I. E. Fodor describes a project in which a group of eight female delinquents was asked to imagine scenes of rape and violence based upon their experiences after having escaped from an institution. This technique of heightening awareness of the consequences reduced escapes from a mean of 2.67 during the six-month period preceding treatment to a mean of .5 escapes during the

[28] Wayne Sage, "Crime and the Clockwork Lemon," *Human Behavior* (September 1974), p. 20.

three months following treatment.[29] The Intensive Training Program at Murdoch Center, Georgia demonstrated reductions in antisocial behaviors by using a combination of behavior modification techniques. An example of the success of extinguishing delinquent behavior is the case of a sixteen-year-old incarcerated delinquent boy described by G. D. Brown and U. D. Tyler.[30] This intimidating and aggressive boy was subjected to brief isolation procedures (time-outs) over a ten month period. The result was less frequent aggressive behavior and an improvement in other behavior.

BEHAVIOR MODIFICATION AS A PANACEA

Can behavior modification in general and aversive techniques in particular really decrease juvenile delinquency? The answer may be either no or perhaps, we just don't know.

Robert Emery and David Marholin II reviewed a sample of behavior modification efforts tried with delinquents which were reported in literature from 1968 to 1976. Of twenty-seven studies reviewed (twenty-two were actually analyzed) only 3.7 percent focused on delinquent behavior as the target behavior. That is, they tried to directly deter delinquency. The others used such targets as social/interpersonal behavior, school behavior, etc. The conclusion was that there was "a failure to show the relationship between successful behavior change efforts and a subsequent reduction in measures of delinquency."[31] In other words, they didn't seem to work.

Behavior modification is also a good example of the panacea phenomenon. It was quickly adopted in juvenile corrections (and adult corrections as well) beginning in the early 1960s. It was adopted based more on what it promised to do than on what it actually did; this was because there was very little experience with its use and almost no research.

Canadians Robert R. Ross and H. Bryan McKay have examined this development, and they postulate several explanations for it. First, behavior modification was new and thus subject to the newism notion

[29] I. E. Fodor, "The Use of Behavior Modification Techniques with Female Delinquents," *Child Welfare,* 51 (1972), 93–101.

[30] G. D. Brown and U. D. Tyler, "Time Out from Reinforcement: A Technique for Dethroning the 'Duke' of an Institutionalized Delinquent Group," *Journal of Child Psychology and Psychiatry,* 9 (1968), 203–11.

[31] Robert Emery and David Marholin II, "An Applied Behavior Analysis of Delinquency," *American Psychologist,* (October 1977), pp. 860–873.

described in the previous chapter. Here we have another instance of novelty overriding established performance. Second, it helped convert the common sense of corrections officials about how offenders should be handled into "scientific treatments." It conveyed the idea that the use of punishment and other aversive techniques was acceptable; these could be justified as being rehabilitative. Third, it did not require these officials to venture alone into uncharted waters. On the contrary, there were many so-called experts (psychiatrists and psychologists) who supported behavior modification techniques. Finally, behavior modification was claimed to be an efficient, cheap, and quick treatment method. It was simple, easy to understand and teach, and easy to do. One did not need a lot of special training or special skills.

Ross and McKay also reviewed the published literature on behavior modification programs and were unimpressed and somewhat dismayed. "Unfortunately," they point out, "the label was applied to many programs which were exclusively punitive. The label was used at times as a euphemism for tyranny."[32] In some cases almost anything that was done to offenders was relabeled behavior modification.

Relative to my panacea phenomenon hypothesis, Ross and McKay conclude: "Perhaps too much was promised . . . we can conclude with confidence that behavior modification is not the panacea it was touted as when it was introduced to corrections."[33] Although they found some evidence of successful use of some techniques, their final words on the subject are: "We should never have promised panaceas."[34]

These conclusions do not offer us a very optimistic outlook for the results of a specific application or adaptation of a kind of aversive technique in which adult inmates try to modify juvenile behavior. Delinquent behavior results from a host of complex and deeply internalized psychological, social, and psychosocial causes. Altering or redirecting it by psychological shock therapy seems to run counter to much of what we know about human behavior. The track record for delinquency prevention programs negates the easy, simple approach.

---

[32] Robert Ross and Bryan McKay, "Behavioral Approaches to Treatment in Corrections: Requiem for a Panacea," *Canadian Journal of Criminology*, 20 (July 1978), 287.

[33] Ibid., p. 289.

[34] Ibid., p. 292.

chapter three

Inmate–Youth Aversion Programs

Because of the frustration resulting from failures to find other effective means to prevent juvenile delinquency, some seekers hit upon the idea of having adult prisoners confront juveniles in encounter-type sessions. One of the early programs of this type was conducted at the Norfolk Prison Colony in Massachusetts under the auspices of two psychiatrists—Ludwick Szymanski and Alice Fleming. In this program, eight delinquent boys aged fourteen to sixteen were counseled individually by three inmates. In their description of the program, Szymanski and Fleming suggest that its objective was to develop a motivation for change. The delinquent, they said, ". . . has to realize that his behavior, from which he derived gratification, will become a source of suffering for him."[1] The rationale for achieving this objective was as follows:

Rejection of delinquency coming surprisingly and unexpectedly from such a knowledgeable person (an inmate), further reinforced by the harsh impact of the prison setting, may constitute a powerful confrontation with reality. As a result, the delinquent may take a "second look" at himself, develop vestiges of self-observation, start

[1] Ludwick Szymanski and Alice Fleming, "Juvenile Delinquent and an Adult Prisoner—A Therapeutic Encounter?" *Journal of the American Academy of Child Psychiatry,* 10 (1971), 308–20.

45

seeing his behavior as not really gratifying after all, and ultimately may become accessible to help offered by the probation officer and the psychiatrist.[2]

Thus was developed a theme of shock and reality-confrontation to be followed, it was hoped, by greater receptivity to the available helping efforts in the community. The juvenile would be more willing to listen and perhaps heed advice and counsel than had been true before the prison experience.

Each boy in the Norfolk project had four or five counseling sessions over intervals of one to three weeks. In a follow-up more than a year later, it was found that three boys had been committed to training schools; one other boy had continued his delinquent activities, but was not committed. The four remaining boys had satisfactory behavior. The authors indicate that "no meaningful conclusions regarding therapeutic effect" could be reached from the project, but they did conclude that, ". . . those who benefited the most from the project were probably the prisoners." Each of these conclusions was to provide an apt description of the results from other similar projects.

The 1960s saw the development in more than twenty states of inmate groups formed to speak to religious, educational, and youth groups on crime and corrections.[3] The speeches were given both inside and outside the prison walls. The procedures followed in these programs were all similar. The inmates usually told stories about their early years and illustrated their escalating involvement from minor offenses to major offenses. The presentations were generally given in a sincere but emotional manner that was intended to produce maximum effect on the youthful audiences. One of the usual goals of these programs was to change the attitudes and behavior of participating juveniles.

This chapter presents a detailed description of a sample of these early programs. For only two, Illinois and Michigan, was there extensive evaluative information. For the rest, evaluation, if there was any, typically consisted of collecting informal remarks and letters. These came from participants, from relatives or friends of participants, from schools, etc.

A typical example is the Colorado State Penitentiary Inmate Teen Program that was described in 1967 as follows:

> The teen teams consist of a group of about thirty inmates. The program involved about forty-seven inmates altogether. There are

[2] Ibid., p. 318.

[3] Stanley L. Brodsky, "The Prisoner as Agent of Attitude Change: A Study of Prison Profiles' Effects," *The British Journal of Criminology,* 10 (July 1970), 280–85.

inside programs conducted by twelve members and programs conducted in various communities by eighteen team members. There are usually four inmates in outside presentations and two to four in inside presentations. The theme of all team programs is Don't Follow Me! The inmates involved give an account of their life, each lasting for twelve to fifteen minutes. There is a question and answer period following presentations. The backgrounds of the team program members range from minor check offenses through narcotics offenders to murderers. Short-termers and lifers are involved, as well as a wide variety of age groups.

The men begin with stories about their early years and show the sequential relationship of minor offenses through major offenses that often become chronic. The presentations are done with a sincere emotional delivery that brings maximum effectiveness. Squirming youngsters become still as mice. Tears often flow in compassion and very likely in guilt also. A question and answer period often follows, and the sophistication of the questions often astound inmate staff and teachers alike.[4]

Stanley Brodsky reported on the letters received by the Colorado program. He said that the program was overwhelmingly rated excellent and was considered to be a deterrent to crime and delinquency. However, he noted that these letters represented less than 1 percent of the estimated audience of the nearly 250,000 which had participated between April, 1966 and March, 1967.

California's San Quentin State Prison inmates organized a program called SQUIRES (San Quentin Utilization of Inmate Resources Experience and Studies) in 1965. This program which depends upon individual counseling and emotionally frank group rap sessions, has been continuously active since then. The sessions are attended by teenagers, convicts, parents and others—inside the prison walls.

SQUIRES is open to boys from a variety of referring agencies. Each group of twenty to twenty-five boys attends three hour sessions on three successive Saturday mornings. Each session involves a rap group which may include a variety of techniques to get the boys involved. One SQUIRE is assigned to each boy and may give some individual attention to the boy in addition to the group involvement. The rap sessions are confrontational, the language is rough, the tours and sharing of life inside the facility are realistically harsh, but there are no scare tactics per se. Until very recently there was little information available on the program's success or lack of it. The results of a recent evaluation of the SQUIRES program will be presented and discussed in a later chapter.

---

[4] Colorado Department of Corrections, "Colorado State Penitentiary Inmate Teen Programme: Don't Follow Me" (1967).

What follows are descriptions and some evaluations of representative programs in Texas, Tennessee, Illinois, and Michigan. Each of these began in the 1960s.

TEXAS—OPERATION TEEN-AGER

The following description of a youth aversion program in Texas makes a number of important points related to the discussion in the previous chapter. First, Johnson suggests that the effect varies with the psychological qualities which the particular adolescent listener brings to the program. Some juveniles may be more conditionable or psychologically receptive to the message conveyed by the inmates. Next, the program seems to lack the reinforcement which is the foundation of conditioning and behavior modification. It is a one-shot, shock treatment which lacks follow-up. In this sense it differs from programs such as Alcoholics Anonymous which depend upon fellowship and continued social interaction for their effect. Finally, the motives for attendance may be insufficiently driving to achieve lasting changes, even though attendance is voluntary.

DOES OPERATION TEEN-AGER HAVE A PLACE IN CORRECTIONS?

Elmer H. Johnson

Several prison systems have experimented with the appearance of inmate-speakers before groups of teen-agers to employ their own life histories as an example to deter others from a life of crime. Luke (16: 27–28) has been quoted as a justification:

> Father, I beseech you to send him to my father's house, for I have five brothers, so that he may give testimony and warn them, lest they too come to this place of torment.

One booklet explains the genesis of Operation Teen-ager in the words of the inmates:

> Operation Teen-ager had its beginning in the consciences of four inmates of the Texas Department of Corrections who came to the conclusion that serving a sentence does not repay a

thing. Surveying our only possession—a dark past—we come to the conclusion that the only original contribution that we could make would be to steer others away from the errors that we have made. As we talked over the genesis of our criminal behavior, an obvious fact emerged: In every case, a decisive turn was taken during the teen-age years, a turn that eventually brought us to the point of extreme crime and imprisonment. Thus, we say that if we were qualified to help anyone, it was the young people, and that only by being scrupulously honest.

Although the approach need not be evaluated solely in terms of treatment purposes, it qualified as one of the repressive-inspirational forms of therapy whereby auditory stimuli (one's own spoken words, in this case) are supposed to suppress anti-social thoughts and to bring inspiration for approved behavior. There are rough similarities to Alcoholics Anonymous, Dale Carnegie courses, and some religious discussion groups.

Similarities to Alcoholics Anonymous include heavy reliance on religious testimony before a group to reinforce the assumed decision of the treatment subject to mend his ways, freedom granted the speaker to select and present materials drawn from his own life, absence of audience participation during the oral presentation, creation of a social psychological environment emotionally supportive of the speaker's evaluation of himself, the rewarding through the speaker role of any exhibitionist tendencies, the lack of formal structuring of the inmate-speaker's role in the audience situation, and talking out of emotional problems in public. Operation Teen-ager differs from Alcoholics Anonymous in that it lacks a subculture, binding audience and speaker together through the common experience of past social deviance. The lack of experiences similar to those of the speaker does not qualify audience members to engage in the debunking process of Alcoholics Anonymous serving as a check against obvious discrepancy between the speaker's rationalizations and the recurrent situations of deviant careers. Because the fellowship and continued social interaction of Alcoholics Anonymous is not present, Operation Teen-ager lacks the core advantages of Alcoholics Anonymous as a therapeutic tool. . . .

The prisoners' speeches typically have themes suggestive of testimony at Alcoholics Anonymous meetings: innocence and purity of the speaker's youth; tale of earlier high accomplishments in business, school, church, family, and other major spheres of life; a drastic fall from this claimed eminence into depths of misery and failure; enthusiastic recounting of the speaker's transgressions against kindly parents, perfect wife, and ideal children, description of cleverness, audacity, capacity for liquor, and success with wild women while eluding detection when the deviant career was in full swing, and the listing of heavy costs in status degradation exacted against loved ones because of their association with the speaker.

Because these themes are applied to lives of crime, the inmate speeches differ from most Alcoholics Anonymous presentations in that greater reliance is placed on descriptions of the unhappy plight of the prisoner: Lonely in forced isolation from loved ones, suffering the physical and psychological privations in a hell of confinement, and forgotten by the outside world. Earlier accomplishments are described in two general classifications. First, early youth frequently is associated with loving parents, high grades in school, constant attendance of Sunday school, and other evidences of social conformity. Second, exploits during the flood tide of the criminal career are described in terms of audacity, skillful evasion of the authorities, clever and bold perpetration of offenses, and courageous reaction against aggression by others. Boasts of earlier exploits are rationalized as indications of the great distance the inmate has fallen to reach his present lowly status. Typically, the inmate will describe current accomplishments in the areas of formal schooling acquired, artistic talents demonstrated, religious good works conducted, and other activities in prison. These accomplishments are supposed to be evidence of his current resolve to lead a good life. However, he says, his current purity has come too late to save him from his present unhappy state.

The major difference from Alcoholics Anonymous presentations is the quality of the audience to which the inmate addresses himself. The Alcoholics Anonymous speaker usually aims his message to fellow alcohol-addicts who have had experiences similar to his own and, as indicated earlier, are qualified to interpret the contents of the message. Alcoholics Anonymous groups tend to be drawn largely from the middle ages and from white collar and professional occupations, whereas Operation Teen-ager is directed toward a group selected according to a younger and more restricted range of ages and by the willingness of some persons to invite the inmate speakers. The invitation is more likely to come from an older group than from the teen-agers themselves. It is probable that the attendance of the teen-agers indicates their interest in the speech, but we cannot be certain because parents may have directed them to attend. Even if their attendance is strictly voluntary, we cannot be certain that the teen-agers' motives for attendance are consistent with a serious interest in learning about matters to be discussed.

The purposes of Operation Teen-ager could be: crime prevention through effect on the audience; therapy for the inmate-speaker; advancement of the inmate's immediate self interests as he sees them; improved public image of prisoners in general; increased public support of prisons as agencies of rehabilitation, and a tool for over-all correctional reform.

The opening paragraphs of this article indicate that crime prevention is the fundamental purpose. Then the target is the audience, rather than the inmate-speaker. What right do the inmates have to appear as experts? They claim the experiences of perpetrating crimes and having undergone the process of becoming criminals qualify them to explore crime causation. As living examples of the results of a criminal life, their physical presence is supposed to deter youngsters from following the same route. An unstated assumption is that teen-agers are in a state of revolt against parents and other adult authorities, accompanied by feelings obscurely defined as inferiority and persecution complexes. Listeners are warned against attitudes of "you can't tell me anything, because I know it all." But, since the teen-agers are supposed to be unwilling to listen to most adults, one wonders why they would listen to the inmates. The answer offered is that the prisoners have had experience in crime and will be accepted as more qualified than parents who lack such direct experience.

The fundamental premise is that fear of punishment is the supreme means of deterring anti-social behavior. In effect, the speakers are defending the punitive ideology which has placed them in prison. They are saying that, since punishment has been beneficial in erasing their criminality, it will be equally effective in keeping non-criminal youths from such behavior. The speech becomes a one-shot form of shock treatment in which the horrible fate of the criminal is brought sharply to the attention of youth. The message is deemed pertinent to every listener because it is assumed that every person is a candidate for prison regardless of social class status and personality conditioning.

Critics of the approach could offer several arguments that the listener is likely to be affected adversely. Criminals may be presented as heroes, victims of persecution, and creatures of their environment, therefore freed of responsibility for their misconduct. The system of criminal justice and correction may be pictured as bungling, cruel, and even corrupt. A spirit of bravado, deceit, and over emphasis on material values may be presented. A false sense of sophistication may be communicated through depicting of unconventional behavior and use of alcohol. Stories of past crimes may suggest to young listeners the possibility of committing certain classes of crime as well as offering instruction on how to commit them. Perpetration of crime may appear to be a normal form of behavior. Because stories are selected for their sensationalism, the listener is encouraged to be a thrill-seeker, rather than evaluating the rational and long-range implications of the events described.

Defenders of the approach may offer counterarguments. The stories may release aggressions among the listeners, thereby serving as lightning rods to discharge dangerous emotions before they stimulate overt anti-social behavior and concurrently suggesting to the listener that he channel such aggressive feelings into more approved behavior. By stimulating the listener's interest, the adolescent may be motivated to examine consequences of crime in a rational manner if he has tendencies toward crime. If he has no such tendencies, the stories will offer him reassurance concerning the effectiveness of our system of justice because the speaker before him attests to the accuracy of the belief that the criminal pays for his crimes. By calling attention to the existence of a crime problem through the physical presence of a convicted offender, the concern of the listener for the problem would be aroused. Defenders might argue that violence and misconduct are part of the everyday world, and that shielding adolescents against the material offered by inmate-speakers would be unrealistic in light of the fare found in the major forms of mass communication.

Probably, the most valid assessment would be to say that the effect on audiences varies with the psychological qualities of the particular listener. Paul G. Cressy has pointed out that the net effect of television, comic books, and other forms of mass communications varies with the social background and personality of the audience member which affect his selection of what he perceives and remembers. The adolescent brings to the audience situation his own set of attitudes which have been determined by a host of factors related to his personality development. The speech is not likely to have major adverse effects if the adolescent has a secure and well-adjusted personality consistent with his effective performance of approved roles. On the other hand, if the adolescent has high potentiality for future crime, the effect of the speech is not likely to be simple and direct. If he lacks insight to equate his present behavior with future consequences, it is unreasonable to assume that a single speech, no matter how dramatic, will bring a drastic revision of perspective. Such revision would require concurrent experiences through factors not subject to the control of Operation Teen-ager.

The approach suffers from the weaknesses of the punitive reaction to crime. In predicting the evaluation of the offender of his punishment situation, the non-criminal advocate of stern punishment is imputing a certain state of mind to the offender which is meaningful only if the offender also has the non-offender's own traits, value system, and definition of the punishment situation. The danger of error lies in the difference between the offender and non-offender in terms of previous personality condition within a particular socioeconomic environment, and in terms of the non-offender's lack of experience in being subjected to the process of criminal justice. Operation Teen-ager reverses roles by expecting the prisoner to impute the motives of non-offenders who have not under-gone his experiences, and age differences may block understanding. An additional weakness is the lack of follow-up in that a one-shot, shock treatment in the unusual social context of coming face-to-face with a prisoner is supposed to achieve a lasting change in attitudes of adolescent non-offenders.[5]

TENNESSEE—OPERATION CRIME PREVENTION

The assessment of Operation Crime Prevention which follows discloses that it was modeled after the Texas program just described. The program's primary aim was "to discourage young people from forming habits which could lead to a life of crime." In a 1965 newsletter from the Tennessee Department of Correction, the then commissioner was reported as saying that results of a program such as Operation Crime Prevention cannot be determined immediately. He said, however, that judging from letters received from school authorities and others he believed the program had merit and that it could deter juvenile crime. Some six months later, he was much less reticent. Again discussing this program in the newsletter, the commissioner said, "For the first time in many years, the percentage of increase in the crime rate has been greatly reduced in Tennessee." In what will seem like a touch of déjà vu, the Tennessee program received national recognition through a film entitled, "I Traded My Freedom." The commissioner explained: "This film is to be used as a pilot program in certain areas of the State of Maryland (the film was said to be cosponsored by Maryland and the U.S. Department of Justice) to discourage crime by youthful offenders. It is in color and sound; it carries a panoramic picture of the City of Nashville and our Main Prison gate, within the 'Walls' of the Main Prison: The inmates who make up our Operation Crime Prevention tell their story. They did a real good job. This has been a wonderful program. It truly has now gained a favorable National reputation."

OPERATION CRIME PREVENTION—STATE OF TENNESSEE

Operation Crime Prevention consists of a group of four inmates who travel about the state, under the supervision of prison guards, telling stories to youth groups of their involvement in

[5] Elmer H. Johnson, "Does Operation Teen-Ager Have A Place in Corrections," *Police*, 11 (September–October 1966), 18–20.

crime, under the untested hypothesis that the program will encourage the young people in the audience to avoid mistakes in life which might lead to criminal involvement.

The inmates' speeches are "canned" presentations, geared to the junior-senior high school level. Though the inmates originally wrote their talks, considerable "polishing" was done by the program's director, who edited them for youthful audiences. One inmate's speech is tape-recorded; the balance are presented orally, presumably by rote.

The inmate team accepts invitations to speak to high school groups throughout Tennessee, fulfilling speaking engagements during most of the academic year. No shortage of invitations has occurred, and the program seems to be popular with school administrators, teachers, and students alike. Favorable letters of endorsement have been received at the prison from several chiefs of police.

In Tennessee, there is little opposition to the program, as it is presently conducted. In fact, Operation Crime Prevention was unanimously accepted by the various administrators interviewed. There has been no determination, however, as to what effects, if any, are generated by the efforts of the inmate speakers. One administrator did indicate that he would rather spend money toward securing a research staff than on Operation Crime Prevention; however, he did not oppose the program. Several volunteered "vague" feelings that the program was enjoying success, and one administrator asserted that the emotional impact upon the audience (in that several persons usually cry during the presentations) demonstrated that the program was effective. He also indicated that the commissioner of corrections, as well as the governor of Tennessee, cried the first time they heard the inmates' speeches, and this result apparently was accepted as a satisfactory criterion of the effectiveness of the program.

Some information, from case histories and from arrest statistics, is cited in support of the program. Several individual cases were noted in which the inmate teams were credited with helping pupils make better adjustments in school. It also was suggested that the program is responsible for a drop in the 1965 crime rate—when compared with the year 1964—for offenses reported by the Federal Bureau of Investigation in areas affecting juveniles. Information for a serious assessment of the relationship, if any, between the program and a decrease of increase in juvenile crime rates is lacking.

Origin. In 1964, the Tennessee Commissioner of Corrections received a news clipping from his sister in Texas; the clipping described "Operation Teen-ager," a Texas prison program designed to send inmates to high schools to tell their stories of involvement in crime, thus urging young people to avoid activities which might eventually land them in prison. The sister suggested that the program might hold considerable potential for the state of Tennessee. Some time later, the commissioner attended the Southern Prison Association Convention held in Texas, where he heard a presentation by an inmate team from "Operation Teen-ager."

Impressed by this program, the commissioner sent the then director of Prison Services in Tennessee to Texas in order to assess the program's popularity and to adapt it to the Tennessee prison system. When he returned to Tennessee, he presented a glowing report of "Operation Teen-ager," stressing the program's popularity with Texas citizens. Thereupon, the commissioner authorized the Tennessee program, instructing the director of Prison Services to begin to select and train inmates for inclusion.

The first five inmates were selected by the director upon his interpretation of how well they could relate to the program. Generally, the men selected were "model" prisoners who were respected by both guards and inmates. No explicit promises of parole benefits were extended to the team members.

Each inmate, upon being interviewed, expressed satisfaction with his role in the program and a feeling of accomplishment with the work. They were pleased to be able to travel throughout the state, eat in restaurants, attend "good" churches, and sleep in clean jails. In general, inmates reported that the program benefits them by making their lives socially meaningful and by breaking the monotony of prison life.

The inmates wrote their own speeches, which were screened for content and length by the director. The field investigator noted a certain continuity among the speeches, perhaps due to the director's personal interpretation as to the causative factors of crime. All inmates trace the origins of their convictions back to childhood activities. In interviews, the director repeatedly stated his thesis that childhood wrongdoings are responsible for adult criminal involvements.

When the inmates were trained and ready, the commissioner contacted the governor and arranged to have him listen to the prepared speeches. The governor, apparently suitably impressed, arranged to have the inmates speak before a special joint session of the state legislature. Following this presentation, the legislature voted unanimously to authorize the Tennessee Department of Corrections to accept invitations to speak in schools throughout the state. The legislature also wanted to authorize funding, but the Department of Corrections already had diverted funds to provide for the program.

In this sequence of events, it is perhaps noteworthy that responsibility for the program was shifted from the Department of Corrections to the governor, to the "people," thus removing the program from "political significance."

Officially the program began in March, 1965, at the Metro Auditorium in Knoxville, Tennessee, when 20,000 young people heard the presentations of Operation Crime Prevention. In its two and one-half years of operation, over 400,000 youths have attended other presentations. The program also has enjoyed nationwide news coverage in many newspapers, national magazines, and on three major television stations. The United States Department of Health, Education, and Welfare has completed a film of the inmate team in action, making it available to schools throughout the Nation.

It would appear that the future of the Tennessee program seems assured. Today, the director of the program is working to structure a female equivalent of Operation Crime Prevention, thus hoping to provide the state with a national "first" when inmates of the women's prison begin speaking at the schools.[6]

ILLINOIS—PRISON PROFILES

Stanley Brodsky sought to evaluate the effectiveness of Illinois' Prison Profiles in changing the attitudes of young people toward the punishment of criminals and toward prisons. He studied attitude changes in high school predelinquents and forestry camp boys, among others, who had participated in the Illinois State Penitentiary program. Brodsky found that there was a slight, but insignificant change toward less punitive attitudes in before and after testing among the groups. His conclusion was that the likely target groups were not strongly influenced.

THE PRISONER AS AGENT OF ATTITUDE CHANGE: A STUDY OF PRISON PROFILES' EFFECTS

Stanley L. Brodsky

The purpose of the present study was to investigate one of the often-cited goals of the prisoner-speakers programmes. It sought to investigate if youth attitudes toward the punishment of criminals

---

[6] Leslie T. Wilkins and Don M. Gottfredson, *Research, Demonstration and Social Action,* U.S. Department of Health, Education and Welfare, Office of Juvenile Delinquency and Youth Development (March 1969), pp. 64–68.

and attitudes toward prisons were modified as a result of being exposed to the programmes.

The eighty-five subjects consisted of eighteen male students and fourteen female students from Southern Illinois University, sociology and criminology classes, nine male and eighteen female students from a criminology class at Principia College in Elsah, Illinois, eleven delinquent boys who were residing in a state forestry camp and fifteen pre-delinquents identified as problem teen-agers in Carbondale Community High School. All of the subjects were taking part in a tour of the Illinois State Penitentiary at Menard, Illinois, a maximum security institution. As part of the tour, they listened to the "Prison Profiles" speakers.

Questionnaires used were the Attitude Toward the Punishment of Criminals, and Attitudes Toward any Institution scale. The Attitude Toward the Punishment of Criminals scale (Wang and Thurstone, 1931) is a thirty-four-item scale in which the subjects check items with which they agree and place crosses next to items with which they disagree. The score is the median of the scale values with which the subject agrees. . . .

The Attitude Toward any Institution scale developed by Kelley (1934) is a forty-five-item scale with two equivalent forms. The subjects place checks next to items with which they agree. . . .

The "Prison Profiles" programmes followed the general format described in the Colorado Inmate Teen Programme. The same four to five prisoners served on each panel. Initially each prisoner reported his offence, the reason for it and personal information such as age and likes and dislikes. Then a discussion of the unpleasantness of being a prisoner followed, with frequent explicit references to violence, fear and sex within the prison. Finally, the prisoner individually met with small groups from the audience to answer questions. A good rapport was developed between the panel and the audience in all of the groups used in the present study.

Both tests were administered to the subjects prior to the beginning of the "Prison Profiles" programme and a second time, immediately following the programme. The administration took place in a large auditorium in which the programme was conducted. Four of the delinquents and pre-delinquents were unable to read at a sufficient level to comprehend the items. Their questionnaires were discarded and are not included in the subjects reported. . . .

A general effect of the "Prison Profiles" was that the audience did demonstrate attitude changes. The listeners tended to become less punitive toward prisoners and more punitive or negative toward prisons. The first finding may suggest that they saw that prisoners were likeable and human, unlike the popular stereotypes of offenders as hostile and unpleasant creatures. The increased negative attitudes toward prisons, which were significant in the case of one college group and not in the other, indicate the possibility that the meaning of imprisonment and prisons became more real to the subjects observing and listening. Bars, lack of freedom and personal restrictions became actual events rather than abstract concepts.

There was more impact on the college students and especially the Principia students than on the delinquents and pre-delinquents. This is of some interest since the pre-delinquents and delinquents are likely target groups for changing attitudes and, hopefully, behavior. The results indicate that they were not strongly influenced. *

The observation that the Principia students' attitudes showed the major significant changes . . . merits some comment. The Principia College student body draws on a much more narrow and limited religious, economic, and social grouping than Southern Illinois University. Southern Illinois University is a major state institution of over 20,000 students from rural and urban areas. It draws on a large variety of the population which presumably may be more involved and exposed to criminals and prison issues. Thus the Principia students may have learned "the way it is" and modified their attitudes in that direction, while the state university students simply had their attitudes confirmed.

There are a number of other possible explanations for the changes found in the Principia students, including the low significance rate among the twelve t tests and the selected nature of the students. [t tests are statistical tests of the differences between two means derived from some measure.] This finding should therefore be viewed as interesting but tentative.

The study did not test the issue of prison profiles as a deterrent to criminal behaviour. An appropriate testing of this issue would require the use of experimental groups exposed to the prison profiles and control groups, as well as follow-ups and establishment of criteria of criminality. For the present study only a small sample of behaviour, namely attitudes, was studied, and this under some relatively limited conditions. There were other factors present, such as being in the prison itself, being part of a tour and, in the case of the students, being part of a class. It is suggested that the present study represents a first step towards qualifying the effects of this widely spreading phenomenon of prisoner-speaking groups. Considerably more research is needed to

*Italics mine.

understand behavioural as well as attitudinal change in different audiences and in varying kinds of presentations.[7]

MICHIGAN

The evaluation of the Ionia Reformatory program that is described below, was the only fairly rigorous study of programs of this type, using further delinquency as the criterion for success. The report is not detailed, nor is it very explanatory, but the findings from this study were unexpectedly dramatic in that they indicated that the program might have been detrimental and actually contributed to further delinquent behavior. This finding can and should be viewed from the perspective of the earlier discussion about boomerang effects resulting from the use of threats or other scare tactics. In this case the issue of a "delinquency fulfilling prophecy" arises for the first time with regard to inmate-youth aversion programs.

A SIX MONTH FOLLOW-UP OF JUVENILE DELINQUENTS VISITING THE IONIA REFORMATORY

Michigan Department of Corrections
Research Report #4, May 22, 1967

In the fall of 1966 a program involving visits of juvenile delinquents to the Ionia Reformatory was resumed and is presently under way. This program, sponsored by the Juvenile Division of the Ingham County Probate Court, and by the Kiwanis Club, with the cooperation of the Michigan Department of Corrections, is intended as an experiment in the prevention of delinquency. This report is a six-month follow-up on individuals making the first two visits in the present series, and is intended to indicate the possible effect of the visits on further delinquency.

The manner in which visits to the prison setting might operate to prevent further delinquency was not pre-defined. The prior question, and the one being considered here, is whether they

---

[7] Brodsky, *The British Journal of Criminology*, 10.

do so operate at all. There has been some feeling on the part of those working with the juveniles concerned that there was a positive effect. It was felt, for example, that the experience of the visit operated as a catalyst to later counseling. The possibility also existed that the confrontation with the ultimate consequences of delinquency could have a more directly deterrent or reformative effect. But the ultimate aim in either case was that of reformation, and the question as to whether this might be accomplished by the program directly, or indirectly through counseling, is secondary to the question which asks whether the hoped for reformation does in fact tend to occur. An affirmative answer to that question would call for further analysis of the dynamics of the process; a negative answer would make such an analysis irrelevant.

The most appropriate method for measuring the effects of an experimental program is the experimental control group design. The most rigorous form of this design, and the one used here, is that in which two groups are selected by random techniques from a single population; one group is then subjected to the program and the other not, and the subsequent results for each group are then measured. In the present case, this was done as follows:

Each visit to the reformatory includes 15 boys; visits occur each six weeks. It was determined that enough boys were available so that for the first two visits the boys making the trip could be matched with boys not making it. This provided, for both visits combined, an experimental group of 30, and a control group of the same size. The court staff furnished the researcher with 60 names, and random number tables were used to select the 30 who would go on the visits. (Two of these did not go, finally, reducing the experimental group to 28.) Six months (182 days) later the court records for both groups were checked at the Juvenile Home to see what further difficulties may have been recorded for each boy during that period. The investigator making this examination was furnished with an alphabetical list of all 58 boys that did not indicate which group each belonged to.

The hypothesis being examined was that those who had made the visits would have been involved in fewer further delinquent acts than those who had not made the visits. "Delinquent acts" were defined to include all cases in which a petition for rehearing had been filed following further difficulties with the law, or in which the probation officer had issued a citation for probation violation.

The commission of further delinquent acts by members of the experimental and control groups within 182 days following the visits is shown in the following table.

The difference between the two groups with respect to further delinquency is statistically significant at better than the .10 level,

Group	Total Number	Involved in Further Delinquency		Not Involved in Further Delinquency	
		N	%	N	%
Experimental Group (visit)	28	12	43	26	57
Control Group (no visit)	30	5	17	25	83
Total	58	17	29	41	71

but in the direction opposite that hypothesized. [.10 level means the finding could have occurred by chance alone only one time out of ten.] The percentage of those committing delinquent acts was about 2 times higher for those who had made the visit than for those who had not.

The efficacy of visits to the reformatory in preventing further delinquency is, to say the least, questionable. A level of significance of .10 is not enough to allow any firm conclusion to the effect that the visits are actually contributing to further delinquency, but this is at least suggested, and the contention that the program is helpful is entirely without support. The recommendation of the researcher is that the program either be abandoned or a second follow-up be made on a new group to see if this finding will be reversed. The "chances are," quite literally, nine in ten, from this data, that the program is detrimental.[8]

AN UPDATE

It is important to remember that each of the above projects was started in the 1960s. Recently corrections officials in these four states were contacted in an attempt to determine the current status of these projects. The Texas program, "Operation Teen-ager," ran out of funds and was discontinued. However, in May of 1970 "Operation Kick-It" was established through the Texas Governor's Criminal Justice Council. In addition to a new title, it has a revamped format. The old Operation Teen-ager was aimed strictly at crime prevention, and the speeches were given by older inmates. Kick-It is aimed at both drug and crime preven-

[8] Michigan Department of Corrections Research Report #4 (May 22, 1967).

tion, and the speakers are younger inmates who are believed to be better able to relate to juveniles.

A Texas Department of Corrections brochure describes the current program as follows:

> A panel of three to five inmates was formed to travel throughout Texas to tell their life stories in an effort to educate, warn, and inform the public, specifically teen-agers, about the dangers and consequences involved in the illicit use of drugs. In 1971, a second panel was formed in order to meet the demand of bookings, so great was the public acceptance of this program. The format was further expanded in 1975, and the program's name was changed to the Community Education Program. . . .
>
> Primarily, the panels appear before junior and senior high school assemblages, but they also speak to church groups, civic organizations, drug abuse workshops, juvenile institutions, and halfway house residents. Additionally, the panels are regularly interviewed by the news media wherever they travel, and they have appeared on numerous TV shows.
>
> The program format, originally designed as a formal assembly presentation, has been expanded to include small group or "rap" sessions. . . .
>
> . . . Measurement of success among the young people of Texas is . . . difficult. However, educators and school administrators throughout the State have viewed the program as a success.[9]

Tennessee's "Operation Crime Prevention" is no longer in existence. The corrections commissioner who started the program acclaimed its success, and tried to keep it going. When a new commissioner took office in 1971, he ended the program. It is alleged, but without documentation, that the project had some problems with inmates trying to escape when they went out to speak. Because the project was deemed a failure, the film "I Traded My Freedom" is no longer in circulation and is presently in the Tennessee archives.

"Prison Profiles" in Illinois was ended in the early 1970s. Although corrections officials say there was no "scientific" basis for the termination of the program, they did cite a few incidents of shoplifting among the kids brought to the prison. It seems that either on their way to a session or on their way back, some kids did some shoplifting in a local candy store. When a new warden came in, he ended the program.

[9] Texas Department of Corrections, "Community Education Program: Operation Kick-It" (May 1970).

Finally, the Michigan project was suspended after the results of the evaluation study reported earlier became known. It too is no longer in existence.

The pre–1976 history of inmate-youth aversion programs of the scared straight genre did not provide very fertile ground in which this concept could be tested anew. There was either no information, only testimonial-type information of questionable validity in the form of cards and letters, information that the program did not work (Illinois), or information that the kids actually got worse (Michigan).

We may wonder how much of this was known to the inmates and their supporters when they started the Juvenile Awareness Project at New Jersey's Rahway State Prison in September, 1976. There is some evidence that they were unaware of this dismal record. An article about the Rahway project in July, 1977 called it, ". . . the first time that young people were ever allowed in a maximum security prison in the United States."[10] A later article in Corrections Magazine (December, 1977) said the Lifers' Group Juvenile Awareness Project ". . . is probably the first of it's kind."[11] We now know that neither of these assertions is correct.

---

[10] James P. Murphy, "Youth and the Criminal Justice System," *Police Chief,* 44 (September–October 1977), 28.

[11] Kevin Krajick, "Lifers Try to Scare the Crime Out of Juveniles," *Corrections Magazine,* 3 (December 1977), 18.

part two

The Prelude

chapter four

The Juvenile Awareness Project

In December, 1975, a small group of inmates serving sentences of twenty-five years or more in New Jersey's Rahway State Prison formed what they called the Lifers' Group. The Lifers' Group was created in part to counteract what these inmates saw as a stereotyped, Hollywood-type image of prisons and convicts held by the general public. This image, they felt,stigmatized convicts as immoral and inhuman. In order to dispel what they saw as a false image, the Lifers wanted to try to prove that they could be useful and worthwhile people even though locked up in a maximum-security prison. One of their early activities in pursuit of this objective was to obtain, repair, and gift wrap Christmas toys for needy children.

Among a number of committees formed among the Lifers was one called the Juvenile Intervention Committee. This particular committee was largely the brainchild of the then president of the Lifers, Richard Rowe. Rowe was serving a double-life term for rape, kidnapping, and armed robbery. He was personally motivated to try to do something for kids over concern for his own then twelve-year-old son who was getting into trouble on the outside. Rowe said: "We were looking for something we could do to keep kids out of trouble, and I thought: . . . bring them in and let them find out what a life of crime is all about, straight from us. A lot of us have kids of our own, and we were worried what was going to happen to them."[1]

The idea of having young delinquents or potential delinquents visit the prison can also be traced to the observation of groups of college students on prison tours. The Lifers thought that if this could be done with college students, it could also be done with younger groups of juveniles. This belief becomes very important because it represents a subtle, but significant shift in what would be the purpose of the prison visits. The college tours were intended to be little more than educational. The ultimate purpose of the juvenile visits, on the other hand, was to be something very different. The purpose, as it turns out, was much more complex and difficult—namely to deter or scare delinquency out of the kids.

This shift from an educational, consciousness-raising type of endeavor to an endeavor aimed at changing attitudes and behavior was an enormous leap into an arena which had witnessed almost nothing but failures, as the earlier discussion has illustrated. In addition, deterring juveniles could be measured; its success could be tabulated; and, the measuring rod used could become the petard upon which the Juvenile Awareness Project might be hoisted.

The Lifers quickly developed their plan for bringing youngsters into Rahway so that these young people could hear about life there from those who knew it best—the convicts who were forced to live it. There were two important steps which had to be taken before the plan could be implemented, however. Because the Lifers are convicts, they are by definition unable to proceed with any activity in an independent fashion. They could not, on their own, simply bring kids into the prison. First, the then superintendent of the prison, Robert S. Hatrak, had to agree to permit youngsters to tour the prison and meet with the Lifers. Second, some official or agency had to be willing to bring the kids to Rahway.

Rowe's wife communicated the plan to a local police chief and a juvenile court judge. The judge, George Nicola, was receptive because he had become a firm believer in deterrence, in what he called "the need for youth to understand and appreciate the nonrewards of juvenile delinquency." Judge Nicola had indicated his support for approaches to controlling juvenile crime that use "shock experiences" to convince youngsters that "crime doesn't pay."[2] Together these officials, impressed with the possibilities, convinced Hatrak to open the door. Hatrak said yes, but he also said, "It was risky, to bring in kids with murderers and

[1] Kevin Krajick, "To Scare the Crime Out of Juveniles," *Corrections Magazine* (December 1977), p. 22.

[2] *Youth Forum*, 1 (June 1977), 3.

robbers. If something had ever happened to one of those kids, it would have been all over, not only for the Lifers, but for a lot of other things here as well."[3]

THE BEGINNING

In September, 1976, the first group of youngsters entered the prison. On September 7, 1976, the very first piece of publicity about the program appeared in a New Jersey newspaper, the *Hackensack Record*. Entitled, "Rahway Lifers Give Juveniles the Unvarnished Facts—Youths Get Lowdown on Jail," the article stated that, "The juveniles are the first under-18's to be allowed into a maximum security prison in the United States." Of course, we now know that this statement was not true. The article was cautious, but generally favorable to the idea.

In the beginning, the plan called for admitting only one group a week. But by January, 1977, the idea had become so popular that the number of visits was increased to two a day, five days a week. Police departments and other youth-serving agencies in New Jersey and elsewhere began clamoring to bring their kids to Rahway in order to get the "cure." Rowe's son was among the first to attend.

At first, the Juvenile Awareness Project was relatively low key. The stress is on the word relatively. The youngsters came into the prison, were briefed by a guard, passed through a metal detector, and then entered the interior of the prison where visitors were seldom permitted. There some of the Lifers at first "rapped" with them as a group or on a one-to-one basis. These rap sessions employed harsh language to discuss prison violence, including assault and murder, homosexual rape, suicide as a fact of prison life, inedible food, the impersonal atmosphere in which there is no unity among inmates, and the need to live "by the bells." The youngsters would ask questions and engage in discussion with the inmates. Finally, there was a brief tour and an opportunity to view the "Hole" or solitary confinement, where, the youngsters were told, inmates might be sent for such things as violating prison rules.

Over a period of time, the Lifers' approach evolved into a form of shock therapy rather than a form of counseling. This occurred because the inmates felt that with the low key, big brother approach, they were not really reaching many kids in the most effective way. There was no overt attempt to intimidate or terrorize the youngsters at first, but this later became a more prominent and dramatic feature of the project. Again, this proves to be a critically important turn of events. Not only were the Lifers

[3] Krajick, *Corrections Magazine*, p. 22.

going to attempt to alter the attitudes and behavior of the juveniles, but they were going to try to do it in a very special and spectacular way—by scaring them straight.

This shock-confrontation treatment was intended to enlighten youth about the effects of involvement in crime. It was authoritarian in style and was supposed to represent the most negative aspects of prison life. Thus, the basic idea guiding the project became the effort to deter juveniles from committing criminal offenses by means of an aversive-type of behavior modification technique. This technique was later approved and sanctioned by the Department of Corrections which said the purpose of the program was, "to deter juvenile delinquency and subsequent criminal behavior." The Lifers describe their project as follows:

> We are showing these young people that the stories about the big house (adult prison) being the places of bad men is in all reality the places of sad men. We are using ourselves as examples to prove the fact of what crime and its involvement is really all about.
>
> We are far from being experts on life and its problems, but we do feel that our prison experiences put in the proper perspective just might turn a young person away from crime and the following in our poor footsteps. In using ourselves as examples we are showing and explaining to them what a life of crime is really all about. This is our main objective. We are explaining to these young people that we who have been through these difficulties and are paying for our misdeeds are both willing to help and are able to understand their problems.
>
> Through our own experiences we feel that these young people might be apt to heed our advice where they might not listen to a parent or someone in authority. We can and do expound freely on this, and we are able to relate to their problems having lived them ourselves. Over fifty percent of our membership has been involved in a juvenile offense or has spent time in a juvenile prison. We are trying to destroy the peer relationship of offenders and non-offenders.
>
> The young people are brought into the institution and are taken on a tour which consists of showing and explaining what an isolation cell is, (the hole, used to house men who have committed rule infractions.) A showing of a regular cell block with explanation. Then they are escorted to the prison auditorium where we have a rap session in which we try to cover the full spectrum of crime and its non-rewards. In these rap sessions we explain using ourselves as examples about prison, crime and its ramifications. We have a group classification of the youngsters who may be taking part in our program. Our conversation is geared to our classification, or what we are told by the authority who may be escorting them.
>
> The Good (those with no involvement in crime)—The Bad (minor infractions with the law or authority)—The Ugly (those who

have been away or are borderline cases.) Our language may be that of the street or prison language or a discussion in a question and answer talk with high school or college students."[4]

The early history of the Lifers and the Juvenile Awareness Project was described in detail in a 1979 interview with me by ex-Lifer Frank Bindhammer. A founder and officer with the Lifers Group, Frank is currently on parole. Portions of that interview follow:

Finckenauer: What was the original purpose of the Lifers' Group? How did it come about?

Bindhammer: O.K. You know, everyone has the impression that the Lifers' Group originated at Rahway State Prison when in fact it did not! It actually originated at Trenton State Prison and a gentleman by the name of Paul Fitzsimmons, I believe it is, and a couple of other convicts, Lifers, got together in an effort to form this organization to help convicts become motivated towards helping themselves. O.K.? I'm sure that you agree that there's no such thing as rehabilitation in our penal system. There is self-rehabilitation and these guys wanted to get other prisoners motivated towards helping themselves—make them consciously aware that they do need to make certain adjustment—get involved in education, vocational training, group therapy, whatever might be available to them—to help them with legal matters, to attempt to change certain laws regarding Lifers, and one in particular was to aggregate consecutive sentences. From there we contemplated fund-raising events for various organizations but that never got off the ground because of the present administration. They were totally against it. When Richard Rowe, who was released from prison, came back on another charge, he was resentenced for . . .

Finckenauer: Meaning he had been paroled once . . .

Bindhammer: He had been paroled. He was, he had several indictments pending—he was found guilty on those charges and sentenced to, if I'm not mistaken, double life. When he returned to Trenton State Prison and became involved in the Lifer's Group he requested permission to be transferred to Rahway. That, it was granted. Shortly after he transferred he approached the superintendent of Rahway, who was Bob Hatrak incidentally, and requested permission to initiate a chapter of the Lifers' Group. For whatever reason Bob Hatrak agreed to allow him to do this. And he did. The bylaws of the Rahway Chapter was basically the same as at Trenton. They were in the process of doing more or less the same thing insofar as changing certain legislation regarding the lifer's work inside. But beyond that they weren't doing anything. When I was transferred to

---

[4] Lifer's Group Brochure, Juvenile Awareness Project Help.

Rahway the program was approximately four months old. Richard Rowe approached me and asked me to become involved in the program. When I say they weren't doing anything, I mean that they weren't becoming involved in community affairs—reaching out into the community— attempting to initiate similar programs as, such as the Juvenile Awareness Project. I was involved in the program approximately a month when I talked to a person by the name of Robert Clements about becoming involved in the Lifers' Group. I explained to him what my ideas were insofar as expanding that program was concerned. He was reluctant to become involved because Robert Clements had been involved in other prisoner organizations that later on proved to be failures for one reason or another, whether it was because the administration deliberately did things to discourage them or because the prisoners themselves lost interest. However, Robert Clements decided that he would give it a try and he signed up to become a member and was immediately accepted and between us we start talking about the possibility of initiating a voice tape project. We wanted to produce voice tapes of various prisoner's experiences as juveniles—that is to say, their experience in crime, with crime, their institutional experiences. We would mail these tapes to law enforcement agencies, public schools—high schools, colleges—with little or no success. And I say that because the people that we were producing them for never gave us any feedback as to the number of juveniles that were getting to listen to them and what their reactions was. Well, we started producing the tapes before we actually secured permission from the present administration. Then we did in fact draw up a proposal, we requested a meeting with Supt. Hatrak and his staff regarding this project. The meeting was postponed on several occasions and one day Chief Deputy James Ucci came into the inmate group center area. He was accompanied by Richard Kern, who was a captain at the time and who is currently Chief Deputy of Rahway. I had previous problems with Chief Ucci, so when the men informed me that they were going to speak to him about this proposal I decided to leave the room so as not to influence his decision. When I returned, Richard Rowe and Robert Clements and Robert Jones, who were all present told me, "Frank, I'm sorry but he knocked down the program." Well, I left the Lifers' Group to find Chief Ucci, and I approached him and I explained to him exactly what we wanted to do. He was totally against the idea and I asked him as a personal favor to give us the opportunity to prove ourselves. And he told me O.K. He says, "You have this one chance. If you blow it, that's it!" So, that's how we actually got permission to begin, officially begin, this voice tape project. But we weren't satisfied with that. We wanted to reach the juveniles directly. We did in fact, eventually meet with Robert Hatrak and Richard Kern and they liked the idea of a juvenile awareness program but they wanted us to confine ourselves to juv . . . well, to young people 18 years of age and up.

Finckenauer: You proposed to them at this time, to bring juveniles . . .

Bindhammer: Juveniles into the institution. And, they refused us to, refused to allow us to bring in juveniles, say, 10 years of age and up. They wanted us to restrict ourselves to people 18 years of age and up and over and they would not allow us to bring them into the actual prison. They wanted us to meet with them in an isolated area. An area that was away from the general population and any activities. We were dissatisfied with that. Now Richard Rowe is from that area. His wife had read an article in a local newspaper regarding Judge George Nicola of Middlesex County and Chief Anthony O'Brien and their effort to help young people. He asked his wife to contact these people and determine whether or not they were in fact sincere about helping young offenders. She did contact Judge Nicola and Anthony O'Brien and they expressed an interest in becoming involved in what we were attempting to do. Judge George Nicola and Anthony O'Brien contacted Robert Hatrak after meeting with us and requested permission to make referrals to this program. And that's how we actually secured permission to initiate the Juvenile Awareness Program. I think I did get a little ahead of myself.

What motivated us to do this. O.K. Speaking for Robert Clements and myself, I know what motivated us. Robert Clements and I have been involved in crime since we were young kids—8 years old. We've been sent to juvenile reformatories. We know exactly what they're like. We know that while we were in these places that they were nothing but schools of crime, homosexuality and hatred—and I'm not saying that the prison administration or the institution administration was responsible for this. I don't think that they set up all night contemplating devious ways of dealing with these young people. I think it was more the result of peer influence, pressures and so forth. It wasn't the administration that was ripping you off, although at that time, there were a number of sick people working in those institutions. They were sadistic, sick people. They were people that were raping young kids in these institutions. But the major factor in the whole thing I would venture to say, was peer influence. It was your associates that ripped you off—exploited you emotionally, mentally, spiritually, physically—and kids were taught to distrust, to hate. And that's what happened to us. And it's out of genuine concern that we were interested in initiating this voice tape project and subsequently the Juvenile Awareness Program. One day when we were in the office, in the Lifers' office, a group of college students, if I'm not mistaken they were from Rutgers University in New Brunswick, were touring the prison and the escorting officer, if I'm not mistaken, was a person by the name of Sgt. Summers, and he asked us to speak to this group regarding the functions of the Lifers' Group. As I recall it, Robert Clements told me, he says, "You know, this is your chance to learn to speak to people." Because I never really learned to communicate with people. He says, "You have the task of telling these young people what the Lifer's Group is about." I was pretty messed up about it. I really didn't know what to say to these kids. So after brief, giving them a brief outline of what we were trying to do, I start trying to give them some real insight into the realities of crime, institution life and everything. And, I wish you could have been there to see the effect that this was having on these young people. They were shocked! And these were straight kids! So when they left, we sat down and discussed the reaction of the students. And if this had that type of an effect on straight kids or allegedly straight kids, what might it do to youthful offenders. And there was no abuse involved—no profanity—none of those things. So that's when we actually start discussing the possibility of initiating a juvenile awareness program—bringing young people in and talking to them—explain to them what the realities of crime is—what institution life is about—discuss with them some of the problems that they're experiencing—try to give them some insight into how they might be able to deal with those problems. We actually started off as being the good, big brother. No man, none of the prisoners, were allowed to use any type of abuse or anything like that. All that they were able to do was share their experiences. When the program was approved the first group of juveniles referred to the program was from Middlesex County, if I'm not mistaken. Middlesex or Woodbridge. Whichever the case. But they were referred by one of two people—George Nicola or Anthony O'Brien. If I'm not mistaken, it was at that time Bill Eastman from the Asbury Park Press was present, and we did nothing but share our experiences with these young people in an effort to give them some insight into what they were opening themselves up to experiencing should they decide to continue a life of crime. We were trying to emphasize the significance of education, vocational training, the necessity for law and order and, yes, we were using hypothetical situations to help these kids understand where we were coming from. Again, no one was allowed to abuse these kids—directly attack any juvenile. We attempted to do this for quite some time as other police departments and youth service organizations became involved. We were doing sessions more frequently and during this period, the early stages of the program, we did not attempt to abuse these kids or humiliate them in any way. I think the program was in existence approximately nine months. When I went to attend a session in the auditorium, Sgt. August approached me. He had a young kid with him and the kid was maybe 12, 13 years of age, and he asked me if I recognized the boy. And I told him I didn't. He said, "Well, you should. He's been here four times." And I asked him, "How was he referred to this program four times?" He asked his youth counselor to bring him. So I asked the kid why. He said, "I think you guys are cool!" Come to find out, there were other young people requesting second, third and fourth visitations. So, it was a result of this we decided to use a hard core approach, more or less, break it down into groups—the good, the bad, the ugly, and stop being the big brother because we felt that we were defeating our purpose. We're trying to make ourselves appear to be the most despicable people imaginable in an effort to turn them away from us and here they're identifying with us. When they left the institution we wanted them to look towards the professional people that were referring them to the program in the first place—for advice, for guidance. Our intention was to destroy that Hollywood stereotype image of criminals and gangsters being cool, tough people, of prisons being the in thing—to attack these young people's own self-image, destroy that image of being a cool, tough person so that when they return to their respective communities they would be more susceptible to opening themselves up to their counselors—the professional people. And, judging from all the reports that we were getting, it did have a positive effect. What we encouraged the various agencies that were making referrals to the program to do was follow-up counseling. Keep track of every juvenile that went through the program. They were suppose to provide whatever type of assistance that these young people required. We're not professionals, Jim, we can't do that. We can't even keep track of the juveniles that participate. From the inception of the program, we attempted to establish a community-based project for that purpose. To follow-up on these juveniles that participate—find out whether or not the organizations that were making referrals were doing their job. Department of Corrections knocked the proposal down. They refused it.

Finckenauer: This was early on.

Bindhammer: It was early in the program—within the first year. They did not want us to establish an outside organization. And, to be perfectly honest, not to attack the Department of Corrections, I think they had reason for that—if you investigate the people that would have probably become involved outside. So from that point on is when we actually began to use that hard core approach. But the purpose of using that was merely to get these young people's attention. Let them know how other people feel to be ripped off. Most of the kids that were being referred in the early stages, I would venture to say, were from local high schools and so forth. But, we were informed in advance that kids from a local high school would be participating in our sessions. So we geared the program towards rap sessions. They would be seated in an auditorium and it would be a question and answer situation.

Finckenauer: As opposed to being on stage?

Bindhammer: Exactly, Exactly. They would not go on a stage and it would be open to question and answer. Again, there was no abusive language and I think it gave a lot of the school counselors and principals some insight into the type of students that they were dealing with. A lot of them said, "These are all good kids. They've never been involved in anything." And then we would ask them, "O.K. How many of you kids have actually done something that you could have been arrested for and possibly sent to jail?" Ninety-nine per cent of the hands would go up. Whether it was pot, drinking, or, you know, petty theft, and the principals are generally shocked. "Not my kids!" O.K.? But that too was good. But as the program expanded the demand became greater and greater and greater and we had to exclude school students—high school, grammar school students. As a matter of fact, we can no longer allow college students to come in and view the program because it's too much of a strain. So we confined ourselves to dealing with just juveniles that were adjudicated juveniles or what were suppose to be adjudicated juveniles. We later found out that some of these organizations were slipping in ringers, so to speak. The kids that had not had actual arrest records. And when we found out about it we would approach the escorting personnel and, you know, asked them, "What's going on?" "Oh, they haven't been caught yet but the parents know they're doing these things." Well, that's one thing for the police to refer somebody to us or youth services—kid, the kids from amongst those case loads—but to just take somebody that they're not actually working with and bring them in is another story. As a matter of fact, we had one group of kids come in that were medicated. They were all on some form of drug. How can you deal with that kid? We had to ask the escorting counselors to take them home! How can we deal with this type of kid? And then it's been my experience that many of the counselors should have been up on the stage instead of the kid. Honest to God! Some of these people are ridiculous.

Finckenauer: I won't ask you to name any of those . . .

Bindhammer: No, please don't. But, I'm telling you for a fact, I can't understand how some of these people become counselors in the first place. They're singling out kids. They're asking you to lean harder on this one and it seems like they're actually taking pleasure in what's going, happening to these young people. And it's not a joke!

Finckenauer: Were you or anybody else in the Lifers' Group, to your knowledge, aware of this kind of approach being used before in prisons? Or, was it something that, as far as you knew, was an original thought?

Bindhammer: As far as I know, Jim, no one was doing it exactly the way that we were doing it. I had heard later on that other prisons have made an attempt to do something like this.

Finckenauer: But you weren't aware of this at the time?

Bindhammer: No, I was not. Well, we weren't allowed to communicate with other prisoners. That is to say, in other states and so forth. So we had no way of knowing that this was being done.

Finckenauer: So as far as you knew, this was an original thought, original approach or effort to . . .

Bindhammer: Yes, it was. As far as I was concerned it was.

THE PUBLIC BECOMES AWARE

As the Juvenile Awareness Project began to take off in early 1977, it attracted the attention of criminal justice and other public officials, also members of the media, and through the media—the public. As interest escalated, more and more the measuring rod of success began to come into play. Some newspaper stories during 1977 illustrated the height of success. For example, on March 17, 1977, the *Bergen Record* (a New Jersey newspaper) reported: "Since the program started seven months ago, the Lifers' Group has talked to 600 juvenile exoffenders. Only nine have been arrested following the talks, all on minor offenses." On April 17, 1977, the *Trenton Times-Advertiser* reported: "Since last September, when the program began, 1,400 youths in trouble with the law have been through the program . . . only fourteen youths who went through the two-hour shock treatment have gotten in trouble with the law, only five seriously." The July 30, 1977, *Newark Star Ledger* indicated that 2,921 juveniles had visited the Project and that, "A preliminary survey shows fewer than 10 percent have been in trouble since their visits."

At least one article in a professional publication was also very supportive and laudatory. New Jersey Criminal Justice Planner, James P. Murphy, writing in the July 1977, *Police Chief* magazine asked, "Does the 'shock therapy' work?" His answer: "In less than six months, the lifers have met with over 155 juveniles. The young people come from urban and suburban areas of New Jersey. Only one has been taken into custody following the visit to Rahway."

Where did these figures come from? For the most part, they were much the same kind of information which was collected on similar programs in other states described earlier. One method of collecting follow-up information is a letter sent by the Lifers' Group to parents or guardians of juveniles who have visited Rahway. The form for this letter is on page 80.

A second source of information is letters received from the sponsoring agencies which bring youngsters to Rahway. The results from these letters have generally been very positive, and it is this information which has been reported in the news media and other publications. The "numbers game" was being played very early, as illustrated in the above articles.

Once again Frank Bindhammer's comments:

Finckenauer: Where did these figures come from? Very early on, if one looks at, one follows the newspapers, the stories as they begin to appear, this is like late fall of 1976 now, the program has only been in operation for a short time, things begin to appear and immediately one begins to read success stories about this number of kids and this many have not been rearrested.

Bindhammer: I think if you investigate it, you find out, that Judge Nicola, immediately after becoming involved, was communicating with any organization that made referrals to the program. O.K.? He was more or less gathering statistics in his own way. We had no actual knowledge . . .

Finckenauer: And he was giving these to the newspapers?

Bindhammer: Let me explain this to you now, Jim. He was writing to every organization that made referrals to our program, requesting a report on the number of juveniles that they referred, and what their reactions, reaction was to the program, and what recidivism rate was amongst the juveniles. Judge Nicola done this for quite some time and before the Lifers even received copies of any of the correspondence we had no idea what was being said to Judge Nicola—communicated to him from, by these various organizations. We had to rely on Judge Nicola to let us know how many juveniles were rearrested out of the number of juveniles that were referred. It's my understanding that the statistics quoted were the statistics of the organizations that were making referrals to the program— not from the Lifers. The Lifers had no control over that.

Finckenauer: What was the reaction when you began to hear about these figures?

Bindhammer: What is the normal reaction? You're elated about it. Here's, you know, you're talking about people, Jim, who have for the most part, been taught to believe themselves to be no good, worthless human beings. People who have never really been involved in anything positive in their lives. Now they've been motivated to do something for somebody else—share their experience with other people in an effort that they might benefit. They see these things—it's the first time in their lives that they actually feel like useful, productive human beings. You throw statistics in front of them like that—80, 85 percent—what is it going to do to that type of person? They're overjoyed! They feel that, "Hey, I'm really doing something—something worthwhile." And who are convicts to question these professional people?

Finckenauer: That's true!

Bindhammer: And when we had requested copies of this correspond-ence it seems that there was always something coming up. I think the first time that we actually received copies of Judge Nicola's correspondence was some time in '78.

Finckenauer: So this might have been going on for, probably was going on for some . . .

Bindhammer: Exactly. Almost two years.

Finckenauer: Without your being aware of it?

Bindhammer: Oh, we were aware that he was communicating with these organizations and whenever he appeared at a banquet or some type of social function he would recite the figures or make quotes from various correspondence that he received. But we never received any of this information.

Finckenauer: What is your feeling about that?

Bindhammer: What is my feeling about it? To be perfectly honest, I'm not taking anything away from Judge Nicola, but I think that all relative information should have been shared with everyone involved—all the organizations that were making referrals, the Department of Corrections, the prison administration, and, of course, the Lifers.

Finckenauer: But that wasn't happening?

Bindhammer: No, that wasn't happening.

What about these numbers—this seemingly incredible success rate? One conclusion seems clear, the figures were and are suspect. They may be so subject to error and inaccuracies as to render them totally unreliable and invalid.

To begin with, a large number of kids participating in the project had admittedly been neither delinquents nor even predelinquents (showing some indications of potential delinquency). Nondelinquents who remain nondelinquent after some treatment intervention—any treatment intervention—cannot be considered program successes.

The information that is collected by means of the form letter mentioned earlier is of the subjective, "to your knowledge" variety, and is thus of questionable validity. Also, letter responses are frequently based upon follow-up periods of only a few days or weeks. Crime-free behavior over a short period of time is not unusual, even for the most hard-core delinquent. Follow-up periods this short are meaningless indicators. Finally, self-selection determines responses to the letters. Because only some parents and agencies respond, the subject juveniles cannot be considered a representative sample of the whole. Perhaps only some who have good things to say, bother to respond.

The scientific name for the measuring rod referred to earlier is, of course, recidivism. This is the "stuff" of the numbers game. In this case, recidivism was neither defined nor applied uniformly by those reporting. Whether it meant rearrest, reconviction, further school problems, or further incorrigibility was not and is not known. It probably meant some or all of these things. Further, recidivism is an inappropriate measure of

```
                        Lifers' Group
                     Rahway State Prison
                        Lock Bag R
                   Rahway, New Jersey 07065


                                      Date:_____

                             Re: Juvenile Intervention


  Dear Parent/Guardian:

  On_____, your son/daughter took part in our Juvenile Inter-
  vention Program here at Rahway State Prison. Would you please answer the
  below questions and return this questionaire to the above address.

  1)  Have you noticed a marked change in your child's conduct since their
      visit to the prison?  Yes:_____  No:_____

  2)  Has there been a slight change in their conduct since their visit to the
      prison? Yes:_____  No:_____

  3)  Do you think that another visit is necessary for your son/daughter?
      Yes:_____  No:_____

  4)  Are there any specific areas you think we might be of some assistance to
      you, or your son or daughter?  Please explain:



  We invite your questions or comments:



                                  Signed:_____
                                         Parent/Guardian:
```

the behavior of a youngster who has had no previous contact with the juvenile justice system.

PUBLIC FIGURES REACT

As the Juvenile Awareness Project attracted more and more public attention, it also attracted the attention of various public figures. New Jersey's Governor Brendan Byrne visited a Lifers' party at Rahway Prison in July, 1977. The Governor was quoted at the party as saying, "The main thing in evaluating it is to determine if it works. That kind of orientation for young people has to have an impact."[5] He seemed to concur in the claims of success, telling reporters, "more and more of our problems are with youth." Byrne credited the Lifers' insight and experience in crime as a valuable tool in "helping us all to learn how to deal better with society." The Governor characterized his visit to the prison by saying it was, "exciting to be here to witness, firsthand, the results of some imaginative thinking . . . making the next generation better than ours." Another official, Robert Mulcahy, who was corrections commissioner at the time, was reported as saying, "We are very excited about the program. This is one time when men on both sides of the bars are working together and accomplishing something beneficial to everyone."

Many police officers, judges, and juvenile corrections officials were in agreement that the program was an effective deterrent to juvenile crime. Juvenile justice officials from many states visited the program or wrote asking for information about it. Superintendent Hatrack and Corrections Sgt. Alan August, who was appointed liaison officer to the Lifers' Group, began to travel around speaking to various audiences about the Juvenile Awareness Project.

Perhaps the most outspoken and vigorous supporter of the program in the criminal justice community was the juvenile court judge who had been one of its founders, George Nicola. Some of his reported comments are indicative of his enthusiastic support. "It's a project worthy of effort. The bottom line, of course, is the rate of recidivism. That's what counts." Of a group of "revolving door delinquents" who were constantly in trouble, Nicola said, "less than 1 percent have gotten into trouble again" after visiting the prison. He said, "New Jersey is becoming a model for the rest of the nation. I am receiving calls from all over the country about the program. I'm thankful for this program, as should the people of New Jersey be thankful."[6] Judge Nicola's philosophy which governs his handling of juvenile offenders is unusual, if not unique. It is also critically important in explaining his strong support of the Lifers' approach. Some of his comments reported in Youth Forum, the newsletter of the National Council on Crime and Delinquency, are instructive in this regard.[7] Discussing his view that locking up juveniles for short periods is the best way to rehabilitate them, Nicola said, "I send them there for shock experience." "We know what the problems are in the reformatories. Kids come out worse than when they go in. All I want that kid to realize is that crime doesn't pay. Now you're in hell. Now, do you want to be with them or outside?"

[5] Governor Brendan Byrne, *Newark Star Ledger* (July 10, 1977).

[6] *Youth Forum*, 1 (June 1977), 3.

[7] Ibid., p. 3.

Nicola's judicial strategy calls for sending four-time losers (kids appearing in juvenile court for the fourth time) to an institution. The purpose is to shock the delinquent, and any followers and companions. The judge insists that he utilizes the recall process to bring out any incarcerated juvenile who shows good progress in a couple of months. The success of this approach is extolled by Nicola's court administrator, Dr. James S. Winston:

Since January of 1975, approximately 105 juveniles have been sent to institutions. Of these juveniles, thirty have been recalled after serving a brief period of time, only five of which have engaged in subsequent delinquent behavior. Many of these recalled juveniles, who once were considered revolving-door delinquents, have remained out of trouble for periods exceeding nine months since being recalled. This has been due to the rapid shock of the incarceration immersion technique which seems to be working quite well in the case of serious offenders.[8]

Judge Nicola's belief in and use of shock treatment to achieve deterrent effects comes through clearly. Also hinted at is his somewhat indiscriminate use of various figures to support his claims of success. But Judge Nicola also showed that he recognized the difficulty which the Lifers' faced in trying to scare crime out of the kids they talked to. He said, "Memories can be short." "Peer pressure is by far the most powerful force at work in juvenile crime. And the Lifers' have a hard time fighting that from behind bars."[9]

THE FIRST EVALUATION

In July, 1977, Deputy Corrections Commissioner William H. Fauver directed that an evaluation of the Juvenile Awareness Project be conducted.[10] This task was undertaken by two departmental interns, Lawrence Gilman and Richard K. Milin, over a period of several weeks during that summer. In their own words, they were not able "to undertake an exhaustive and comprehensive analysis of the Lifers' Group Program due to staff limitations and time constraints." They were only able to make "a limited attempt" to evaluate the effect of the program on recidivism. They did review literature on the program, conduct inter-

[8] Dr. James Winston, "Reducing Juvenile Delinquency by Judicial Action in New Jersey," *Journal of Juvenile and Family Courts* (February 1978), p. 23.

[9] Krajick, *Corrections Magazine*, p. 23.

[10] An Evaluation of the Lifers' Group Juvenile Awareness Project, New Jersey Department of Corrections, Trenton, N. J. (July 1977).

views and a telephone survey, observe sessions in the prison, and consult with department of corrections officials.

The purpose of the evaluation was: "to determine the program's strengths and weaknesses; to assess its impact on the youngsters who participate in it; to gain an understanding of its organization and operation; and to evaluate its effectiveness from the point of view of the attitudes of the adults who bring the juveniles to the institution in order to expose them to the unique experience the Lifers' Group offers them."

Gilman and Milin recognized the kinship of the project with both shock therapy and deterrence theory. About the former they said, " 'Shock therapy' has a long history, but it has been controversial for most of that history. Some psychologists have challenged its effectiveness on the grounds that a single frightening experience cannot change an individual's lifestyle. . . . Even if 'shock therapy' can have positive results, the criticism that it uses bad means to good ends must be answered." On its relation to deterrence, the researchers said: "Since the Lifers' JA Program conveys information specifically aimed at increasing the perceived magnitude of the probability and losses of imprisonment for juveniles, the deterrence theory provides it with a strong theoretical basis."

After their rather brief and limited survey, the two researchers reported a number of findings and recommendations. Some of these findings included the following:

"Only 43 percent of the group leaders surveyed agreed that juveniles in their groups saw inmates as heroes before attending the Lifers' program. However, of those who did agree, all felt that the Lifers' destruction of this hero image had a favorable effect in changing the juveniles' behavior. Unfortunately, there is no hard data on this point . . ."

". . . The most prevalent reaction to the program among the juveniles interviewed was that they 'did not want to end up in prison,' which suggests that the Lifers' successfully increased the juveniles' perception of the losses they would suffer if they were imprisoned. Some juveniles also seemed to have been convinced that they would inevitably be caught and imprisoned if they continued their criminal activity, suggesting that the Lifers' successfully increased some juveniles' perception of the probability of arrest and incarceration as well."

"Eighty-six percent of the group leaders surveyed thought that the effort to frighten the juveniles' increased program effectiveness. . . . The leaders' support was not based on hard data, and few leaders offered theoretical grounds for their belief. . . . Since actual costs of scare tactics have been demonstrated [reference here is to some children reportedly being unable to sleep after visiting the prison] while benefits are only believed to exist, concern over these costs must take precedence. These costs may be eliminated by temporarily discontinuing the use of scare tactics pending a demonstrable loss of program effectiveness. If the use of scare tactics is to continue, it should at least be demonstrated that the juveniles will not listen unless threatened, and that there are significant reductions of the recidivism rate as a result of the effort to frighten the juveniles."

"The current screening and classification of groups by Lifers and group leaders does not appear to be sufficient . . . the Lifers tend to gear their presentation towards the 'hardest core' members of each youth group. An improved screening and classification procedure could greatly diminish the adverse effects of the JA Program."

"For the most part, the group leaders surveyed were enthusiastic about the overall effectiveness of the JA Program. . . . Those respondents who saw no change in behavior felt that the effects of the program wore off within a few days. Two respondents who did notice a change in behavior expressed the same concern. Although little 'hard' recidivism data were available, 57 percent of the respondents stated that the recidivism rate of the juveniles who attended the program was lower than they ordinarily would have expected . . ."

Gilman and Milin concluded their report by saying, "Although there is no conclusive data, the program seems to be effective in changing juveniles' behavior, and few modifications seem necessary."

This evaluation was a commendable effort despite its recognized deficiencies and shortcomings. The report raised a number of pertinent and important issues. One was the recognition that the program could have adverse and counterproductive effects because of its scare tactics. Their recommendation that the use of these tactics be suspended, at least temporarily, was never followed. Another issue raised was the inadequacies in the screening and classification process (a practically nonexistent process). This too became an issue which was never addressed. Finally, the emotional commitment to the program on the part of its sponsors came through very clearly in the report, but in almost every instance there were no data to support their belief and their enthusiastic support. It was almost as if people wanted so much to believe it was so, that therefore it was so. Even among professionals who might have been expected to be more skeptical, there was unquestioning support. The researchers themselves seemed to get caught up in this euphoria when they concluded that the program was effective in changing the youngsters' behavior, despite the absence of any data to support their conclusion. There were, however, some undercurrents of doubt and some second thoughts that came out in the report for the first time, and these became more prominent in the following months as events unfolded in 1977 and early 1978.

SOME OTHER THOUGHTS

Not all the media coverage was as glowing as that reported earlier. For example, on April 19, 1977, the *Home News* of New Brunswick, New Jersey, described a visit to Rahway by some high school boys who had previously been to the juvenile court. It said, "Although some of the students later conceded somewhat half-seriously that they were frightened by the presentation, few appeared to be really disturbed by the vivid description of prison life the program depicted." A December, 1977 article in *Corrections Magazine* quoted from a letter to the inmates from a fourteen-year old girl which closed with the following: "P.S. Yall didn't scare me because I already knew what was going to happen." This made apparent the dangers of overexposure on TV and in the newspapers which could reduce the factor of fear of the unknown and lessen the program's potential for scaring kids.

The *Corrections Magazine* referred to the Department of Corrections evaluation report and the problems disclosed in it. One of these was the lack of effect (however measured) upon the hard-core, "ugly" juveniles. Yet these kids were the most obvious and intended targets. The article also referred to reports that some less mature kids seemed to be affected too much in that they had trouble sleeping for weeks after their experience.

A troubling incident occurred in November of 1977; troubling more in terms of its implications than in what actually happened. On November 16, 1977, a group of twenty-two eighth-grade boys was taken to Rahway to participate in the Juvenile Awareness Project. Following the boys' participation, complaints were received from parents that several boys had been kissed and fondled by the Lifers. This incident was extensively investigated by school authorities and by the Internal Affairs Unit of the Department of Corrections. The department report concluded that it was possible that some of the boys were kissed and one may have had his long hair touched by an inmate. It also agreed with parents' complaints that the school authorities had not properly informed them (the parents) of what the project was all about and what the sessions entailed. Finally, the report indicated that nothing more happened in the session than usually happens. "In fact, less happened than usual," the report said. "All this could have been avoided if . . . the students had been selected more appropriately. . . ." We should keep in mind that this happened some four months after the department's evaluation report which addressed the inadequate selection and screening process.

An investigation by the principal of the school which the boys attended concluded that there was "a foul-up in communication with the prison concerning the type of youngsters being brought in that morning." He said, "The boys on this trip were very frightened by what they experienced and when they returned to school . . . stories became exaggerated." His recommendation was that the school not continue that program, "not because I do not believe it has value for our students, but because I felt it could create further turmoil in the community which has already produced elimination of certain aspects of the Lifers' Program which were extremely vital to its success in steering youngsters from pursuing criminal activities." In other words, this was a potential "hot potato" which should be left untouched.

The Department of Corrections promulgated program modifications after this incident. Among them was the following rule which we should file away for future reference:

> Only juveniles with a criminal or police problem background will be permitted to participate in the sessions on the auditorium stage. Juveniles that do not have a previous criminal or police problem background will observe the session in the audience with the adult escorting personnel.

Several implications can be drawn from all this. First, this is a sensitive and volatile technique which can be easily abused, with possibly negative consequences for children inappropriately exposed to it. Maybe it didn't really happen this time, but certainly the potential was there. Second, the department was either ignoring its own report or the Lifers were operating autonomously, out of the control of the corrections authorities. In either event, the scare tactics and the lack of classification and screening were obviously still present.

January, 1978 saw the third major turning point in the developing history of the project. Comparable in importance to the decision to run a program whose acknowledged purpose was to deter juvenile delinquency and the decision to try to accomplish this purpose by scaring kids, was an article which appeared in that month's edition of *Reader's Digest* (*Reader's Digest* sells 30 million copies monthly in twelve languages.) This was not a local newspaper story, nor even an article in *The Police Chief* magazine. This was the big time. The article, by Roul Tunley, was entitled, "Don't Let Them Take Me Back!"[11]

---

[11] Roul Tunley, "Don't Let Them Take Me Back!" *Reader's Digest* (January 1978), pp. 96–100.

One of the millions of readers of Tunley's article was one Arnold Shapiro, director, motion pictures and special projects for Golden West Television in Los Angeles, California. It was this article which planted the seed that was to become the famous television documentary "Scared Straight!" Because of its important pivotal role, and because it provides a concise, but informative description of a Lifers' session, it is here reproduced in its entirety.

DON'T LET THEM TAKE ME BACK!

Roul Tunley

Nine youngsters stood outside the main gate of Rahway State Prison. Aged 12 to 17, none had seen the inside of a maximum-security lock-up before; until recently, in fact, no minor was ever allowed in one. But these kids had all been in some trouble with the law—car theft, mugging, arson, shoplifting, drugs. So they were literally perched on the door step of prison, ready to go in either direction.

But today they weren't worried about that. The 2½-hour prison visit meant a full day off from school. They joked and feinted blows at each other, cocking their hats at rakish angles. They were sure it was going to be fun.

At the sound of an earsplitting bell, the main door swung open. The kids filed through and into a long corridor the color of sour cream. "Line up against the wall!" ordered a sergeant. They obeyed.

"You may think this is a sightseeing trip," he continued. "It isn't. When you went through the door, the man who brought you lost jurisdiction over you. You're in our hands. You'll do as we say. The first thing is to stop smoking! And don't chew gum! And take off those hats!"

The festive air vanished.

Another buzzer; another door opened. They filed into a small, concrete room, deeper into the prison. The door banged shut. "Take a look through here at our game room," invited the sergeant. The boys peered through a glass opening at an arsenal packed with the instruments of riot control: guns, gas, truncheons, helmets. Another officer told them to empty their pockets of cigarettes, knives, metal, anything "contraband." One by one, they filed through a metal detector. The sergeant stamped each wrist with a color-coded, invisible ink.

Then came more doors, leading ever deeper into the prison. Each one clanged behind them with a steel finality that echoed through the building. Now they were passing the "hole"—a wing lined with tiny cells, each windowless, with metal walls, a cot, a toilet bowl. From one, a man yelled: "Get me outa this place!" A guard told him to shut up.

The boys climbed steep, steel steps to yet another barred door—the seventh. It too banged shut behind them. They found themselves in a small auditorium, where they were led to a stage and seated on a hard bench. In front of them were eight of the toughest convicts in the prison system—men serving life or "life plus" for murder or other major crimes.

A black inmate, his arms like tree trunks, stepped to within several feet of the boys. They squirmed uneasily as he peered into each face without saying anything. Finally he spoke:

"We're gonna tell you turkeys what prison life is really like, not what you've seen in the movies or on TV. These men are gonna tell you things that are not easy to tell. If I find any of you smiling or looking around or not paying attention, I'll break your goddam jaw."

Not a foot shifted. And for 90 minutes the "lifers" described existence behind the 30-foot walls.

"Do you know how I got here?" asked a 31-year-old con who'd been in Rahway for 13 years. "Doing the same crap you're doing. At eight, I stole bikes. By ten, I was shoplifting. In my teens, I was breaking into houses. I thought I was too smart to get caught. I wanted to be like the older guys in my gang, my heroes. One day I went with one of them to break into a house. We'd rung the doorbell and the phone. There was no answer and we thought we were safe. But when we got upstairs, we found the owner facing us with a pistol. We ended up killing him. That's why I'm here, and it could happen to any of you punks."

Another inmate then took over. "You're scared all the time in prison," he said. "Nobody on the outside ever tells you about the things that go on here—the murders, the suicides, the rapes. Sure, the rapes."

He pointed to a fair-skinned boy with long, blond hair. "You're goodlooking," he said. "We like boys like you. You'd be raped within 24 hours of landing here, and I'd be the first to try. And there's nothing you could do about it."

The boy looked as though he were going to be sick.

"Oh, sure, you could rat and go to the Man and tell him what happened," the prisoner continued, "and for your own sake you'd be put into Protective Custody. We call it Punk City. From then on, there'd be no visits, no movies, no association with any other prisoner. You'd be locked up 22 hours a day, allowed out only to exercise by yourself. You'd never go back to the prison population. Because if you did, you'd be dead.

"Of course there is another alternative. You could become some strong con's 'woman.' But you'd have to have sex whenever he wanted, wash his socks and underwear, clean his cell and run errands. And when he wanted to share you with someone else, you'd have to do it."

As the boy began to cry, the con sneered. "You wouldn't like that, huh?" he asked. "My, oh, my. And I thought you was a real hard guy."

Another prisoner stepped forward. He told the boys they hadn't seen the real "hole," just the double-lock cells. He'd been sent to the real one: no light, no bed, one tray of food a day, and no one to talk to. After a few days, he reached a point where he'd do anything to get out, and one night he tried.

"I banged my head against the wall until it was a bloody mess," he said, "all the while yelling for the guard. But he didn't come until he was good and ready. I was handcuffed and carried to the prison hospital. The doctor sewed me up as though he were trussing a chicken. Then I was carried right back to solitary, only this time to a padded cell where I couldn't injure myself. I still had to do my time."

The smallest boy in the group—a 12-year-old whose feet didn't touch the floor—was told to stand up. A convict then ordered him to tell the biggest boy to stand with his nose against the wall. The small boy hesitated, then gave the command. The convict told the big boy to obey. Then the youngster was told to order another boy to get down on all fours. The order was given, and the second boy also did as he was told. Another youngster was ordered to crawl under the bench. When all had been given and obeyed some command, and were finally back in their seats, the convict asked each one how he liked it. They all shook their heads.

"Well," said the inmate, his voice rising to a yell, "that's what it's like in here every day! I'm 45 years old. How do you think I like it when some punk 18-year-old guard tells me to clean out a filthy toilet? But I do it."

The average pay at Rahway is $1.25 a day—for work in the laundry, the shops, the yard. A man is rich if he has two dollars in his prison account. "Do you know what my most precious possession is?" asked a convict. He extracted a metal spoon from his rear pocket and held it up. "This. I eat with it, sleep with it, go to the shower with it." He explained that prisoners aren't allowed knives and forks, and that when a man loses his spoon, he eats with his fingers until the guards, convinced he has not made a weapon of it, issue him another.

The last speaker was tall, thin, unsmiling, and his blue eyes blazed like laser beams. He told the boys he'd give anything to change places with them. They could go home at the end of the morning. He had to stay at least 20 more years.

A 14-year-old shifted uncomfortably on the bench and looked away for a second. The con turned on him. "I don't think you believe what we've told you," he said. "You think you're too smart to get caught." The con's face almost touched the boy's. "But let me tell you something," he shouted. "You're one of the stupidest guys I've ever seen!"

Suddenly, unexpectedly, the boy spat in the prisoner's face. And time stopped on that stage in Rahway. No one moved. Not a sound was heard. The boy on the bench sat frozen, his eyes wide with the horror of what he'd done. Like everyone else in the room, he knew that the prisoner had killed for less. Finally, spittle running down his face, the con stepped back. He took a handkerchief from his pocket and wiped his chin. Then he spoke in a low voice:

"If that's what it takes to get through to you, to make you realize what a mess you're making of your life, I'll take it. At least it shows you have guts. Why not use them for something better?"

The session was over.

Without a word, the boys got up and filed out one by one— through the seven steel doors, through the room where the invisible ink on their wrists was checked with black light to make sure it matched the day's code, through the corridor past the riot-equipment room. Finally, they emerged into blinding sunlight.

There were green trees in front of the prison—a sight some convicts hadn't seen in decades. The 12-year-old impulsively threw his arms around the juvenile officer who'd brought them. "Don't ever let them take me back there!" he pleaded.

No one was embarrassed by this. Walking silently to the bus, the boys showed no jauntiness, no joking. Later, the driver who took them back to their community said it was the quietest bunch of teen-agers he'd ever taken anywhere.

This dramatic and powerful depiction of the Lifers so impressed Shapiro and his California colleagues that it stimulated the initiation of a series of events resulting in a film, in numerous awards, but finally in controversy.

chapter five

Scared Straight:
The Making
of a Myth

Newspapers and magazines were not the only media to become involved in disseminating information about the Juvenile Awareness Project. Perhaps the most powerful medium of all, television, soon became interested. Television crews from the major networks and other American stations, and from overseas networks visited the prison. It was quickly recognized that the Lifers' project would make for great television viewing. It was appealing, dramatic, and exciting. Viewer appeal seemed to stem in part from the obscene language, the erotic and explicit sexual references, and the sado-masochistic content. In mid–1977 Channel 13, the New York Public Broadcasting System affiliate, aired a documentary film on the project.

Sometime after reading the *Readers' Digest* article, Arnold Shapiro conceived the idea of producing his own documentary film about the Juvenile Awareness Project.[1] He contacted the Lifers at Rahway Prison and did some preliminary research to familiarize himself with the subject of juvenile crime. Shapiro reviewed materials sent to him by the Lifers. He was also informed by them of the earlier television documentaries which had been shown by New York area television sta-

---

[1] U.S., Congress, House, Subcommittee on Human Resources of The Committee on Education and Labor, *Hearings, Oversight on Scared Straight,* 96th Cong., 1st Sess., June 4, 1979, p. 52.

tions. One of the best of these was produced by Richard Hughes for WPIX-TV. Shapiro requested a video cassette tape of the film which was entitled, "I Am My Brother's Keeper," from WPIX. This moving and informative documentary had been first shown in New York in December, 1977.

Arnold Shapiro showed the *Readers Digest* article and the cassette tape to his colleagues and superiors at Golden West Broadcasters and television station KTLA in Los Angeles. He was given permission to visit New Jersey and interview the Lifers, Rahway officials, and some youth agency representatives to determine the feasibility and the possible cost of making a documentary film.

In April of 1978, Shapiro met with Superintendent Hatrak and Sergeant August at the prison. He accompanied a group of youngsters into the prison and got a first hand taste of what a Lifers' session looked, sounded, and felt like. At a meeting with the Lifers after the session, Shapiro determined that they would cooperate and participate in the filming of a documentary.

Ex-Lifer Frank Bindhammer described this meeting in his interview with me as follows:

Finckenauer: How did the movie come about?

Bindhammer: What actually happened was Arnold Shapiro requested an interview with the Lifers' executive staff to discuss the possibility of his, for making or producing a documentary.

Finckenauer: You did not know who he was at this time.

Bindhammer: Oh yes. Yes. He had communicated with one of the staff members for some time before he actually came in to meet with us. So we did have some insight into who Arnold Shapiro was. When Arnold Shapiro visited Rahway he explained to us what he would like to do. The Lifers agreed to allow him to film the sessions and to work with him. And, that's how he actually became involved. After talking with Arnold Shapiro I learned that he did in fact read an article that appeared in *Reader's Digest* and this article stimulated his interest and that's why he contacted us in the first place.

Finckenauer: Well, what did he tell you that he wanted to do?

Bindhammer: He told us that he did, in fact, want to do a documentary based on the program. And, of course, we cooperated with him. He felt that he could in fact, produce a quality film. He had, if I'm not mistaken, already contacted the various TV stations that had done documentaries and had an opportunity to view their work and felt that he could do something that was superior to that. And at the same time do the program some type of a justice.

Arnold Shapiro met with several persons from agencies that were routinely referring youngsters to the Juvenile Awareness Project. All, according to Shapiro, were cooperative, helpful, and even enthusiastic about the idea of his making a film. Two of them (Det. Sgt. Charles Martini of the Ridgefield Park Police Department and Tony Rivera, a youth counselor from Passaic, New Jersey) agreed to propose to juveniles with whom they were working, that they consent to be filmed for the documentary. Martini and Rivera were confident that their youngsters would cooperate.

Shapiro planned his filming for early May. Filming was to include showing the faces of the juveniles—which had not been done before—and interviews with them. It would portray them before, during, and after their Rahway visit. One potential problem discussed at Golden West during the planning was the realization that the film would probably have to contain explicit language never before heard on Los Angeles television. For that matter, with few exceptions, such language had never been heard in any telecast anywhere. It was decided, according to Shapiro, that the public interest potential of the film would outweigh its necessarily coarse language.

This issue of language was not only a sensitive one because of the possible repercussions from censors or from religious or conservative figures, but it was also an attractive one because it could be anticipated that it would add to the shock effect of the film. Obscene language is shocking to those who are not used to it; and, if nothing else, it gets just about everybody's attention.

Shapiro maintained telephone contact with the Lifers, and with Martini, Rivera and others during April. He also spent some time in Passaic, Ridgefield Park, and again at the prison during this period. Sgt. Martini described his involvement with the documentary at that time as follows:

In April of 1978 I received a phone call from Mr. Shapiro. Mr. Shapiro gave me an indication of the idea that he had perceived in reading this article in *Reader's Digest*. At that time I explained to Mr. Shapiro that the only way I can get involved in such a program of filming that would be that he would have to contact the juvenile presiding judge who would have to give permission to me to be allowed to have the kids filmed and taken to Rahway.

At that time Mr. Shapiro to my knowledge contacted Judge Harvey Sorkow, presiding juvenile judge in my county, and with his permission we took 13 kids from our community to Rahway. Parental permission was signed for myself and Mr. Shapiro. My involvement with the parental permission for Mr. Shapiro, he sent me a folder of permission slips with the letter statement or release form. At that time I had handed them to the kids that had been chosen to go to Rahway. I told them to take them home, to review them with their parents and return them as soon as possible as Mr. Shapiro will be in town 2 weeks later.

Approximately April 28, 1978, Mr. Shapiro appeared in my office. We rode around and he viewed areas of the county he wanted to film. On April 30 he filmed the 13 juveniles which are in that "Scared Straight" documentary.[2]

Arnold Shapiro says he had no responsibility for choosing the particular youngsters who appeared in "Scared Straight!" In fact, he says he did not actually meet them until the day they were filmed. He does claim that a stipulation was made to Martini and Rivera that each juvenile to be filmed must have "broken the law." They did not necessarily have to have been arrested, just have broken the law. Shapiro also says he wanted a mixture of kids—by age, race, sex, and offense type. As it worked out or was planned to work out, Ridgefield Park—a suburban, mostly white middle-class community—provided the white kids, boys and girls who were less serious "law breakers." Passaic, an urban community, provided the black kids who could be considered "hardcore." Shapiro distinguishes between what he calls softcore and hardcore juvenile offenders.

Shapiro says he did not have access to the police records of any of the juveniles, but he was given assurances by the people in Passaic and Ridgefield Park that each of the juveniles was a lawbreaker. This assurance was reinforced, says Shapiro, when he personally interviewed all the kids on film. He states that no juvenile told him that they had not broken the law, although some did say they had not been arrested.

The film interviews were conducted on April 29 and 30. According to Shapiro, the youngsters were not told how to act, what to say, nor what to do. He says they were told only to answer his questions in complete sentences and to be totally honest. Neither the youngsters nor their counselors were given any of the questions beforehand, says Shapiro. He is also of the opinion that the kids did not exaggerate their crimes or their attitudes during the filming in order to display a more bravado image. To the contrary, he thinks that if anything the kids were

[2] Ibid., p. 117.

conservative, cautious, and generally "toned down." The filming of the kids brazenly entering Rahway State Prison, the actual session, and of the contrite departure took place on May 1, 1978.

To accompany the showing of the film, a brochure and other publicity materials were prepared for distribution. These materials included the following statements:

- Fact: Half of all serious crimes in the United States are committed by Youths 10 to 17! Violent juvenile crime between 1960 and 1975 tripled!
- Fact: Existing deterrence programs or punishments seem ineffective as the number of juvenile crimes increases every year—twice as fast as adult crime!
- Fact: "Kiddie crime," as it's sometimes called, includes murder, rape, armed robbery, violent assault, mugging, robbery, arson, vandalism—hardly "kids stuff."
- Fact: Virtually all adult criminals were juvenile offenders. IF ONLY THEY COULD HAVE BEEN STOPPED THEN!
- Fact: 80–90% of the kids in THIS unique program are 'Scared Straight.' Take an hour and watch this powerful approach work.[3]

And the following:

SCARED STRAIGHT

A most unlikely group of men have begun a most unusual program to combat the alarming epidemic of juvenile crime.

The unlikely group of 50 men—calling themselves "the Lifers"—are all hardened criminals serving life sentences for murder and other major crimes. And the program they started is unusual and different because it *works*!

... This "shock therapy" approach is frightening, yet compelling to watch, most importantly—it's effective.

The cameras follow and profile a group of seventeen juvenile offenders—aged 14 to 18—before, during and after their half-day at Rahway. All their experiences, emotions, and attitude changes are captured on film. Full-face to the camera, these kids are candid in describing their criminal ways and equally candid in relating how they felt after their grueling hours inside the prison. The content is startling and powerful. There's even a three month follow-up on the remarkable progress of the kids.

Crime-fighting convicts are unique, and so are the results they're achieving: 80 to 90% of the kids who visit Rahway go

[3] Ibid., p. 213.

straight! It's a startling and encouraging statistic. If just one child were "scared straight," the program would be worthwhile, but thousands of young criminals have already experienced "the Lifers" program, and most of them have reformed![4]

These promotional statements can be read in the context of the characteristics of the panacea phenomenon, described earlier. We should ask ourselves if they seem to fit the definition of such a panacea. The particular antidelinquency program—in this case the Juvenile Awareness Project—is promoted as a cure-all, as some kind of magic answer to the delinquency problem; and, it is "hyped" accordingly. The fit would seem to be reasonably good.

More important and influential evidence suggesting that "Scared Straight!" exemplified the panacea phenomenon is heard in the narrative of the film itself done by actor Peter Falk. Some examples follow:

> Over 8,000 juvenile delinquents have sat in fear on these hard wooden benches. And for the first time they really heard the brutal realities of crime and prison. The results of this unique program are astounding. Participating communities report that 80 to 90 percent of the kids that they sent to Rahway go straight after leaving this stage. That's an amazing success story, and it's unequalled by traditional rehabilitation methods. . . .
>
> The Lifers' program is saving many kids from a life of crime. And at the same time it's helping the convicts too. . . . America has 450 prisons but only a handful of programs like this one. It's not easy to make allies of convicts and those people who locked them up, but in New Jersey former enemies now work together. . . .
>
> But while we're attacking the causes of crime, we can still allow those convicts who care about kids to start programs inside their own prisons. It doesn't cost the taxpayers any money, and it can stop thousands of prison-bound delinquents in their tracks. For that, parents, police, judges, victims and all the rest of us will be very grateful. Prisoners can help in the fight to save today's children from becoming tomorrow's convicts.

Finally, the film closed with this statement from Judge George Nicola:

> When you view the program and you review the statistics that have been collected, there is no doubt in my mind, and in the

---

[4] Ibid., p. 214.

mind of anybody who has seen this program, that the Juvenile Awareness Project at Rahway State Prison perhaps is today, the most effective, inexpensive deterrent in the entire correctional process in America.

There is little way that these statements can be misinterpreted or misunderstood. They clearly promise a new "cure" for juvenile crime.

"SCARED STRAIGHT!" GOES PUBLIC

The film was first aired on November 2, 1978 by KTLA, Channel 5 in Los Angeles. *TV Guide* for that evening carried the following blurb: "SCARED STRAIGHT! Special: Inside a maximum security prison. This hour-long program follows 17 juvenile offenders as they learn, at firsthand, about the realities of prison life. Using brutally frank and frequently obscene language, 'Lifers' at Rahway (N.J.) State Prison tell the young people about the ultimate pay-off for their criminality." Actor Peter Falk's narration of the documentary seemed to enhance the authenticity and drama of the film. After all, would Columbo mislead his audience?

"Scared Straight!" was received by a large and very enthusiastic audience. There had been few, if any, television documentaries like it. It not only had "street" language, but it had vivid descriptions of sex and violence, powerful and frightening caged men, and the sights and sounds of a fortress prison. It was, in short, a sensational media event. The elements of "good" television—stimulating color, emotion, and sound—were there in dramatic abundance.

Some mental health professionals—psychiatrists and psychologists—are of the opinion that a major part of the mass appeal of this film rested in its sexual content. This content is explicit in its descriptions and threats of sexual violence such as homosexual rape. The language is sexual and shocking. But this content is also implicit or present on a subconscious level as well! The film is very physical, and it portrays human relationships in which powerful figures emotionally and physically subjugate those who are powerless. The inmates do not come across as sad or weak creatures. Instead, they are very dynamic and super-masculine. The subtle effects of these images on the undeveloped or confused sexual identities of adolescents are open to speculation.

"Scared Straight!" became an overnight smash. Its success was recorded by the Los Angeles press. For example, the *Valley News* called it, "One of the most riveting hours of television ever produced!"[5] Los Angeles' most influential newspaper, the *Los Angeles Times*, said it was, "One of the most unusual and powerful television programs ever broadcast!"[6] KTLA was quickly flooded with over two thousand letters, almost all of them supportive, including one from the mayor of Los Angeles.

After the film's overwhelming success in Los Angeles, The Signal Companies, Inc., which sponsored the film as a public service, decided to show it nationally. Thus, during the week of March 5, 1979, "Scared Straight!" was shown in two hundred major cities from coast to coast. Many local television stations also aired a half-hour sequel to the film hosted by Dick Cavett. Cavett discussed the Juvenile Awareness Project with Frank Bindhammer, Robert Hatrak, Alan August, and three juveniles who had visited Rahway. S. James Coppersmith of WNEW-TV in New York described the reaction to that station's broadcast:

"Scared Straight!" was broadcast on our Station WNEW-TV on March 8, 1979. . . . The overwhelming reaction we received from our viewing audience certainly supported our judgment. Seldom have I known a program to receive as much favorable comment, to wit, almost 700 letters, of which approximately 94% were laudatory. . . .

The size of WNEW-TV's audience was another interesting phenomenon. According to the Nielsen Rating Service, on March 8 from 10:00 to 11:00 p.m., "Scared Straight!" was the highest rated show in the time period—39% of the total viewing audience. . . . Translated into numbers, that means over 3 million people in the New York/Northern New Jersey metropolitan area were watching. . . .[7]

Not all the reaction to the documentary was favorable however, as witness this commentary from a reviewer for the *Kansas City Raytown News*:

If you like filthy language and think convicts are glamourous, you'll like 'Scared Straight!' If you think juvenile delinquents should be treated "like the animals they are," you'll love 'Scared Straight!' If you believe criminals are the best doctors for a sick society, 'Scared Straight!' is for you.

---

[5] National Center on Institutions and Alternatives, *Scared Straight: A Second Look* (n.d.), p. 4.

[6] Ibid., p. 4.

[7] U.S., *Hearings, Oversight on Scared Straight*, p. 183.

This is a propaganda presentation which sets forth a persuasive argument for the setting up of a 'Lifers' program in your state. . . .

The program is shocking—not because of dirty language; we've all heard that. It's shocking to realize that we have so many crime-hardened children in our society and yet have no more effective way to reform them than with what amounts to emotional electroshock.[8]

Bald and bare as it is, the language isn't even the most offensive part of "Scared Straight!," which purports to offer news of an almost surefire panacea for juvenile delinquency: convicts.

Confronted with a phenomenon, the American instinct is to institutionalize it.[9]

Still, "Scared Straight!" had an impressive array of influential supporters. It was endorsed and recommended by the National Education Association. The vice president for Mental Health Materials Center gave his endorsement: "This strong film deserves wide use by educators, guidance counselors and others who work with potential delinquents. A powerful and convincing argument for this treatment of juvenile delinquency."[10] A film reviewer for the *Saturday Review* called it, "One of the most powerful and disturbing documentaries to hit the screen. It has a raw eloquence no viewer will forget."[11]

"Scared Straight!" also reaped a number of prizes and awards. These included the George Polk Award for television, the Gold Camera Award, and the choice as best film of 1979 by the National Council on Family Relations. The prizes were capped in April, 1979 when it was awarded an Oscar by the Academy of Motion Picture Arts and Sciences as Best Documentary Feature for the year. This was followed by a prestigious Emmy award later in the year.

THE CRITICS SURFACE

Despite the accolades from the entertainment world, and a great deal of interest and support in the criminal justice community, not everyone was sanguine about "Scared Straight!" or the Juvenile Aware-

[8] Patricia Levine, "Scared Straight: Bad Language, Glamorous Cons," *Kansas City Raytown News* (February 21, 1979), p. 5.

[9] Patricia Levine, "Caution: Contains Explicit Balderdash," *Kansas City Raytown News* (February 21, 1979), p. 5.

[10] Jack Neher, in *Film News* (n.d.).

[11] Pyramid Films, *Scared Straight*, film advertisement (n.d.).

ness Project. It was at this point that it became increasingly difficult to separate the two. The Lifers' project had in effect become the Scared Straight program.

Perhaps the most persistent and ultimately telling criticism of "Scared Straight!" came from the Washington-based National Center on Institutions and Alternatives beginning in March, 1979. The NCIA President is Dr. Jerome G. Miller, the respected former commissioner of youth services in Massachusetts who made his reputation by closing down that state's juvenile institutions. Writing in the NCIA investigative newsletter for March, Miller said:

> We followed the documentary first with curiosity and interest. But as the claims, testimonials, and true believer simplicity developed, our curiosity turned. Indeed, there has not been such a "successful" program in the last 100 years of treatment of juvenile delinquents as this "Scared Straight." One becomes inured to hearing such claims from assorted religious zealots and the occasional reformed addict, but here we are hearing claims of historic consequence made for a program in delinquency treatment—claims "hyped" to a degree unprecedented with an audience of tens of millions.
>
> But it didn't stop there. The program was followed by discussion groups virtually unanimous in their praise. Normally incisive interviewers such as Dick Cavett, seemed totally enthralled and titillated with the program. . . . It was a fitting culmination to the hype, the result of highly professional press agentry. . . .
>
> Ultimately the program tells us more about ourselves and the current state of our society than anything else. Having been deluged for the last number of years with media events depicting children as devils, witches, and anti-Christs, it should not be surprising that we now bless a panacea designed to scare the hell out of our children.[12]

Jerry Miller says he became interested in "Scared Straight!" because of the publicity and notoriety promoting the film; publicity which turned a relatively obscure project—obscure at least on a large scale—into a national panacea. Miller and his associates conducted an investigation of "Scared Straight!" and reported the following:

> The film and promotional materials surrounding it give the misleading impression that the youth pictured are "chronic, life long hell-bent offenders." On the contrary, the group had "relatively minor or non-existent involvement with the law."

[12] U.S., *Hearings, Oversight on Scared Straight*, pp. 9–17.

At least one of the youngsters appearing in the film had visited Rahway previously, contrary to impressions given in the film.

The filmmakers perceived the youngsters as being more delinquent than was actually the case. Some reported having committed some minor offenses, including setting off firecrackers, smoking marijuana, and filching cookies and candy bars. They were not, however, "hard core" delinquents by any stretch of the imagination.

There were indications that the youngsters were encouraged to act in a particular manner, i.e., boisterous and cocky going in, but contrite and scared coming out.

Permissions were obtained from parents who were told that the film would be shown on the West Coast and thus not subject their children to ridicule or stigmatization.[13]

Miller's criticisms were widely reported by the media, raising a storm of controversy. Newspaper accounts of the charges used such words as misleading and faked to describe the documentary. For example, the TV Screen Editor for the *Milwaukee Journal* wrote the following:

> I'm afraid we've all been had with the recently shown documentary "Scared Straight." . . . a "documentary," produced for profit, that probably had no particular social significance, undoubtedly scared no one straight, unfortunately got a lot of people planning cuss sessions to scare their delinquents with and, for the most part, tediously assaulted the ears with the kind of language that TV stations, in saner moments, wouldn't dream of permitting.[14]

These charges against the film culminated in the filing of a ten-million dollar lawsuit against Arnold Shapiro, Golden West Broadcasters, Peter Falk, Police Sgt. Charles Martini, and New York's WNEW-TV in September, 1979. The suit asked for punitive and compensatory damages on behalf of a majority of the Ridgefield Park juveniles appearing in the film. The lawsuit contended the youngsters and their parents were misled; that the youths were wrongly portrayed as juvenile delinquents; that they suffered permanent psychological damage; and, that the families suffered mental anxiety.

---

[13] Ibid., pp. 3–7.

[14] Wade H. Mosby, "Questions Won't Scare Channel 4 Straight," *Milwaukee Journal* (May 6, 1979).

THE FILM'S DEFENDERS RESPOND

Producer/Director Arnold Shapiro defended "Scared Straight!" in an April, 1979 interview with *The New York Times*.[15] He denied charges that the documentary misrepresented the youngsters' degree of criminal involvement or the success rate. Shapiro formally responded to the charges at Congressional hearings before the House Subcommittee on Human Resources on June 4, 1979. He said:

From the very beginning of this project, I have understood my responsibility as a communicator of information to be as honest and accurate as possible. I did not want to make the Rahway program something that it wasn't. I also did not want to underplay what it was. My initial production research convinced me that the program was effective and did work, and, therefore, we were presenting an important documentary. We said that this program is effective. We do not say in the script or anywhere else in the documentary that every juvenile should go through this program, that it works for every juvenile. Nor do we say that it has a one hundred percent success rate. . . .

I have produced numerous informational and documentary television programs over the last 15 years. I have received five Los Angeles area Emmys for other programs I have done. I am known by my colleagues as a very responsible and cautious documentary producer who will often avoid a dynamic piece of material if I feel that it is sensationalistic or inaccurate. There is nothing in "Scared Straight," either visually or in the narrative, that I feel is inaccurate, irresponsible, misleading or that I would want to change if I were rewriting the script today.[16]

Mr. John T. Reynolds, Executive Vice President of Golden West Broadcasters also defended "Scared Straight!" at the Congressional hearings. He said:

When we decided to produce "Scared Straight!" we didn't do it frivolously [sic] or with a feeling this was something that would be exploitable because obviously we knew we were going to produce a very controversial film. We did because we believed as broadcasters we have a responsibility to communicate to the world some of the things that go on in the world. . . .

[15] Arnold Shapiro, "Producers Defend Scared Straight," *The New York Times* (April 29, 1979).

[16] U.S., *Hearings, Oversight on Scared Straight*, pp. 45–46.

We decided to make this product and to do this film and to put it on the air after much thought because we thought it was an important message. The matter of degree of success is why we are here to discuss it today. If nothing else, people all over the country are talking about juvenile delinquency.[17]

Later in an article published in *p.d. cue* magazine, Mr. Reynolds accounted for the massive public response to the film as follows:

. . . after much review and discussion, it is our conclusion that the country was ready for and receptive to a television documentary dealing with the terrible increase in juvenile crime. In addition, contrary to most documentaries, "Scared Straight!" had a beginning, a middle and a positive ending. It had an ending which left viewers fulfilled and with a feeling of great hope that indeed there may be a means of effectively deterring the youth of America from a life of crime.[18]

One of the girls in "Scared Straight!" also testified at the hearings in defense of the documentary. She denied that there was any fabrication in the film and described her initial reactions as follows:

. . . when they said—you know, we were told to act and we had to—I ain't an actor, you know, that is what I am trying to say. That is why I got so mad when all that stuff came up because the only thing that was repeated because they wanted to film us walking in. We got there and they were not even ready for us yet. They didn't know we were there when we got there so that is the only thing we filmed over. When we walked in I thought, you know, this is great but what am I doing here. You know, I am never going to go to no prison.

When asked what she thought of the program she said:

A lot of them said that, you know, they saw it on TV. See, in our town at 10 o'clock the parks close and the night that "Scared Straight" was on the police didn't even have to chase no one, they all ran home at 9:30 to watch it. But they said like you have to watch it, it was a put-on. Who are you kidding?
You can ask them now and they will tell you it was not a put-on because, see, if they thought—a lot of people think that maybe

[17] Ibid., p. 67.
[18] John T. Reynolds, "The Scared Straight Phenomenon," *p.d. cue* magazine (August/September, 1979), pp. 20–22.

we were told to do certain things and how to act and what to say and all but when you go there and you are not on film and it is the same thing, then they know the truth. So you just have to go there, experience it and then you will know. . . .[19]

Finally, I asked ex-Lifer Frank Bindhammer about his own involvement with the film. That portion of our interview went as follows:

Finckenauer: What's been the aftermath of the film both in terms of your own involvement and in a kind of general sense?

Bindhammer: It was shown in Los Angeles the first time. If I'm not mistaken that was in October of '78 and the response was so overwhelming that they decided to attempt it here nationally.

Finckenauer: You mean that was not an original purpose?

Bindhammer: No. Oh no! Not that it wasn't the original purpose but they simply did not believe that they could sell it to other markets. O.K? It was only after it was aired in LA that they approached the Signal Company.

Finckenauer: You're not involved in this law suit, by the way, are you?

Bindhammer: Not to my knowledge.

Finckenauer: Because I want to ask questions about things that have to do with . . .

Bindhammer: You can ask, Jim. If I can't answer the question, I can't answer it.

Finckenauer: One of the issues has to do with the location or the areas in which the film was shown. I've not seen the briefs, but it's my understanding one of the complaints being made against the film people is that they were given assurances it would not be shown—

Bindhammer: No, that's not true, Jim. That is not true. I distinctly remember talking with Arnold Shapiro about that prior to the, his making this film. And the Lifers had inquired about it. Would this program be aired nationally or in any other area and Arnold's response to the best of my knowledge was, "It will probably only be shown in California because the New York markets and so forth have produced documentaries on this program, so there's a possibility that it will not be shown there." But the man did not make a commitment to the Lifers. There's absolutely,

---

[19] U.S., *Hearings, Oversight on Scared Straight,* pp. 99–100.

honestly, Jim, I'm not lying to you when I say this. I don't know what the Lifers said, I don't know what the parents or anyone else says, but I know for a fact that Arnold said this. I was present. And, you know, I can understand someone attacking the man if they have some justification but, and in that regard they do not. Now, I can only speak for what was said in my presence. Whatever happened with the parents or somebody else outside of that institution, I have no knowledge of that. But I know for a fact that he did not promise that the film would not be shown nationally.

Finckenauer: At what point in there did you leave the institution and become involved with that?

Bindhammer: Well, I was released September 19, 1978.

Finckenauer: So the film was actually completed?

Bindhammer: It had been completed. As a matter of fact, not only had it been completed but Arnold Shapiro brought the film into the institution to give a premiere and shortly thereafter I was released. When Arnold Shapiro found out that I was in fact released from prison, he contacted me and he asked me if I would be willing to come out to California to do a screening of "Scared Straight" and to talk about crime, institutional life, etc. and I agreed to do that. Golden West held the screening on their lot and I did in fact address a pretty large audience after viewing "Scared Straight" and their response was really tremendous. The President and Vice President of Golden West was rather impressed with my presentation and the following day when Arnold Shapiro drove me to the airport he mentioned that they expressed an interest in possibly asking me to come back to do some promotional work, and wanted to know if I would agree to do that. And I told him I would. Ten days later, I believe it was, I returned to California to do promotional spots for "Scared Straight." And, it was at that time that the management of Golden West and Signal Company asked me if I would, in fact, be interested in working with Golden West and I agreed to do that. As a result of, well, you're aware of the fact that I had traveled around the country promoting "Scared Straight" and talking to various people about initiating some of the programs in correctional institutions. As a result of the Congressional Subcommittee hearing the Signal Companies and Golden West decided to, not to promote the Juvenile Awareness concept. So, I wrote to John Reynolds, who is executive Vice President of Golden West and explained to him exactly what my situation was—what my thoughts and so forth were regarding the program and we agreed that I should do my own thing—which is to promote similar programs. So, I left their employment to do exactly that.

Finckenauer: In the period then, between roughly September and June, you were then traveling to various cities and the film was being shown and you were speaking to organizations and groups around the film as portraying the program?

Bindhammer: Well, my purpose of, yes, was to fill in all the gaps that "Scared Straight" left out.

Finckenauer: What kind of reaction did you get? Were you surprised at the reaction that this film got? And that you got?

Bindhammer: I think that most people are really ignorant to what crime and institution life like this is really about, Jim. And to hear somebody get up and talk about it, not simply attack Department of Corrections, but to try to be objective about it and give them some real insight into what it's about. It's something that they never heard before and they do respond favorably. I think that people should be made educated or they should be enlightened as to what is actually happening in these places.

Finckenauer: What was their reaction to the film? You saw people's original reactions?

Bindhammer: They were shocked! Because again, they were ignorant to what institution life is really about. They never heard anybody talk about these type of things.

Finckenauer: But they got the impression that this would be a thing to do?

Bindhammer: Not simply based on the film. Again, because there's so much more to the program than the documentary "Scared Straight." And that, I think, is what they were responding to more readily than to "Scared Straight."

Finckenauer: By and large they were supportive?

Bindhammer: Yes.

Finckenauer: What kinds of groups? College groups?

Bindhammer: No. No. These were all professional people. You're talking about youth services organization, law enforcement, juvenile judicial system, attorneys, mental health.

Finckenauer: What do you think is going to happen now? And when I say that, I mean, what do you think is going to happen in terms of the film, because I think a lot of people's knowledge about this whole thing has to do with the film. It doesn't go a lot beyond that.

Bindhammer: With regards to the film?

Finckenauer: Yes, what do you think is going to happen to that?

Bindhammer: I would personally like to see it back on the, I'd like to see it shown a number of times in every area with explanations. I think that if it is shown and the public is given a bit more insight into what the program is about, how the program, the faults of the program as well as the benefits, and let them decide whether or not the programs like this should be initiated in other institutions. I think you should share with the public not only your success but your failures. Let them know what the pitfalls of the program are.

Finckenauer: But I guess now if your judgment is correct, that they're now not advocating showing this film?

Bindhammer: As far as I know, they're not going to show it again. I don't know.

The postscript cannot yet be written on "Scared Straight!" The disposition of the law suit may determine its ultimate place in the history of film-making. However, it does seem clear that the documentary has misled the American public into thinking this is some kind of miracle cure for juvenile crime. The scare tactics in the Juvenile Awareness Project were overemphasized. This can result, and as we will see, has to some extent already resulted in encouraging the brutalizing, terrorizing, and traumatizing of youngsters across this country and elsewhere. Inmates may be exploited, and other kinds of inmate efforts to prevent delinquency may be discouraged or destroyed. For example, shortly after "Scared Straight!" was shown in California for the first time, inmates in San Quentin's SQUIRES program complained to KTLA about their program not being chosen as the subject for the documentary, since theirs is a California program. Inmates from a Rahway-type project at the Susanville prison in California criticized the publicity surrounding "Scared Straight!" for undermining the effectiveness of their own Dead-End Center program. Inmates from both California institutions indicated that the glare of publicity and controversy would severely damage the spontaneity, credibility, and authenticity of their own efforts.

Almost simultaneous with the events just traced in this chapter, other activities were taking place not far from the walls of Rahway State Prison. The location was the Rutgers University School of Criminal Justice in Newark. These activities, comprising my evaluation of the Juvenile Awareness Project, are detailed in the following three chapters.

part three

The Study

chapter six

How to Find Out
If The Project "Works"

My evaluation of the Juvenile Awareness Project was conceived in the late spring of 1977. The JAP had been in operation for some eight or nine months at that time, and approximately two thousand kids had participated in it. Public awareness of the project was still rather limited—this was before the extensive newspaper and magazine coverage; before the TV coverage; before the Department of Corrections' study; before the somewhat infamous "fondling incident" described earlier; before the *Readers' Digest* article; and before "Scared Straight!" The idea for the study came to me from the Assistant Dean of the School of Criminal Justice, who relayed a conversation about the Lifers' project between New Jersey's Chancellor of Higher Education and the then commissioner of the Department of Corrections. Corrections Commissioner Mulcahy expressed interest in there being an outside study or evaluation of the project. I was asked if I would be interested in such an undertaking and finding the idea fascinating, I readily agreed.

Since one can study little without financial support, my first step was to seek money to support the research. In order to present my ideas for evaluating the project, I decided to prepare a brief concept paper and a proposed budget. Before writing the paper, I arranged to visit Rahway Prison. There I spoke with Richard Rowe, who was the president of the Lifers' Group, observed a session while sitting on the stage, and discussed the project at length with Sgt. Alan August. I was also given descriptive information about the Lifers and about the project.

My first impressions from this visit remain vivid in my mind. I had been in the prison a number of times, so this part was not new. I had also worked in a juvenile correctional facility (Oceanfields, New Jersey) which used group confrontation techniques, and was thus very familiar with "shock-confrontation" as a treatment mode. Still, the Lifers' session made me uneasy. The particular group which I observed consisted of eight to ten girls and one boy. They all seemed to be very young (eleven to thirteen years old) and did not fit my conception of "hardcore" delinquents. The disturbing parts of the session were the unrelieved harshness of the inmates' approach and the belittling and berating of individual kids; but above all there was the sexual nature of the inmates' message to the girls. The latter consisted of explicit descriptions of the homosexual attacks which would be made upon these girls once they were confined in a female prison. The value to the girls of repetition of these scenes seemed debatable; further, I recall thinking that I would not want my own teen-age daughter subjected to this sort of treatment. I left the prison somewhat troubled and admittedly somewhat skeptical, but still intrigued with the idea of determining whether or not it "worked," and whether or not the claims of success were valid. Sometime later, I also attended a meeting of police juvenile aid officers at which Judge George Nicola described the project and expressed his belief in its effectiveness.

The concept paper which emanated stressed that, "the basic idea guiding the project is an effort to deter certain juveniles from committing offenses." I pointed out that the Juvenile Awareness Project would provide an excellent opportunity for trying to test the efficacy of the deterrence concept. The size of the sample of kids to be studied would be determined by the availability of resources and to some extent the length of the funding period. The questions that could be addressed in the proposed study were:

1. How is the "shock-confrontation" treatment modality received by the youth?
2. Which youth are deterred, if any?
3. Are any youth negatively affected with regard to both psychological effects and future behavior patterns?
4. Does the experience have a lasting, constructive influence on the participating juveniles?
5. What contributing factors such as age, sex, race, socioeconomic status, criminal history, peer influences, etc., influence receptivity to this approach?
6. Is there a typology of juveniles which can be defined in accordance with potential amenability to involvement in the project?

The proposal was sent first to the Victoria Foundation, Inc. and The Fund for New Jersey on July 28, 1977. The Victoria Foundation response was unpromising. The response from the Fund for New Jersey was equally unpromising, but did raise some interesting points. The answering letter said in part, "I have one major problem with the proposal and that is whether the questions you seek to answer can be answered in any reliable manner. . . . It is not clear to me that there is anything in your proposed research design which is capable of establishing a connection between a two- or three-hour visit to Rahway prison and the avoidance of arrest in the months and years which follow the visit. Conversely, it would be equally difficult to trace a subsequent arrest to the experience at the prison."[1] The perceptiveness of this letter rested in its questioning of the implicit causal assumptions of the JAP linking the prison visit to subsequent delinquent behavior.

The proposal was also sent to New Jersey's State Law Enforcement Planning Agency in the summer of 1977. This agency provided federal money for a variety of projects in law enforcement and criminal justice, including projects pertaining to juvenile delinquency and juvenile justice. SLEPA's first informal reaction to funding the study was also negative. The stated reason was that SLEPA was not mandated to support what they called pure research projects. Subsequent to this initial response however, the Lifers' Group also submitted a proposal to SLEPA for funding of the project itself. This action placed the agency (SLEPA) in a difficult position. There were those in SLEPA who were not enamored with the idea of giving public funds to a group of inmates, no matter how ostensibly worthy the cause. Resistance in some law enforcement circles was adamant. At the same time, SLEPA officials recognized that the Juvenile Awareness Project had become very popular and that the Lifers had many influential supporters. Thus, a flat turndown also did not seem particularly palatable. Financial support of my study, on the other hand, was seen as defensible because it was a necessary step before any consideration of direct funding could be given. This move would permit SLEPA to do something without treading into a potentially risky area.

This link which developed between my proposal and the Lifers' proposal was to cause later problems in the evaluation. The denial of funding directly to the Lifers coupled with approval of my application left the impression that I had, in effect, gotten their money. Although it seems clear that the Lifers had little or no chance of receiving funds, whether or not there was an evaluation, they and their supporters saw things differently. This did not make for a smooth working relationship, and it made the necessary cooperation that much more difficult to come by.

[1] Letter from Gordon A. MacInnes, Jr., Director, The Fund for New Jersey, August 2, 1977.

During the preparation of the application, questions arose about what agency should actually receive the funds, that is, Rutgers University or the Department of Corrections. SLEPA preferred the Department of Corrections, and the department agreed to house the study for administrative purposes. This decision also had implications for the study and its aftermath. Several were immediately clear. The department was going to be responsible for a study which it had not designed and maybe only partially understood, which was physically located in a university and run by university personnel, and which was going to be independent and autonomous in its implementation.

SLEPA approved the grant on October 27, 1977, after budget revisions to bring the SLEPA share below $20,000 which seemed to be some kind of necessary ceiling. The final total budget, including matching funds, was $21,272 for ten months (December 1, 1977—September 30, 1978).

It is important that neither SLEPA nor the DOC is a research-oriented agency. In neither agency was there much consideration of the design of the research, of the possible findings, nor of their potential implications. Also, there was no clear understanding of the possible pitfalls confronting the study. These and the failure to comprehend the fact that research is often a high-cost, high-risk activity were to bring problems later on. These problems were in part due to inadequate communication on my part, but they also seem to be inherent in evaluations undertaken in conjunction with operational criminal justice agencies.

DEALING WITH THE COURTS

One objective of the research was to secure information regarding arrests and adjudications of juveniles in the study sample. In accordance with the provisions of the New Jersey juvenile code, juvenile court judges in those counties which were the biggest referral sources to the Lifers' Project were immediately contacted by letter to gain permission for access to the desired information. This occurred at the end of October. In early November, one judge agreed to meet with me and Ms. Janet Storti, who was to be the full-time project specialist. (Janet was a second-year graduate student in the School of Criminal Justice.) The judge who asked for the meeting was somewhat suspicious of the Juvenile Awareness Project because the fondling incident described in Chapter 4 had just recently occurred and involved children from his jurisdiction. The judge was very supportive of our evaluation. However, he and several other judges indicated that we should gain the formal approval of the New Jersey Administrative Office of the Courts for the study. This body is the administrative arm of the New Jersey Supreme Court.

On November 16, 1977, a letter making such request for approval was submitted to the chief of the Juvenile and Domestic Relations Court Services of the AOC. The request included the SLEPA-approved privacy certification protecting the confidentiality of the juvenile subjects. There was no formal response to the request. There was a telephoned suggestion that we meet with Judge Nicola to introduce ourselves and brief him on the nature of the evaluation. This suggestion was made in the context of the Juvenile Awareness Project being Judge Nicola's "baby."

After several delays and problems with scheduling, the meeting with Judge Nicola took place in his office on December 19, 1977. He was, to say the least, not supportive of the study. He felt the Lifers should have gotten the SLEPA money. He was critical of the academic community which, according to him, knows little or nothing about the "real world." He saw no need for an evaluation since he already had collected hundreds of letters attesting to the success of the Juvenile Awareness Project. Judge Nicola offered us his letters, and he offered to pick the sample which should be studied.

Several days later, the AOC juvenile chief requested a written plan for gaining parental/guardian permission for sampled juveniles to participate in the evaluation. This plan was sent to them on December 23, 1977.

Over a month later, on January 25, 1978, I was advised by telephone and later by letter that the Supreme Court had met in administrative conference on January 19th. The Court had "requested that Judge Nicola discuss the . . . proposal with the other . . . judges and then submit to the Supreme Court for its approval a plan agreeable to all the judges for you to access the juvenile records."[2] The letter went on to suggest "that Ms. Storti cease attempting to obtain lists of the juveniles who attended or who will attend the Lifers' Program unless and until the Supreme Court approves your proposal."[3]

I spoke with Judge Nicola about the so-called plan on January 31, 1978. He invited Janet and me to the monthly dinner meeting of the juvenile judges to be held the following February 8th. The purpose of this was to explain what we were doing and answer any questions. The judge indicated he had confidence in his program and that not to do an evaluation would be a mistake. He conceded that Rutgers University was a "pedigree" institution. He said he endorsed the evaluation, and he

---

[2] Letter from The Supreme Court of New Jersey, January 25, 1978.
[3] Ibid.

felt the dinner would speed-up the process for the plan to be presented to the state Supreme Court. He added, significantly, that he was not stalling the procedures. Nicola did question again my "theory hypothesis" that the program does not work (he was referring back to my earlier discussion with him of what my null hypothesis was). He said other judges would question this as well.

Janet and I attended the judges' dinner and meeting. Judge Nicola, acting as host, was charming and supportive. One might have gotten the impression that this whole thing was his idea. He presented the proposal; we said nothing; there were no questions; the judges approved overwhelmingly.

Despite surmounting what I thought was the final obstacle, nothing happened for the next six weeks. Then on March 21, 1978—exactly three months and three weeks into the study, and exactly four months and one week since the first request was made—a letter was received indicating that ". . . the Supreme Court has granted your request . . ."[4] This meant that the sample selection originally scheduled for January could finally begin in full in April. It meant that nearly 40 percent of the allotted time and almost that much of the budget had been expended, but the real work of the study had not begun.

Whatever the cause or causes of the delays, and whether or not they were justified, the effects were not helpful—to say the least.

THE STUDY DESIGN AND THE REALITY

The Plan

The research design proposed to evaluate the Juvenile Awareness Project was explanatory; through an analysis of relationships among various aspects of the project and its results, it would be possible to find reasons why particular events and reactions occurred. The specific goals of the research were to evaluate the psychological and behavioral reactions the juveniles experienced as a direct result of their involvement in the project, the recidivism rate of these juveniles, and the extent to which the initial exposure and the effects therefrom were manifested in the lives of the participants. These were to be quantitatively and qualitatively measured to demonstrate both short- and long-term results.

The objectives of the approved study plan were as follows:

1. Select and interview a random sample of approximately fifty juveniles who have participated in the project since its inception in September, 1976. These interviews will have two components: (1)

[4] Letter from The Supreme Court of New Jersey, March 21, 1978.

administration of an anonymous self-reported delinquency instrument, of which there are a number available, e.g., Porterfield, Short and Nye, and Gold; (2) structured questions to ascertain impressions of and reactions to the project. Some of the juveniles in this sample will have attended the project more than a year before.

2. As a supplementary verification of the self-report information, efforts will be made to secure information regarding arrest and adjudication of the sampled juveniles. Section 24 a. (6) of L. 1973, c. 306 provides that "Records shall be made available to any person or agency interested in a case or in the work of the agency keeping the records, by the order of the court for good cause shown." The appropriate courts will be petitioned for access to the desired information.

3. Correlation of the dependent variable of outcome measures, obtained as indicated above, with the independent variables of age, educational level, sex, race, socio-economic status, and previous criminal history.

4. Selection of a sample of approximately one-hundred juveniles designated for attendance at the project. Random assignment of fifty of the juveniles to an experimental group and fifty to a control group. The experimental group will attend the project; the control group will not.

5. Standardized psychological tests will be administered to both the experimental and control groups on a before and after basis. The only intervening variable not controlled for by random assignment will be attendance at the project. Possible tests being considered for this purpose are the Attitudes Toward Punishment of Criminals scale developed by Thurstone and Wang, and the Attitudes Toward any Institution scale developed by Kelley. These scales were used in a study by Stanley Brodsky of attitude changes among delinquent and predelinquent groups who were exposed to a "Prison Profiles" program at Illinois State Penitentiary. Other possibilities include the California Personality Inventory or a semantic differential measure.

6. Self-report delinquency instruments will be administered to both the experimental and control groups from four to six months after the experimental group has visited Rahway. The experimental group will also be questioned about impressions of and reactions to the project.

7. Other behavioral measures for both groups will be sought as described above.

8. Correlations of dependent and independent variables will be made as described in (3) above.

The plan also included a discussion of alternative methods to be followed if the original design did not work out for some reason. The possibilities were outlined as follows:

Alternatives to the classical experimental design proposed include a quasi-experimental design, in which a similar comparison group—but not a control group—is tested and assessed. This type of design is less rigorous in that the absence of random assignment leaves open the possibility of other uncontrolled variables entering into the outcome. Comparability of groups can also be a problem. It is, however, probably the best alternative method to be used if necessary. It is relatively convenient, flexible, and can allow for quick decisions by working backward in time.

Another alternative is an ex post facto or "after only" design. This type of design does not employ control or comparison groups and, therefore, limits the confidence that can be placed in any findings and conclusions.

A combination of the before/after and after only designs could also be used. The juveniles attending the Rahway sessions could be pre- and post-tested to give a before/after psychological measure. A sample could then be followed-up in the community to obtain an after only behavioral measure. The absence of a control or comparison group would again limit the validity of any findings.

The experimental design is considered to be the best and most rigorous method of conducting evaluative research. It is the research design of first choice, but if for some reason it proves to be infeasible, a quasi-experiment will be designed and implemented.

Adjustments in the Plan

As indicated, one objective of the evaluation was to select a sample of approximately one hundred juveniles designated for attendance at the Juvenile Awareness Project. These juveniles were to be randomly assigned to experimental and control groups—fifty youths to each.

In order to select a sample representative of the type of juveniles attending the project, monthly reports of sponsoring agencies visiting Rahway during September, October, and November, 1977, were obtained from the Lifers. Out of state agencies and agencies serving a national population such as the Job Corps were excluded. The remaining forty-nine agencies were classified by agency type. These types were: counseling (youth services bureaus, Big Brothers, family services, etc.), police, educational (high schools, etc.), drug treatment (NARCO, Inc., D.A.R.E., etc.), employment (youth employment services, vocational rehabilitation, etc.), and recreational (YMCA, YWCA, Boys Clubs, etc.). It should be noted that only one of these agency types (the police) is a law enforcement agency. Only two (the police and drug treatment) could be expected to be handling almost exclusively juvenile offenders. The others, with the exception of probation departments which were classified as counseling agencies, handle all kinds of kids, most of whom are nondelinquent.

A stratified random sample of twenty-eight sponsoring agencies was selected to represent agency type. I wanted to insure that the agencies were represented in our sample in the same proportions in which they were represented in the total referral group of forty-nine. The reason for this was a suspicion that the types of kids being referred to Rahway were in part dependent upon the types of agencies which were referring them. In other words, I suspected that the police might be referring a different type of kid than the YMCA was referring, and that a probation department might be referring a different type of kid than a high school was.

Each of the agencies in the sample was contacted and asked if they would be willing to participate in the evaluation. If willing, they were asked to provide the names of juveniles proposed to visit Rahway. They were told to use whatever selection procedures and criteria they were normally and routinely using to select juveniles for participation in the Lifers' project. The juveniles nominated were not to include any who had already visited Rahway.

The above process began in December, 1977, but was seriously stymied and delayed by the court permission problems described. From the agency sample, only eleven agencies (two cooperatively) actually provided us with the names of juveniles that were included in our sample. This represented a comparatively large attrition problem, the reasons for which were numerous and varied. These reasons included:

1. Agency refusal to cooperate with no particular reason given.

2. Agency advised not to cooperate with the evaluation. An example of this was the fact that no agencies in Judge Nicola's jurisdiction were willing to work with us. A probation officer from Judge Nicola's county asked for a private meeting. He explained that he had serious questions about the Lifers' project and Judge Nicola's role in it, but said he could not cooperate with us because it might jeopardize his employment.

3. Personnel problems, that is, the agency had no one to transport the kids to the prison.

4. Failure to gain parent/guardian permission before releasing names of juveniles to us. Two police departments had this problem. Our letter to the particular parents asking for signed consent came as a great surprise and shock to some previously uninformed parents. They became angry about what they viewed as an unauthorized disclosure of their child's name and refused permission. The police departments asked us to destroy the lists and to forget the whole thing.

5. Provided names of juveniles who had already attended the Juvenile Awareness Project. This was discovered accidentally in a review

of the attendance rosters at Rahway. Although this could have been done inadvertently (which says something about the referring agency's record-keeping system), I suspect that in some cases it could have been done purposely. Knowing that this was an evaluation, some agencies—wanting the project to look good—simply gave us a sample of known successes. In any event, each name had to be checked against the roster at the prison.

6. Inability or unwillingness to go along with the need for random assignment of some juveniles to a control group. This is not an atypical or unusual problem in criminal justice research. It often militates against the use of pure experimental designs. Some agencies had participation in the project mandated by the court as a condition of probation for their clients. Thus, they could not hold back any kids to be used as controls.

This agency attrition problem consumed a large amount of Janet's time, in particular. Numerous and repeated telephone contacts were made with sponsors; letters describing the evaluation were sent; copies of the privacy certification were sent; and meetings were held. More often than not, after a considerable investment of time and resources, the sponsoring agency did not come through for the reasons already enumerated.

The eleven agencies which ultimately participated included six counseling agencies, two police departments, one high school, one neighborhood employment service center and a YMCA. The kids came from urban areas, for example, Newark and Trenton, as well as from smaller communities. One agency participating was the Ridgefield Park Police Department, which also furnished subjects for the "Scared Straight!" documentary.

The design called for random assignment to experimental and control groups within the designated lists received from each agency. This was done by simply alternating assignment of subjects to the two groups. Two pairs of agencies made joint referrals because they had a cooperative arrangement. This meant that eleven agencies in effect made nine sets of referrals.

Attrition continued to be a nagging problem. Once the names were obtained, each parent or guardian had to be contacted to give informed, written permission for their child to participate in the study. Only a few overtly refused, but many simply failed to respond which meant these kids could not be included. It also meant considerable lost time waiting to see whether or not they would respond and how. Human subjects concerns such as this are another common problem in criminal justice research, particularly where juveniles are involved. Although important and necessary, the need for written consent does not facilitate evaluation efforts. Some of the further attrition was also attributable to the juveniles themselves, although sometimes due to events beyond their control. Juveniles who had been pretested on the attitude tests failed to appear for their visit to the prison (agencies were responsible for transportation of these kids as with any others). Pretested juveniles went to Rahway, but failed to appear for their posttest. Both pre- and posttesting was done in the agencies by Janet and myself. Kids in the control group—who had not been anywhere or done anything despite knowing they were in a study—failed to show up for the posttest. Their motivation was obviously less than that of the experimental kids. Some kids got locked up, or moved, or simply disappeared somewhere in the process. Consequently, although hundreds of kids were involved at some early point, the hoped-for fifty experimentals and fifty controls was not achieved.

A different set of problems was presented by the agencies in the sample—problems which resulted in yet more attrition, and in the experimental design becoming a quasi-experimental design in which assignment to experimental and control groups was not purely random for all agencies.

After the assignments, despite instructions and admonitions to the contrary, two sponsors took both experimentals and controls to Rahway, thereby losing the controls. This reflects their failure to recognize the nature and importance of a control group. In one of these cases, a subsequent group designated for attendance was held back and used as a comparison group. Two other sponsors failed to take their experimentals to the project as scheduled. One agency sponsor twice failed to show up at Rahway after being given dates and waiting two months on the waiting list each time. He was called several times to remind him of the dates. Because he had no good reason for the no shows, the Lifers refused to reschedule the visit. One other agency sponsor, with a large number of pretested juveniles, simply changed his mind and backed out. It was decided to use these pretested juveniles in the comparison group. Thus, for five agencies the assignment was purely random; for one agency the experimentals and controls were selected separately; for two agencies (the high school and the YMCA) there were no experimentals; and, for one agency (a police department) there were no controls.

Although dictated by reasons of feasibility, the design was still considered to be sufficiently rigorous to protect against the effects of extraneous variables on the outcome measures. Each juvenile in the sample was designated by the referring agency for participation in JAP in accordance with the selection criteria employed by that agency. The problems that occurred in maintaining the experimental design did not reflect any uniform pattern which might seriously bias the sample. Also, the sponsors did not know which juveniles were designated as experimentals and which as controls. However, the experimentals and controls cannot be assumed to be comparable. Instead, this needs to be confirmed and the differences accounted for. A total of forty-six experimentals and thirty-five controls was finally included in the study.

Looking for More Money

With all the problems and delays, it became apparent in the spring and early summer of 1978 that the evaluation could not possibly be completed by the end of September. Therefore, as is all too often the fate of researchers, other options including additional funds and time had to be sought if the study was to be brought to a successful conclusion. A meeting was held with representatives of the Department of Corrections to propose that Janet's position be absorbed into the department's regular budget after September. Unfortunately, the proposal was rejected. On April 14, 1978, I received a letter from an assistant commissioner of the department which said in part:

> I am extremely concerned over the news that you now feel that your evaluation of the Lifers' Group program will not be completed with the time constraints of the grant period. . . . I am aware that you encountered some difficulties in obtaining access to the juvenile court records. However, since the initial delay in obtaining permission to use Court records was approximately three months, I question why a six month continuation is now requested.
> You have suggested that the costs of Ms. Janet Storti's position be assumed by the State in order to complete the evaluation. I must advise you that, because of present budgetary constraints, there are no State or SLEPA funds available for continuation of this project. I must also point out that the request is rather extraordinary in light of your first commitment to complete the project in 10 months and for $20,000.[5]

A research proposal for just under $6,000 was submitted to the National Institute of Mental Health small grants section in May. These funds would have supported some part of the field research after September. It too was rejected. Why? ". . . the Committee questioned whether a post-test only control group design with such a poorly assessed treatment will yield any treatment effect after a 4–6 month lag, a lag that at the same time is probably too short in terms of dependent

[5] Letter from The State of New Jersey, Department of Corrections, April 14, 1978.

variable behavior."[6] This was not a post-test only design. Also, it had been hypothesized that there would be no treatment effect no matter how long the follow-up. However, the funds sought would have permitted the longer follow-up period suggested.

Three private foundations or individuals were contacted about supporting the continuation of the evaluation. Two turned it down because of limited funds and one failed to respond.

The Federal Juvenile Justice and Delinquency Prevention Administration was approached on July 1, 1978. Our proposal to them was also rejected, but not until January 17, 1979. The reasons were that the paper was said to be weak on "adequacy of the research design and methodology" and on "scope of proposed research."[7] Finally, we went back to SLEPA asking for a ten-month continuation for approximately $12,000. Their response was to extend the study period through January 31, 1979, but without additional funds.

Beginning on October 1, 1978, the evaluation had to proceed as a part-time endeavor with a mixed bag of limited support from SLEPA, the Department of Corrections, and the university. The detailing of this part of the history of the study is not intended as an excuse nor as an effort to criticize the agencies mentioned, but simply as an attempt to inform would-be researchers and evaluators of some of the realities and pitfalls which confront those who work in this business. The discussion is to clarify some of the difficulties and the obstacles which must be overcome in attempting a program evaluation of this kind. Two of the major failures on my part were in not anticipating the drawn-out court permission process and thus planning accordingly, and in not adequately communicating the nature of and inherent risks in research to two organizations which are by and large not sensitive to these risks.

CRITICISMS OF THE STUDY METHODS

I think it is important to describe those criticisms of the study that were focused on considerations of how it was done before further discussing the results. These criticisms came largely from two sources which can be conveniently grouped first into what might be called the lay critics (those who are not research scientists and were thus reacting more on common sense or intuitive grounds to what was done). This group includes some persons who work in juvenile or criminal justice agencies.

---

[6] Letter from The National Institute of Mental Health, n.d.

[7] Letter from The United States Department of Justice: Office of Juvenile Justice and Delinquency Prevention, January 11, 1979.

Next are the critics who are researchers and/or statisticians. These persons are generally well-versed in research and evaluation methods.

The Lay Criticism

The lay critics include mainly the Lifers themselves, members of the Lifers' Group Advisory Committee, some referral agents to the JAP, and many just plain believers and supporters in general. Some examples of the criticisms from this group are the following:

> The program does not need defending . . . What has to be done is that this research has to be questioned. Let's stop accepting research based on very limited data. They have come out with broad, broad conclusions based on a follow up of only 81 juveniles out of a total of 13,600 who have gone through the program.[8]

> Judge George Nicola
> (quoted in *The Sunday Trentonian*,
> April 29, 1979)

> We question the motives of dilettantes who compromise their intellectual integrity by thrusting themselves into the national limelight with meaningless statistics deceptively presented as the product of scientific study. Out of fourteen thousand youngsters who have visited Rahway, the Rutgers' scholars surveyed a mere eighty-one, of which thirty-five made up a "control" group. Should a serious reputable scholar take this inadequate study to *The New York Times* and pompously declare our program doesn't work, and, most incredible of all, that it may actually cause crime? No right thinking academician of any stature would condone such unprofessional conduct. We dismiss the Rutgers' study for what it is— Nonsense!"[9]

> Robert J. McAlesher
> Staff Advisor to the Executive Committee,
> Rahway Lifers' Group
> (Prepared statement for U.S. Congress House
> Subcommittee on Human Resources,
> May 29, 1979)

> I don't like the way they did it. The control group did not match up. Some of the teenagers had no records . . . Finckenauer

---

[8] Ken Carolan, "Is 'Scared' Straight?" *The Sunday Trentonian*, April 29, 1979.

[9] Statement to U.S. Congress, House Subcommittee on Human Resources of The Committee on Education and Labor, *Hearings, Oversight on Scared Straight*, 96th Cong., 1st Sess., June 4, 1979, p. 148.

was here one time in three years. He had his mind made up before he started.[10]

Lieutenant Alan August
(quoted in *The Rutgers Daily Targum,*
January 23, 1980)

This criticism also included assertions that Janet Storti was unqualified to work on the study; that I personally spent too little time on it; and, as shown above, that I visited the project only a few times in the course of my study. My response to these criticisms is that they are absolutely without merit.

Although these particular criticisms are not really substantive, some others are. For example, Lt. August's statement reflects a view that I had a negative bias against the project from the beginning which slanted the evaluation. The proposal which SLEPA funded clearly stated the null hypothesis to be tested in the evaluation as follows: "The basic or key hypothesis underlying this evaluation is that the Juvenile Awareness Project has no effect, either psychologically or behaviorally, on the juveniles attending. We hypothesize no significant differences on pre- and post-testing experimentals, nor between experimentals and controls on post-testing. We also hypothesize no significant differences in behavioral outcomes between experimentals and controls."[11] The basis for this criticism perhaps rests in part in a lack of understanding about what a null hypothesis is. But, it also seems to derive from an absence of trust in evaluators. There is some feeling that evaluators simply concoct data and statistics to support some preconceived notion. Unfortunately, there are instances in which this has occurred. In any event, it is certainly possible. Perhaps the best response to this lack of trust issue that I can make was contained in my prepared statement delivered before the House subcommittee which investigated "Scared Straight!"

I assured both the New Jersey State Law Enforcement Planning Agency (the funding source) and the New Jersey Department of Corrections that I would conduct an evaluation which would be as thorough, complete and fair as possible within the limitations of time and resources. And, most important, I would let the chips fall where they might in terms of findings. If the Project worked, I was prepared to say so; if not, I was also prepared to say that. In my judgement, to have done otherwise would have been to foolishly jeopardize my credibility as a social scientist. There was

[10] Frank Argote Freyre, "Reality of Prison Life Detailed by 'Lifers,' " *The Rutgers Daily Targum* (January 23, 1980).

[11] Proposal to evaluate Juvenile Awareness Project Help.

no particular gain to me personally or professionally, say in terms of publishing articles or reports, which would have been enhanced by faking the study. However, the losses from such a fraud, if discovered, would have been professionally catastrophic.

Another point made repeatedly by the lay critics was that the sample studied was too small to provide a meaningful assessment of the project. This criticism was echoed by the New Jersey Corrections Commissioner, who was quoted in *The New York Times* as saying he was not completely satisfied with my report because only eighty-one juveniles were studied.

Sample size is usually a function of the time and resources available to do a particular study. The issues of time and resources have already been discussed in considerable detail earlier. There are numerous research examples of the use of relatively small samples to generalize about considerably larger populations, for example, the Gallup, Harris, and Roper opinion polls. The secret, of course, rests in the science of sampling and the extent to which a sample is representative of the population that one wishes to describe.

It is also a fact of research methodology that small samples increase the difficulty of finding statistically significant differences between groups. This should be kept in mind when reading the findings in Chapters 7 and 8. It is apparent from these chapters that my interpretations of the data were deliberately conservative so as to account for the relatively small sample size. Some more will be said about sample size specifically in the next section. None of the aforesaid should be interpreted as meaning that we would not have preferred a larger sample if that had been possible. All other things being equal, researchers almost always prefer larger samples to study.

Yet another criticism of the sample was that the group studied was not representative of the kinds of kids routinely attending the project. I think this issue has been adequately addressed in the earlier discussion of how the sample was chosen. The attrition of agencies and juveniles did not reflect any uniform pattern which should bias the sample. On the other hand, it is possible that the lack of cooperation on the part of some agencies could be interpreted as possibly limiting the more likely failures among both experimentals and controls. That is, agencies less than confident in how their outcomes would look might have been more inclined to not want to be involved in the evaluation. If this were so, the effect would be to inflate the results in a positive direction. This we should bear in mind when the findings are reviewed.

Last, there was the criticism that the experimental and control groups were not comparable, and thus my comparisons were unfairly prejudiced against the experimental group. This important point has been raised as well by the critical professionals. Since their challenge is a much more sophisticated one, it will be discussed in the next section and again in Chapters 7 and 8.

The Professional Criticism

A number of critical responses to my research from fellow researchers have been chosen as representative of the types of criticisms which were made. These particular comments proved to be helpful because they stimulated new and additional data analyses in an effort to respond to the questions which were raised. First is a letter from a psychologist which was written to Corrections Commissioner William Fauver:

As a social science researcher and methodologist, and as a strong supporter of New Jersey's efforts on the part of juveniles, I want to alert you to a very serious methodological flaw in Dr. Finckenauer's evaluation of the Juvenile Awareness Program. Unfortunately, *this* flaw is serious enough to render the evaluation uninterpretable and obvious enough to discredit it in the scientific/academic community.

In order to insure the unbiased evaluation of any treatment, that is, to insure that treatment-control group differences are due to the treatment alone and not to extraneous factors, it is necessary that research participants be randomly assigned to treatment and control groups. Random assignment is the only procedure available to scientists that assures treatment and control group equivalence and comparability. So central is this procedure to experimental evaluation methodology that evaluations which do not use it cannot appropriately be called "experiments."

. . . it is clear . . . that the 81 juveniles he studied were not randomly assigned to conditions. And despite Dr. Finckenauer's claims that the two groups were similar prior to treatment, there is ample evidence already available which suggests that the two groups *did* differ prior to treatment, and that they differed along at least one critical dimension. The *Times* reports "Of the experimental group, 27 had arrest records, 19 did not. In the control group, 14 had arrest records, 21 did not." These figures strongly suggest that the treatment or experimental group contained more delinquents, proportionately, than did the control group. As social scientists (and people in every walk of life) have long known, the best predictor of future behavior is past behavior. It is much more likely that the treatment group members . . . were arrested more frequently after the treatment than the control group members . . .

because they were from a different, more delinquent population to begin with than that the Juvenile Awareness Program somehow "caused" them to commit crimes. Unfortunately, the cause of the treatment-control group differences found by Dr. Finckenauer are unknowable. Because we know that the groups were different to begin with—and may have differed on a countless number of other important characteristics as well as the one noted, it is actually *not possible* to make *any conclusions* about the effectiveness of the Juvenile Awareness Program on this study.[12]

This letter raises the comparability of groups issue and asserts that the absence of random assignment to experimental/control groups discredits the results. The problem of lack of randomness has already been discussed—the methods used to compensate for this problem will be described in the chapters on findings.

A letter to the editors of *Psychology Today* following that magazine's publication of my August, 1979, article entitled "Scared Crooked," made some of these same points, but further elaborated upon them. This letter, coauthored by the chairman of the Panel on Research on Rehabilitation of Criminal Offenders of the National Academy of Sciences, said in part:

In reporting his own research on the effects on delinquents of the Juvenile Awareness Program ("Scared Crooked," August), James O. Finckenauer asserts that his so-called experimental and control subjects were comparable in age, sex, race, delinquency potential, and prior criminal history. By "comparable," Finckenauer apparently means that the groups did not differ in statistically significant ways. But prior to treatment, 59 percent of the experimental group had a history of delinquency, whereas only 40 percent of the control group did. The experimental group had a higher delinquency "seriousness" score, more boys, and more minority youngsters than did the control group. All these differences, though not large, are in the direction of predicting higher risk of posttreatment delinquent behavior in the group exposed to treatment—exactly the result that was found. If the outcomes were tested against the existing data for each group before treatment, the change in delinquency would not have been significant, either.

We believe it entirely possible that kids with greater tendencies toward delinquent behavior, whether it was manifested in a prior record or not, were more likely to be sent to Rahway for treatment. The reason for demanding randomization is that there

[12] Letter to William H. Fauver, New Jersey Commissioner of Corrections, May 28, 1979.

are so many ways in which subtle biases can enter into group-assignment decisions made on any other basis. Randomization is the cornerstone on which experimentation rests, and is essential to the drawing of unequivocal inferences of cause. Finckenauer states that individuals were assigned randomly to the treatment or control groups. However, we received early reports on this research from Finckenauer's office that indicated that efforts at randomization were not wholly successful, and that frankly label the study design as quasi-experimental. How it became a randomized design, meriting the interpretations it has, deserves explanation.

We do not believe that Finckenauer's study provides a basis for any conclusion about the effectiveness of the Juvenile Awareness Program other than that it will not be easy to find out how effective the program may be.[13]

In addition to the issues of comparability and random assignment, the letter implies that agencies were exercising some kind of selection bias in determining which kids went to Rahway. As explained earlier, that was clearly not the case. The agencies themselves had no say over which kids were experimentals and which were controls.

Next is part of an appraisal of my work by the director of research for an Arizona juvenile court center. This writer also proposes wrongly that the agencies controlled the selection process.

First of all, there is the matter of attrition. Forty-six instead of 50 are in the experimental group and 35 instead of 50 are in the control group. The loss of 4 candidates in the experimental group could easily have happened by chance. Perhaps one or two moved; another may have refused to participate, etc. But it is highly unlikely that chance factors would cause the attrition of 15 subjects from the control group.[14]

This same evaluator said the following about the issue of sample size:

The original intent of the study was to have 50 experimentals and 50 controls. For reasons which I have not yet been able to determine, only 35 juveniles appear in the control group and 46 in the experimental group. Dr. Finckenauer argues that statistically samples larger than 30 are adequate for estimating population

[13] Lee Sechrest, Robin Redner, "Letter to the Editor," *Psychology Today* (November, 1979).

[14] Letter from Gene A. Fisher, Director of Research, Juvenile Court: Superior Court of the State of Arizona, May 21, 1979.

averages and differences between groups, and he is quite correct in that increasing a sample from 30 cases to an infinite number of cases reduces the sampling error by only 4 percent. But the practical difficulties of doing a study like this argue strongly for a larger sample.[15]

This writer did concur that the general finding of my study, ". . . that the program has no effect, is valid."

Finally, the staff director of the U.S. House Subcommittee on Human Resources submitted my reports, along with the Department of Corrections' 1977 study and Golden West Television's informal survey, to the Congressional Research Service of The Library of Congress. The three questions asked and the responses pertinent to my research were as follows:

Question 1. Was Dr. Finckenauer's sample size large enough to be representative of young people who had been through the JAP at the time of the study?

There are two aspects of this question to consider. In order to draw reliable conclusions about the 8,000 young people who had participated in the Juvenile Awareness Program, the sample must be large enough, and it must be chosen so that it is representative of the group.

In the case of the Finckenauer study, the sample was large enough to determine if the Juvenile Awareness Program had a large impact on the recidivism of the young people, but not large enough to determine effects of lesser magnitude. For example, if the program improved the recidivism rate of the participants by 30 or 40 percent, the sample size used by Finckenauer would show that the program had a significant effect. However, if the program actually improved the recidivism rate by about 10 percent, a sample of this size would probably show the program's effects to be insignificant.

For purposes of evaluating the JAP, the sample size used in the Finckenauer study was adequate to test the claims of those who viewed the JAP as a phenomenal success, but was probably inadequate to test the more moderate claims that the program is a good addition to an overall effort against juvenile delinquency. . . .

There are serious questions about the representativeness of the sample used in the Finckenauer report. There are two primary areas of concern. First, although care was taken to insure that the sample would be drawn from a representative group of the agencies which participate in the JAP, the actual sample was drawn from less than half of this group of agencies. Second, out of the 100 youths chosen for the study, only 81 actually participated. No tests

[15] Ibid.

were performed to determine if there were any significant differences between those who did and did not participate in the study.

For these reasons it is not possible to have confidence that the
Finckenauer sample was representative of the 8,000 youths who
participated in the JAP. It should also be noted, however, that it is
not possible to say for certain that the sample was not representative. The problem is simply that one cannot be confident that
the sample was representative.

Question 2. Is the methodology used sufficient to support the
conclusion that "The juveniles in the group which attended the
Juvenile Awareness Project were somewhat more delinquent than
the comparison juveniles, but not significantly so"?

The particular method used to test for real differences
between the two groups was appropriate and consistent with
standard statistical procedures. . . .

Question 3. Compare the reliability of the Finckenauer
studies and the information found in The New Jersey State
Department of Correction's "An Evaluation of the Lifers' Group
Juvenile Awareness Program," and in Golden West Television's
"An Informal Follow-up Survey."

. . . . The Finckenauer reports claim to be rigorous statistical
analyses and can be evaluated as such. . . .

. . . . With respect to the success or failure of the JAP on the
recidivism rate of the youths who went through the program, the
Finckenauer reports are considerably more statistically reliable
than either of the other reports. However, as noted above, the
Finckenauer reports themselves are not without their problems.[16]

This appraisal points out that there are certain methodological
flaws in my research, and these will be addressed in succeeding chapters. At the same time, the critique seems generally positive in its overall appraisal.

This interchange and discourse on the pros and cons of evaluation
research was basically as it should be, healthy and informative. There
have been those on occasion who seemed to hit below the belt and/or,
in my judgment, assumed a condescending and even sarcastic posture;
but by and large the dialogue was very professional and enlightening.
The latter, I think, represents the search for knowledge at its best. We
will next explore the findings which have been alluded to in these
various discussions.

---

[16] Memo to U.S. Congress, House Subcommittee on Human Resources of The
Committee on Education and Labor, *Hearings, Oversight on Scared Straight,* 96th Cong.,
1st Sess., June 4, 1979, p. 241.

chapter seven

Changing Behavior

The Juvenile Awareness Project seemed to me to provide an excellent opportunity for testing the usefulness of fear and intimidation in deterring juvenile delinquency. The Lifers' Group and their supporters have emphasized this objective in so many words.

This part of my evaluation was grounded in deterrence theory, based upon the premise that it is deterrence that provides the project with its theoretical base. The project's guiding theme seems to be to deter juveniles from committing criminal offenses, whether or not they have previously committed them. All of this had to be only a premise on my part because there were no explicitly stated causal assumptions for the project. As was the case with most of the delinquency prevention efforts discussed in the first chapter, no one seemed to have clearly thought through, or presented the case in any definitive way showing why this particular approach should be expected to work.

As already indicated, a number of substantial differences exist between the available research on deterrence and this study of the Juvenile Awareness Project. However, if one mentally constructs a three-legged deterrence model based upon perceptions of swiftness, certainty, and severity, it seems reasonable to assume that the Lifers'

Group cannot influence perceptions of swiftness and certainty. These legs in the model are dependent upon the actual or perceived reactions of the juvenile justice system—the police, intake, the juvenile court, probation, and finally training schools and reformatories.

That leg of the deterrence model remaining is perceptions of severity, of harshness. How awful are the consequences? How bad can prison and punishment be? The Lifers' Group, and others who emulate the scaring technique, must deal with the constraint of being limited to this one leg, and must attempt to convince youths who are amenable to convincing that confinement in a maximum security prison is a reasonably likely consequence of their future involvement in delinquent behavior. [Not only did this seem to be a difficult if not impossible task, but its potential for success was limited by the results of previously cited research evidence which showed that perceived severity has no particular deterrent effect.] It doesn't matter how bad it is; if the targets, whether juveniles or adults, are not convinced that there is a reasonable certainty—an unacceptable risk—of the punishment occurring, they are not likely to be scared straight.

The goals of the research reported in this chapter are to evaluate the subsequent behavior of juveniles exposed to the Lifers and the prison, and to compare this behavior with that of the control group.

THE METHODS FOR ASSESSING BEHAVIOR

Juvenile court records in the six New Jersey counties from which the eighty-one juveniles came were surveyed for a period of six months after the experimental group visited Rahway, and after the control group was pretested. This was done to determine whether or not there was any recorded delinquent behavior for either experimentals or controls. It should be noted that these court records contain only information that has been officially reported to the juvenile court. The information may exist in the form of complaints, arrests, or adjudications (convictions). The records were similarly obtained for all cases using the same criteria.

Where records of delinquency were found, they were reviewed for type of delinquency (before and after visit or pretest) and number of delinquencies (before and after). Type of delinquency was weighted according to seriousness by classification as a juvenile in need of supervision (JINS) offense or a juvenile delinquency (JD or criminal) offense. The former classification consists of what are known as status offenses. These include such behaviors as running away, truancy, and incorrigibility which are not crimes if committed by adults. They are unique to the juvenile status, thus the phrase status offenses. This weighting permitted a rough determination of not only whether one group committed more offenses than the other, but also whether these offenses were more or less serious. For comparative purposes, a mean seriousness of delinquency score for each juvenile was developed. Nondelinquency was weighted as zero, JINS offenses as one, and JD offenses were given a weight of two. The score resulted from multiplying each offense by its weight and then adding them for each youth. For those experimental juveniles having prior offenses, subsequent offenses could be considered an indicator of recidivism.

INITIAL FINDINGS

Initial examination of juvenile court records revealed that nineteen of the forty-six youths in the experimental group (41 percent) had no record of prior offenses. This finding was a surprise because I, and presumably many others, had been led to believe that all referrals to the Juvenile Awareness Project were delinquents. Certainly the Scared Straight! documentary very strongly gave this impression. Among those who had visited the prison, the number of offenses for those with prior records ranged from one to as many as eleven. The seriousness of delinquency scores ranged from zero for those with no priors to twenty-two. The mean seriousness score was 4.26; excluding the nineteen non-delinquents, it was 7.26. Among the controls, twenty-one of the thirty-five juveniles (60 percent) had no prior record. But, keep in mind that all these youth (experimentals and controls) had been selected for referral to the project by their sponsoring agencies. The number of offenses for control kids ranged from none to nine; seriousness scores from zero to eighteen. The mean seriousness score was 2.51; excluding non-delinquents it was 6.29.

This background information on prior records raised some concern about the comparability of the two groups in terms of their criminal histories, and I decided that this should be tested. The results which are shown in Table 7-1 indicate that the two groups do not differ in a statistically significant difference between the mean seriousness score of delinquency.

It was decided to further test their comparability by using the mean seriousness of delinquency scores. A difference of means test showed no statistically significant difference between the mean seriousness score of the experimental group and that of the control group ($t = 1.43$, $df = 79$).

Table 7-1

Comparability of Experimental/Control Groups
By Prior Delinquency Records

	Priors	No Priors	Total
Experimentals	27(58.7%)	19(41.3%)	46(56.8%)
Controls	14(40.0%)	21(60.0%)	35(43.2%)
Total	41	40	81

$x^2 = 2.785$; 1 df; n.s.

These results lead to the conclusion that overall the two groups were comparable. When the nondelinquents were excluded from the analysis, the difference between the mean seriousness scores for experimentals and controls was even further from being significant ($t = .37$, $df = 40$). The juveniles in the group that attended the Juvenile Awareness Project were somewhat more delinquent than the comparison juveniles, but not significantly so. Others disagreed with this judgment, however, and this important point will be dealt with shortly.

Outcomes: Success or Failure?

Each juvenile's court record was tracked for six months after the visit or after pretesting in the case of the controls. Using further recorded offense regardless of disposition as the definition of failure, the results are shown in Table 7-2.

This table indicates that a significantly higher proportion of the juveniles who did *not* attend the project did better in terms of subsequent offenses than did the group which attended. The relationship between the variable of group and outcome was a moderately strong C = .44. This surprising and unexpected finding seemed to call for further examination and analysis of the data.

Table 7-2

Comparison of Experimentals/Controls
By Outcome

	Success	Failure	Total
Experimentals	27(58.7%)	19(41.3%)	46(56.8%)
Controls	31(88.6%)	4(11.4%)	35(43.2%)
Total	58	23	81

$x^2 = 8.73$; 1 df; $p<.01$; C = .44 (corrected)

Among the experimental group, the success rate was twenty-seven out of forty-six (58.7%). This was certainly a far cry from the 80–90 percent success rates being claimed by the Lifers, by the supporters of the Juvenile Awareness Project, and being touted in the film. Among the twenty-seven youths with prior records, fourteen (51.8%) were successes; conversely, the failure or recidivism rate was 48.2%. This was not only not better than, but in some instances was worse than recidivism rates from other programs designed to prevent or treat juvenile delinquency.[1]

An interesting outcome with the experimental group was that six of the nineteen youths (31.6%) with no priors had subsequent records of delinquency. This result could be explained by several possibilities. First, there is something about the project that actually stimulates rather than prevents or deters delinquency. Or second, these kids were simply hidden, closet delinquents who happened to get caught after attending the project. The result could also be used to test the assumption that it is with this nondelinquent or hidden group that the Lifers can perhaps be most successful. A comparison of their outcomes with those for the nondelinquents in the control group lead to the results illustrated in Table 7-3.

The nonattenders obviously did much better, but treating these data conservatively because of the very small numbers of cases led to a nonsignificant finding.

It seemed that more of the nondelinquent controls were successful than their counterparts in the experimental group, but not significantly so. The Lifers were more successful with nondelinquents alone than with their overall group (68.4% vs 58.7%) successes. However, this success rate was still considerably short of the claimed success rates. It was even less favorable when compared with the success rate of the nondelinquent controls (95.2%). As noted earlier, the Lifers have a rough typology of the juveniles referred to their project in which the youths are classified as the "good," that is those with no involvement in crime; the "bad," those with only minor infractions; and, the "ugly," those who have been incarcerated or are in serious danger of being locked up. Does the Juvenile Awareness Project scare the so-called "good" kids straight? The answer appeared to be no.

What about the "bad" and the "ugly" kids? A comparison of only those with prior records of delinquency is shown in Table 7-4.

---

[1] See for example the work of: Robert Martinson. "What Works?—Questions and Answers About Prison Reform," *The Public Interest* (1974), pp. 22–50; David F. Greenberg. "The Correctional Effects of Corrections: A Survey of Evaluations," in *Corrections and Punishment* (California: Sage Publications, 1977); and Michael C. Dixon and William E. Wright. *Juvenile Delinquency Prevention Programs: Report on the Findings of an Evaluation of the Literature* (National Science Foundation, October, 1974).

Table 7-3

**Comparison of Nondelinquent Experimentals/Controls
By Outcome**

	Success	Failure	Total
Nondelinquent Experimentals	13(68.4%)	6(31.6%)	19(47.5%)
Nondelinquent Controls	20(95.2%)	1(4.8%)	21(52.5%)
Total	33	7	40

$x^2 = 3.3$ (corrected for continuity); 1 df; n.s.

Table 7-4

**Comparison of Delinquent Experimentals/Controls
By Outcome**

	Success	Failure	Total
Delinquent Experimentals	14(51.8%)	13(48.2%)	27(65.8%)
Delinquent Controls	11(78.6%)	3(21.4%)	14(34.2%)
Total	25	16	41

$x^2 = 2.76$; 1 df; n.s.

Again, more of the controls were successful than experimentals (78.6% vs. 51.8%), but the difference was not significant. The conclusion seemed to be that the Lifers were relatively more successful with the "good" kids than with the "bad" or "ugly" kids, but that overall the project was not particularly successful with any of these youth when outcomes were compared to those of the control group.

Outcomes: Seriousness

The next step in the comparative analysis of the outcomes of the experimental and control groups was a difference of means test for the mean seriousness scores of the two groups. Whereas the first findings dealt with the proportions of successes and failures, these results would tell us something about the number and seriousness of subsequent offenses. The scores were for subsequent offenses committed within the six month follow-up period. The results shown in Table 7-5 compare mean seriousness of delinquency scores for all experimentals and controls and for the nondelinquents only (those with no priors). The latter comparison again tested the assumption that these youths were perhaps the best targets for the Lifers' efforts.

The results illustrated in the above table reinforced the earlier finding that the experimental group did significantly worse than the control group in terms of outcomes. More experimentals than controls committed subsequent offenses and their mean seriousness of subsequent delinquency scores was significantly higher. As a subsample, the nondelinquent experimentals did worse than their nondelinquent counterparts in the control group. Once again, the project did not have better results in a comparative sense with those who seemed most likely to be deterred.

Table 7–5

**Comparison of Experimentals/Controls
By Seriousness of Outcomes**

	Mean	t value	df	2-tail Probability
Experimentals (N = 46)	1.2			
		2.67	78.19	.009
Controls (N = 35)	0.3			
Nondelinquent Experimentals (N = 19)	0.8			
		1.84	19.42	.08
Nondelinquent Controls (N = 21)	0.09			

CRITICISMS, SUBSEQUENT ANALYSES
AND RESULTS

The negative findings discussed above were in a report dropped off at the New Jersey Department of Corrections on a Friday in April, 1979. In less than a week, these results were in circulation and engendered an immediate outpouring of response that rolled across the state and country. That portion of the story will unfold later in the text. At this point I want to discuss the major criticisms leveled at my research and the way in which it was done.

As stated in Chapter 6, deficiencies were pointed out by persons who reviewed or read about the study and offered criticisms of it. Most of the criticism that was received questioned the results on the grounds that the methodology was flawed. In order to correct for any deficiencies and to be responsive to the questions that were raised, I undertook several additional analyses of the data just presented. One of the points raised earlier pertained to my failure to maintain pure random assignment of all the juveniles to either the experimental or the control group. This is a procedure, known as an experimental design, which I agree is critically important and should be sought whenever possible in evaluation research. However, because of events beyond our control the randomization broke down in the case of three of the referral agencies. One police agency took all of their eleven juveniles to Rahway instead of just the six who were supposed to go. Two other agencies, with eight and three juveniles respectively, did not take their experimentals to the prison.

I subsequently removed these particular cases (twenty-two), and reanalyzed the data. The result was a failure rate of 31 percent among the experimentals and only 17 percent among the controls. This finding is not statistically significant, but the earlier conclusion that nonparticipants do as well or better than participants continued to hold when the cases which could be questioned were removed.

Another comment reported earlier referred to the loss of four juveniles from the experimental group and fifteen from the control group. The reasons for those losses were detailed in Chapter 6. Here I decided to use what might be called a hypothetical "worst case example" to partially compensate for the attrition and to see what effect this might have on the findings. The way the example works is as follows: Suppose in the worst case (worst from the viewpoint of my conclusions) that all four of the lost experimentals had been successes and all fifteen of the lost controls had been failures. Although this may seem improbable and somewhat like a stacked deck, it was certainly not impossible. What would the results look like? There would have been thirty-one out of fifty successes in each group—an identical 62 percent success rate in both. Two conclusions would then have been warranted. First, 62 percent is still considerably short of the claimed 80–90 percent, particularly when one-half or more of the juveniles were nondelinquent to begin with. Second and more important, the absence of any difference in outcomes would lead to the conclusion that the project had no effect. Again, the basic conclusion would still stand.

Finally, a major reanalysis of these data was undertaken, using a more sophisticated statistical technique. This technique enabled me to statistically control and account for the effects upon subsequent delinquency of differences between the two groups on prior offense history, age, sex, race, and delinquency probability. There were significant differences in subsequent delinquency between the attenders and nonattenders once all these background characteristics were accounted for; and, *the experimental group still does worse than the control group.*

Specifically, I found that prior offenses, age, and sex are significantly correlated with subsequent offenses. This confirmed what some of the commentators had suspected. However, once the effects of all other variables, including these three, have been accounted for, the experimental-control group factor is still significantly correlated with subsequent offenses. (see Table 7-6) This means that any differences in the characteristics of the two groups are not causing the differences in outcomes between them. It simply reiterates the conclusion that those juveniles who visited Rahway and confronted the Lifers behaved considerably worse after their visit than did the juveniles who did not visit. A further finding is that sex accounts for the greatest amount of variation in subsequent offenses, that is, 6.3 percent. Group (experimental or control) accounts for the next largest proportion, 5.6 percent.

Table 7-6

Anova for Subsequent Offenses

Variable	Degrees of Freedom	F	Significance
Sex	(7,73)	2.96	<.01
Race	"	0.94	n.s.
Low Risk	"	1.14	n.s.
High Risk	"	0.31	n.s.
Prior Offense	"	7.87	<.01
Age	"	7.40	<.01
Group	"	5.43	<.01

* The analysis of variance tests the correlation coefficient against a hypothesized correlation of zero.
** Variables were entered into the equation in a predetermined order.

Table 7-7

Regression Analysis of Subsequent Offenses

Variable	Multiple Corr. Coefficient	R^2	RSQ Change	Corr. Coeff.	Unstd. B	Std. (Beta)
Sex	.251	.063	.063	−.251	−.393	−.200
Race	.256	.065	.002	.162	−.195	−.122
Low Risk	.276	.076	.010	−.126	−.364	−.217
High Risk	.284	.080	.004	.061	−.203	−.113
Prior Offense	.365	.133	.053	.273	.967	.341
Age	.429	.184	.051	−.133	−.171	−.312
Group	.491	.241	.056	.217	.394	.250

* Variables were entered into the equation in a predetermined order.

Table 7-8

Anova for Subsequent Seriousness of Delinquency Scores

Variable	Degrees of Freedom	F	Significance
Sex	(7,73)	3.17	<.01
Race	"	2.33	n.s.
Low Risk	"	0.82	n.s.
High Risk	"	0.19	n.s.
Prior Delinquency seriousness score	"	17.58	<.01
Age	"	4.89	<.01
Group	"	7.06	<.01

* The analysis of variance tests the correlation coefficient against a hypothesized correlation of zero.
** Variables were entered into the equation in a predetermined order.

Prior offenses and age explain 5.3 percent and 5.1 percent respectively as shown in Table 7-7.

Prior seriousness of delinquency scores, age, and sex are also significantly correlated with subsequent seriousness of delinquency scores. However, the experimental or control group factor is still significantly correlated with this outcome when the other variables are controlled (Table 7-8). Prior seriousness explains 15 percent of the variance in subsequent seriousness; and, group explains 6.7 percent (Table 7-9). These results also affirm the earlier conclusions.

The results from these reanalyses, particularly the last, effectively refute the criticism that the evaluation is seriously flawed,

Table 7-9

**Regression Analysis of Subsequent Seriousness
of Delinquency Scores**

Variable	Multiple Corr. Coefficient	R^2	RSQ Change	Corr. Coeff.	Unstd. B	Std. (Beta)
Sex	.248	.062	.062	−.248	−.743	−.197
Race	.251	.063	.001	.148	−.560	−.183
Low Risk	.259	.067	.004	−.084	−.566	−.176
High Risk	.263	.069	.002	.035	−.292	−.085
Prior Delinquency seriousness score	.468	.219	.150	.415	.131	.483
Age	.493	.243	.024	−.006	−.255	−.241
Group	.557	.310	.067	.274	.823	.271

* Variables were entered into the equation in a predetermined order.

uninterpretable, and discreditable. There is certainly a basis for reaching conclusions about the effectiveness of the Juvenile Awareness Project.

PREDICTING DELINQUENCY

One of the potentially more important background variables we decided to include in the study was something we called delinquency probability. This factor permitted us to assess the chances of any juvenile in the study becoming a delinquent. The variable was created by using the well-known Glueck's Social Prediction Table. Admittedly, I decided upon this particular aspect of the study with some concern and a little trepidation.

This trepidation arose in part from my awareness that prediction of criminal behavior is a rather risky business. People, it seems, are such ornery creatures that they don't want to behave in any predictable manner. Prediction of criminal and delinquent behavior has been notoriously unsuccessful. More than ten years ago, in a paper entitled "Assessment and Prediction Methods in Crime and Delinquency," Don M. Gottfredson said: "Despite the painstaking studies, item analyses, and validation studies . . . all currently available prediction methods still have only relatively low predictive power."[2] That statement is as true today as it was then. It means that prediction methods do not predict very

[2] Don M. Gottfredson, "Assessment and Prediction Methods in Crime and Delinquency," President's Commission on Law Enforcement and Administration of Justice, *Task Force Report: Juvenile Delinquency and Youth Crime* (Washington, D.C.; U.S. Government Printing Office, 1967), p. 181.

well. For example, Stephen E. Schlesinger recently tried to predict dangerousness in juveniles, using in part some thirty different factors (predictors) identified from nine different studies as being "statistically related to violent behavior in children."[3] He found no systematic relationship between the predictor variables and such criterion (predicted) behaviors as violent offenses, burglary, or larceny, running away, or being a so-called person in need of supervision (PINS). Schlesinger's conclusion was: "Predictors of violent behavior identified by previous researchers were not substantiated by this study. Future efforts to predict dangerousness will probably meet similar success,"[4] or, in this case, lack of success.

The ability to predict delinquency is grossly imperfect, irrespective of the particular technique or combination of techniques that might be employed. So why make the effort in this study? There were several arguments or reasons for doing so. The first is that we have learned a great deal about prediction, despite its shortcomings, and we can learn more only by continuing to experiment with various prediction methods. Thus, employing the Social Prediction Table would enable us to determine how well it predicted delinquency for this particular sample. Second, apart from its usefulness as a delinquency prediction tool, the Social Prediction Table permitted us to classify our experimental and control groups according to their risks of future delinquency. The two groups could then be compared to see whether or not they differed in any significant way on this classification. Because of these potential benefits, we decided that this would be a worthwhile endeavor.

The second source of my concern was the Social Prediction Table itself. This Table was developed by Sheldon and Eleanor Glueck from their famous *Unraveling Juvenile Delinquency* study completed in 1950. This work of the Gluecks is considered to be one of the pioneering efforts in the prediction field. The husband and wife, Harvard-based team attempted to identify potential delinquents at a very early age; to identify "delinquency-prone or delinquency-endangered children." The original scale was developed from a sample of 451 delinquent boys in correctional schools, and a matching sample of 439 nondelinquent boys. From a mass of social, psychological, medical and anthropological data, the Gluecks selected five factors that sharply distinguished the two groups. These five factors were: discipline of boy by father, supervision of boy by mother, affection of father for boy, affection of mother for boy, and cohesiveness of family.[5] The Gluecks used the percentage of delinquents in each sub-

---

[3] Stephen E. Schlesinger, "The Prediction of Dangerousness in Juveniles," *Crime and Delinquency* (January 1978), 40–48.

[4] Ibid., p. 48.

[5] Sheldon and Eleanor Glueck, *Unraveling Juvenile Delinquency* (Cambridge, Massachusetts: Harvard University Press, 1951).

category of the five factors as a weighted failure score.[6] These scores were then grouped and group failure rates were calculated.

The procedures used by the Gluecks and their conclusions have been both "strongly supported and severely criticized."[7] Most of the controversy has centered on their sampling methods, which resulted in samples that were not representative of the delinquent and nondelinquent populations. Nonetheless, there is evidence from a ten year validation study conducted by the New York City Youth Board, that the scale can be "a good differentiator between potential delinquents (serious and persisting) and nondelinquents.[8]

The particular version of the scale used here was adapted by Samuel A. Kramer in 1961.[9] Kramer's adaptation used the five family items developed by the Gluecks; but, he had the subject juveniles rate themselves on each of the factors. The Gluecks, on the other hand, had evaluated family situations by means of appraisals made by home visitors trained in social work techniques of observation.

Kramer modified the wording of the Glueck items to make the statements clear to the boys in his study. His revisions were carefully reviewed by teachers and others to make certain there were no changes in meaning or concept.[10] This conversion of the scale into a self-administered instrument made its use feasible in my study. The scale used by Kramer and the one used in the present study, including weighted failure scores, looks as follows:[11]

Five statements are given in the following section. For each one check the idea that seems the best way to describe most of your life at home.

Weight

1. The discipline given to me by my father (or person acting for my father) was:

     ( ) Very strict   71.8

---

[6] Sheldon and Eleanor Glueck (eds.), *Identification of Predelinquents* (New York: Intercontinental Medical Book Corporation, 1972), p. 4.

[7] Gottfredson, *Juvenile Delinquency and Youth Crime,* p. 178.

[8] Maude M. Craig and Selma J. Glick, "Ten Years Experience with the Glueck Social Prediction Table," *Crime and Delinquency,* 9 (July 1963), 249–61.

[9] Samuel A. Kramer, "Identifying Juvenile Delinquents Among Negroes," *Identification of Predelinquents,* Sheldon and Eleanor Glueck (eds.) (New York: Intercontinental Medical Book Corporation, 1972), pp. 22–35.

[10] Ibid., p. 25.

[11] Kramer reported a test-retest correlation of .92 on his modified Glueck items. This result indicated a high degree of reliability.

( ) Strict, but usually fair 9.3
( ) Sometimes strict, sometimes easy 71.8
( ) Usually easy 59.8
( ) Very easy 59.8

2. My mother (or person acting for my mother) gave me supervision that was:
( ) Very helpful, with close watch over me 9.9
( ) Usually helpful, although sometimes she failed 9.9
( ) Helpful only when I asked for help or advice 57.5
( ) Most likely to let me do anything I pleased 83.2
( ) Completely useless, because she did not care what I did 83.2

3. My father (or person acting for my father) usually showed that he:
( ) Liked me a great deal 33.8
( ) Liked me about the same as he liked his friends 33.8
( ) Neither liked me nor disliked me 75.9
( ) Disliked me most of the time 75.9
( ) Did not want me around 75.9

4. My mother (or person acting for my mother) usually showed that she:
( ) Liked me a great deal 43.1
( ) Liked me about the same as she liked her friends 43.1
( ) Neither liked me nor disliked me 86.2
( ) Disliked me most of the time 86.2
( ) Did not want me around 86.2

5. My family (parents, brothers, sisters) has made me think that we:
( ) Stick pretty close together in everything 20.6
( ) Would help each other more than we would help friends 61.3
( ) Can be equally happy at home or away from home 61.3
( ) Would rather be with friends than with relatives 96.9
( ) Have almost nothing that we like to do together 96.9

Kramer found in his study that "the Glueck index, dealing with family situations as perceived by the boys, proved to be exceptionally powerful in its discriminating effect."[12] He concluded that, "the Glueck scale is a powerful differentiating tool . . . in determining delinquency proneness."[13] Kramer's results convinced me to use his version of the Gluecks' index in this study.

One other issue which arose surrounding the decision to use the Glueck's scale was the fact that both the Gluecks and Kramer (as well as many others) had used the scale with boys only. My concern was whether it could be used with girls as well, since there would be girls in the

[12] Kramer, *Identification of Predelinquents*, p. 26.
[13] Ibid., p. 28.

Juvenile Awareness Project samples. Fortunately, I found a report by Hermann Elmering which led him to conclude that, ". . . the table is applicable to girls, even though it was initially constructed on boys only."[14] Therefore, I felt it would be applicable for use with girls.

The weighted items that make up the scale enable us to classify juvenile subjects into low (below 250 points), medium (250–299 points), and high (over 300 points) probability of delinquency categories. The results of this classification of the juveniles in my study is shown in Table 7-10.

Table 7-10 indicates that the two groups did not differ significantly on their probability of being delinquent. Thus one of the reasons for using the Glueck scale to assess comparability, was successfully accomplished. But beyond that conclusion, the large size of the low probability category raised serious implications for the outcome measures, that is, attitude and behavior changes. If the Glueck scale was a valid predictor of delinquency—and that remained to be seen—it indicated that a large portion (more than 70 percent) of the kids involved in the Juvenile Awareness Project were not likely to be or to become delinquents, whether or not they visited Rahway. If this were so, it raised several interesting issues: Why did these particular kids need to attend the project? Why were referring agencies not sending more high risk juveniles who might be more in need of deterrence? Finally, if the low risk of delinquency kids did not in fact become delinquents, could the Juvenile Awareness Project legitimately claim credit for this "success"?

Because there was a total of only twenty-one cases falling into the medium and high risk categories combined, these two were lumped together to make a "higher" risk group which was compared to the "lower" risk group. The groups were compared first on the basis of whether or not they had a prior delinquency record, and these results are shown in Table 7-11.

Tables 7-11 and 7-12 clearly indicate that the Glueck Social Prediction Table, as adapted and used in this research, was not a very good predictor of delinquency. This is true regardless of when that delinquency occurred. Also, the Glueck scale did not predict pre-or postdelinquent behavior any differently or more validly for the experimental group than it did for the control group. There may be many explanations for this result, including the fact that this was a revised form of the scale that was self-administered. In any case, whatever the reason, the scale was not a particularly useful predictor here.

[14] Herman Elmering, "Retrospective Validations of Glueck Table to Identify Delinquents in Various Countries," *Identification of Predelinquents,* Sheldon and Eleanor Glueck (eds.) (New York: Intercontinental Medical Book Corporation, 1972), p. 15.

Table 7-10

Probability of Delinquency By Group

Glueck	Experimental	Control	Total
Low	31(70.5%)	24(75.0%)	55(72.4%)
Medium	10(22.7%)	5(15.6%)	15(19.7%)
High	3 (6.8%)	3 (9.4%)	6 (7.9%)
Total	44	32	76*

$x^2 = 0.68$; 2df; n.s.
* Five juveniles did not complete the scale.

Table 7-11

Prior Delinquency Record By Risk

	Prior Record	No Prior Record	Total
Lower Risk	25(45.4%)	30(54.5%)	55(72.4%)
Higher Risk	13(61.9%)	8(38.1%)	21(27.6%)
Total	38	38	76

$x^2 = 1.64$; 1 df; n.s.

Table 7-12

Subsequent Delinquency Record By Risk

	Subsequent Record	No Subsequent Record	Total
Lower Risk	12(21.8%)	43(78.2%)	55(72.4%)
Higher Risk	5(23.8%)	16(76.2%)	21(27.6%)
Total	17	59	76

$x^2 = .03$; 1 df; n.s.

SOME INDIVIDUAL REACTIONS

As indicated in the discussion of my plan for the study, one objective was to question kids who had visited Rahway some four to six months after their visit about their impressions and reactions to the project. A total of fifteen of the kids in the experimental group were interviewed. Seventeen control group subjects were also interviewed.

Five of these experimental group juveniles were from the Ridgefield Park High School which furnished most of the juveniles for the "Scared Straight!" documentary. When asked who decided that they should visit the Lifers' Project, all of them said it was Sgt. Charles Martini who also had been instrumental in recruiting kids for the film. One of these kids, a sixteen-year-old girl, said she thought Martini had decided to send her because she ran away a lot, and because she had problems with her parents. She said she wanted to visit Rahway because her sister had gone and she was curious about it. Asked what she thought of her visit, she said, "Everybody was kind of quiet and was talking about how they were scared." Asked whether she thought the visit was helpful to her, she said: "Running away ain't a crime. The Lifers' Group didn't say nothing about running away!" She repeated this same thought when asked whether she thought the visits were helpful to other kids. "I don't know—it's hard to say. I ain't committed a crime," she said. She seemed to be saying that the shoe didn't fit, and therefore she wasn't going to wear it.

A number of surveys over the years have arrived at the conclusion that the rate of undetected delinquency is high. Large amounts of misconduct and lawbreaking seem to remain hidden in terms of the identities of the offending juveniles. The offenders are simply in the right place at the right time and do not get caught; or if caught, they are released without any official record. In addition, the surveys clearly reveal that all adolescents seem to be delinquent to some degree—at least as far as minor offenses are concerned.[15]

After their visit, each of the young people was also asked about their own delinquent behavior. This particular method of collecting information about delinquency is known as a self-report study. Anonymous self-administered questionnaires or confidential interviews have been used to uncover hidden or undetected delinquency. In our interviews, we assured the juveniles of the confidentiality of any information given to us. The importance of answering fully and accurately was also stressed. Still it must be recognized that there is some possibility of reporting error and of inaccuracies with this method. Curiously, error may arise from the possibility that some kids deny offenses which they have committed, but others may claim credit, so to speak, for things that they have not in fact done. Despite these short-comings, this method has a considerable history and, if used judiciously, has been found to be a valuable supplement to official records as a source of information about the extent and nature of delinquent behavior.

[15] See for example the work of: Austin Porterfield. "Delinquency and its Outcome in Court and College," *American Journal of Sociology*, 49 (1943), 199–208; Martin Gold. "Undetected Delinquent Behavior," *Journal of Research in Crime and Delinquency*, 3 (1966), 27-46; Martin Gold and David Reimer. "Changing Patterns of Delinquent Behavior Among Americans 13-16 years old: 1967–1972," *Crime and Delinquency Literature*, 7 (1975), 453–517; and James Short and F. I. Nye. "Extent of Unrecorded Juvenile Delinquency: Tentative Conclusions," *Journal of Criminal Law, Criminology and Police Science*, 49 (1958), 296–302.

Each juvenile was asked about twenty different offenses, ranging from the very minor, that is, doing things their parents had told them not to do, to some that were very serious, that is, robbed someone by threatening them with a knife, or a razor or a gun.[16] Again, the time frame was the period after their participation in the Lifers' Project. The aforementioned girl, who emphasized that running away is not a crime, admitted disobeying her parents or other authorities numerous times (five or more); running away once; skipping school twice; and buying or drinking liquor at least a half dozen times. These are not particularly serious. However, she also admitted three petty larcenies (under $2), using dope (probably marijhuana) numerous times, and selling dope at least three times. The latter offenses are obviously more serious, and do constitute juvenile delinquency. She apparently was not deterred by her visit to the prison.

A second Ridgefield Park girl, this one seventeen-years-old, said she also was curious about the Lifers' Project and wanted to go. She said she was scared, but she hadn't been in trouble so she knew she wasn't like the others. This is a similar reaction to the first girl's. She said if she had been in trouble, she would stop after visiting the prison. On the self-report survey, she too admitted to skipping school, buying and drinking liquor, and using dope after her trip.

A third girl from Ridgefield Park, also seventeen, spoke about the corrections officers involved with the project. She said: "The guards were pushing and shoving—they yelled at me three times for smiling." "I knew they weren't gonna hurt me," she said. She also said, "I think it would be better if we [girls] went to women's prisons." This girl referred to getting mixed signals from her visit. She said they yelled at you, then shook your hand. "It was weird!" she said. Asked whether the visit might be helpful to other kids, she said: "It works for people who want it to work—for those who let it sink in. Some kids got put in there for light stuff." This girl admitted disobedience, driving without a license, skipping school, and using and selling dope after her visit.

The fourth Ridgefield Park case was the only boy interviewed from that particular town. This seventeen-year-old said he too was curious about going but didn't really know why Sgt. Martini had referred him. He said the guards were more scary then the inmates. Asked if the visit had been helpful, he said if a radio was sitting in a car, he wouldn't think twice before taking it. However, he would think twice if somebody asked him to rob a bank. He too reported disobedience, numerous instances of driving without a license, and buying and drinking liquor. Also admitted were

[16] See appendix for interview schedule.

three larcenies ($2–$50 in two cases and over $50 in one case). He admitted destruction of property on three occasions, and numerous instances of using and selling dope. Obviously he was not scared straight by his experience!

The final Ridgefield Park juvenile, another seventeen-year-old girl, said she wanted to go to Rahway because she too was curious, but also because she could get out of school for the day. Her generally negative comments were: "After it was over, I thought it was a crock. After screaming at us for an hour, then they wanted to talk nice to us . . . The guards were more obnoxious than the inmates. I doubt if I were in trouble that I would be affected—it seemed like such a put-on. There should be more explanation of what's going on." Despite this reaction, this girl reported only driving without a license, skipping school, and drinking after her visit.

The next group of interviewees were all from an urban setting (Passaic, New Jersey); three black boys—two fifteen-year-olds and one thirteen-year-old. The thirteen-year-old, a seventh grader, said he thought he had been referred to the Lifers' Project because he had been caught in two B & E's (breaking and entering). He wanted to go, but said he didn't like the guards and didn't like "how the prisoners and guards treat other people." Asked if he thought the visit was helpful to him, he said, "Yea, I do not want to go to prison. I'm being OK on probation." He said the visit "may be" helpful to other kids. "If you want to go to prison, they can't help you," he said. "If you don't—they can!" What about his own reported behavior after his visit? He chalked up three petty larcenies (one of value, $2–$50); one destruction of property; three times using dope; and, one fist fight. Curiously, he said he was doing "OK on probation!"

The first fifteen-year-old said he had been referred because of fighting and two B & E's. He said he "wasn't scared until the doors closed. The guy doing double life scared me the most." He also said the visit was helpful because, "I haven't been in trouble—don't know no one who went that has." His self-report almost bears this out. He reported only some disobedience and using dope on three occasions. Not too bad!

The other fifteen-year-old was a seventh grader, living with his mother who was on welfare. He said he went to Rahway because everybody in his group went. He admitted he had been stealing, but said no one knew about it. He felt he would stop stealing because it "ain't worth getting into trouble for." He said, "Nobody wants to go to Rahway." He seemed to take his own words to heart, reporting only some disobedience of his mother after his visit. He seems to be a success, if his own report is accurate.

The final seven kids from the experimental group who were interviewed were some of the toughest and most delinquent juveniles in my sample. They all come from the city of Trenton, New Jersey or its environs. These particular kids fully met the Lifers' characterization of being the "Ugly" delinquents. Because of their "hardcore" delinquent histories, they provide a real test of the effectiveness of the Juvenile Awareness Project.

The first of this group was a sixteen-year-old boy. He was referred to the Lifers' Project by the Juvenile Aid Bureau of the Trenton Police Department because, he said, "they said I was bad—I was shooting dice and smoking reefer." He did not want to go to Rahway because he "didn't think I was that bad. I wasn't bad enough." He also said he wasn't scared because, "I didn't think they were going to hurt me." Asked what he thought of his visit, he said: "It was alright . . . I didn't like the place. I was cool and waited to see what would happen. They didn't bother (hurt) me!" He said he was going to be more careful in the future as a result of his visit. He also felt the visits would be helpful to other kids because, "It'll straighten 'em out a little!" However, this boy reported a number of offenses and violations following his visit. These included twice driving without a license, a half dozen times buying and/or drinking liquor, a petty larceny (under $2 value), using and selling dope (at least three times for each), and beating up an innocent person. Depending upon the facts and circumstances, the latter may have been a felonious assault and battery. He does not seem to have been deterred by the project.

The second case was a seventeen-year-old white boy who had quit school and was working full-time. He was referred because he was on probation. He thought his visit was helpful to him, saying "Yea, I ain't stole nothing since!" He also recommended the trip for others because, "Them people scare you to death!" His self-report reflected that he had not stolen anything, as he said. However, he had numerous liquor law violations; and, more serious, he reported destroying property and having many fist fights and beating up innocent people. Perhaps the drinking and the fighting were related, but in any event, there appears to be a continuing problem.

The next boy, sixteen-years-old and black, had been in the county youth house for several months at the time he was interviewed. He too had been referred by the Trenton Police Department. He offered some very interesting observations about his visit. Did he want to go? "I didn't mind. I had been there before and I was O.K. for awhile—then I got into some trouble again with this cop. So I thought going again would be good—I would be good longer." What did he think of the visit? "It's O.K. It's not too scary. It stinks in there. I thought they might have remembered me—they didn't. I think some guys got picked on bad." Was the visit helpful? "Yea. You stay straight for awhile—but I ain't bad enough to go there. When I can go there, I'll just cut this out." What about other kids? "If they scared they ain't gonna get into trouble—if not they will." He seems to be a believer in the deterrent effects of fear, but what about its effects upon his own behavior? Subsequent to his visit he reported the following list of offenses:

1. Disobeying—5 or more times.
2. Driving w/o license—Once.
3. Skipping school—3 times.
4. Drinking liquor—3 times.
5. Stealing something worth $2-$50—5 or more times.
6. Stealing something worth over $50—5 or more times.
7. Destroying property—3 times.
8. Stealing a car—Once.
9. Breaking and entering—5 or more times.
10. Using dope—3 times.
11. Selling dope—3 times.

This boy obviously was not scared straight, even following two visits.

The fourth boy was also sixteen-years-old, black, and in the county youth house. He was referred by his probation officer for stealing and for a breaking and entering. He was interested in visiting Rahway because he had heard about it from some other kids, and he wanted to see what it was like. His impressions were that the place was noisy. He said, "I thought they might kill me—some of the things they said scared me." He thought the visit helped him to stay straight for a while; but asked why he got into trouble again, he said, "Some things just happen!" He was noncommittal about whether the project might help other kids. He too reported a string of postvisit offenses: disobedience, drinking, stealing, using and selling dope, and fighting.

The next boy had previously been at the Highfields Residential Group Center, indicating he had been a failure on probation. He too was sixteen and black, and had been referred by his probation officer. What did he think of his visit? "We were pushed and shoved. The guards were real nasty. They snatched our lunches away and we couldn't eat until we got on the bus." He thought the experience was "kind of helpful." He said the "guards were rough, but pretty fair. It might help unless you're really bad." Did it help him? On most offenses he was clean, but unfortunately he reported three breaking and enterings since his visit.

Another youth house resident was the sixth interviewee. It should be emphasized that none of the youth house kids were in the youth house immediately before their Rahway visit. A fourteen-year-old boy, who was also black, had been referred by the police department's juvenile aid bureau. He said he was "not scared—but kept cool." He "saw other boys shook up physically," but decided that he "was not going to get hurt." Asked if he thought the visit was helpful to him, he said: "No! It made me think, but fighting is different. They didn't talk about what happens when you get into fights, and I ain't killed nobody." He also did not believe the visits are helpful to other kids because, "most of the kids weren't that bad." He reported disobedience, destroying property, using dope, and fighting following his visit.

The final interview was with a sixteen-year-old white boy, referred to the Juvenile Awareness Project by the Trenton Police Department. He said he didn't want to go to Rahway, but was told he had to go to "teach me a lesson." He said the visit did teach him a lesson "for a while." He thought the project was helpful because it showed him and others "what it's like" and "how it is." His self-reported behavior doesn't seem to indicate he learned the lesson the Lifers were trying to teach. He reported disobedience, driving without a license, running away, skipping school, buying and drinking liquor, property destruction, and using dope after going to Rahway.

By and large, these results are pretty dismal. There were certainly not any glowing successes to report. On the contrary, in almost every one of the fifteen cases described there were subsequent delinquencies, some more serious than others. The "Ugly" delinquents seemed particularly impervious to any deterrent effects from their confrontations with the inmates and the prison environment at Rahway.

Given the past findings of others, my expectations were that self-reported offenses would exceed officially recorded offenses over the same period; and, that more juveniles in both the experimental and control groups would report being delinquent than had been disclosed in the juvenile court records. Let us look first at the court records of the fifteen juveniles who reported the delinquencies just presented.

Of the five young people from Ridgefield Park High School, only one had any record of a subsequent offense. The one sixteen-year-old girl was charged with incorrigibility, a noncriminal or status offense. Because this occurred more than six months after her prison visit, it was not included in our outcome data reported earlier. Officially, these five juveniles were all successes. However, unofficially at least three of them could be considered serious delinquents based upon their own reports.

Of the three Passaic boys—two age fifteen and one age thirteen— only the youngest reported any serious criminal behavior, and he was the only one who had a court record. This boy's record showed three JINS (incorrigibility) offenses, but no criminal offenses during the six month follow-up period. The juvenile justice system seemed to have the right boy in this case, but for the wrong things. The self-reported and officially recorded behavior seem pretty consistent in these three cases.

The seven boys from the Trenton area, all reported a string of minor and serious offenses during their postvisit period. All of them also had official records during the six month follow-up, although the number of official offenses was far less than the number of self-reported offenses. Two boys recorded one arrest each; four boys had two arrests each; and one boy was arrested three times in the following six months.

Seventeen juveniles in the control group were similarly questioned about their delinquent behavior during the preceding six months (the same follow-up with the experimentals and with the official records check). The results from official records and self-reports are as follows:

Case Number	Official	Self-Report
1	None	3 or 4 times driving w/o a license; 3 or 4 times buying alcoholic beverages and drinking; and 3 or 4 times smoking marijuana
2	None	Twice skipped school
3	2 JINS	3 or 4 times disobey; twice petty larceny (under $50); one property destruction; and 5 or more fist fights
4	Possession stolen property	None
5	None	3 or 4 times skipped school; 3 or 4 times destroying property; and one fist fight
6	None	One disobey; twice skipped school; and 3 or 4 petty larcenies (under $2)
7	None	None
8	None	3 or 4 times drinking
9	None	One driving w/o license; twice skipped school; two petty larcenies (under $50); and twice smoked marijuana
10	None	3 or 4 times destroying property

11	None	twice drinking; 3 or 4 petty larcenies (under \$2); and, twice destroying property
12	None	one fist fight
13	None	5 or more times skipped school; twice bought alcoholic beverages; and, 5 or more times drinking
15	None	3 or 4 times disobeying; 3 or 4 times skipping school; drinking; 3 or 4 petty larcenies (under \$2); once destroyed property; 3 or 4 times smoked marijuana; 3 or 4 times sold marijuana; and 3 or 4 fist fights
16	None	3 or 4 times disobeying, driving w/o license, skipping school, and buying and drinking alcohol; 5 or more petty larcenies and one theft of money (less than \$50); 5 or more property destruction; 2 B & E's; 5 or more times smoking marijuana, and 3 or 4 fist fights
17	None	once disobeying; driving w/o license; 3 or 4 times skipped school, drinking alcoholic beverages and smoking marijuana

These results confirm both my expectations, and also substantiate previous findings from self-report surveys. With only one exception (a boy in the control group who had a known arrest for possession of stolen property) all the juveniles reported engaging in more misconduct and actual lawbreaking than was officially known. Only three of the thirty-two juveniles interviewed—including the boy mentioned above—denied any misconduct. Thus, just over 90 percent admitted to being at least minor delinquents. Many more juveniles in both groups reported delinquent behavior than had records for such behavior. This rate of hidden delinquency is high, as other surveys have found, but similarly it involves minor offenses more than serious ones.

Our original intent was to interview all eighty-one juveniles in the sample, however money and time ran out. Because only partial samples could be interviewed, experimental/control group comparisons would not be valid. However, these results leave the impression that the experimentals were more seriously delinquent than the controls. This impression fits with the previous conclusions.

chapter eight

Changing Attitudes

As indicated earlier, one of the goals of my research was to look also at the psychological reactions of kids participating in the Juvenile Awareness Project. In order to do this, we decided to try to measure any attitude changes which occurred as a result of visiting the prison and confronting the Lifers. We made no attempt to look at the effects of any follow-up treatment which the juveniles might receive from their referring agencies. Such follow-up was and is either minimal or nonexistent in the history of the project. Where it did occur, we assumed it was similar for both experimentals and controls. Our assumption was based upon the fact that with a couple of exceptions, the kids came from the same agencies and would thus be treated equally.

We did not assume that changes in attitudes are necessary and sufficient conditions for changes in behavior. However, we did assume that attitude changes might be an important intervening link to behavior changes. In other words, you don't have to have changes in attitudes in order to have changes in behavior, but frequently the two do go hand in hand. We further assumed that the absence of any attitude changes would diminish the likelihood of finding changes in behavior.

Findings from this phase of the study of the project need to be understood from two perspectives. The first concerns the importance of measuring attitude change as a means of determining whether or not the project "works." There were those who loudly concluded, and perhaps some who will still conclude, that the project is not trying to change attitudes, but is rather trying to prevent or deter delinquent behavior. Therefore, this thinking goes, measuring attitude change is nothing more than an academic exercise that bears little relationship to the real world. After all, they say, isn't behavior what it is all about? Isn't that what is really important? The answer to these questions is that behavior is indeed important; but, there must be some way of getting from here to there. Behavior is the "proof of the pudding," so to speak. But, behavior is often a function of attitudes, and of the immediate situations in which an individual finds himself or herself at different times. Attitudes affect behavior, as well as perception, learning, etc. Since people who work with juvenile delinquents are generally not in a position to alter the environments in which delinquents or potential delinquents live, they usually concentrate upon the attitude part of the equation in attempting to prevent juvenile delinquency. Mobilization for Youth was one attempt to prevent delinquency by altering environmental influences; without much success, as we have seen. We usually try to change behavior by changing delinquent attitudes. This is in fact the approach being followed by the Lifers' Project. Therefore, evaluating its effectiveness seemed to us not only appropriate, but necessary.

The conceptual foundation for JAP rests in deterrence theory, whether or not this was intended. I previously indicated that the recent research on deterrence has increasingly pointed to the importance of the perceptual properties of punishments and other sanctions. The argument increasingly being made is that potential offenders are deterred by what they perceive to be the certainty, swiftness, and severity of punishment, whether or not that perception is accurate. The goal of the Lifers' Project, which is to heighten the awareness or perception of the attending juveniles, is linked to that idea.

One can see, therefore, a complex series of interrelationships among attitudes, perceptions, deterrence, and behavior. Attitudes can influence behavior; attitudes can influence perceptions; perceptions can influence deterrence; deterrence can influence behavior, and so on. I therefore considered it critically important that we measure attitude change as an initial catalyst in this entire process.

Operating on this premise, the second perspective on the evaluation findings must focus on the question of whether or not the Juvenile Awareness Project in fact changes attitudes. This perspective will constitute the heart of the discussion in the remainder of this chapter.

The preceding thoughts on attitudes and behavior were commented upon by a reviewer for one of the criminal justice journals. This reviewer said: "He [meaning me] . . . argues, but not too effectively, that the mechanism of change is through alteration of attitudes. Indeed . . . we find a long (and erroneous) harangue on why attitude change is necessary prior to behavior change." The reviewer referred me to the literature on operant conditioning in psychology as "an antidote to [my] overstated position."

I hope that the preceding discourse clears up any confusion or misinterpretation of my intent. I did not and do not now claim that attitude change is necessary prior to behavior change, but rather that it may simply be an intervening link. That changes in behavior can occur without changes in attitudes is neither denied nor ruled out. Behavior modification, discussed earlier, is a prime example of that. Also, the so-called harangue is merely an attempt on my part to illustrate the complexity of the connections among attitudes, perceptions, deterrence, and behavior. I hope this position is not seen as overstated.

GROUP COMPARISONS

We were unable to adhere strictly to our intended experimental design with pure random assignment as I have already indicated. As a result, I considered it necessary to look at the similarity of the experimental and control groups. Such comparisons are generally recommended, even in cases where random assignment has been successfully accomplished. One way of looking at comparability is to test for statistically significant differences between the groups being studied on any relevant background factors. The two groups were compared on such factors as sex, race, age, and time lapse between pre- and post-testing. The purpose here was to make sure that there were no big differences between the groups which would have an effect similar to comparing apples with oranges.[1]

In the experimental group, there were thirty-eight boys and eight girls; in the control group, twenty-seven boys and eight girls. There were twenty-seven blacks, seventeen whites, one Hispanic, and one other in the experimental group; there were fifteen blacks, sixteen whites, two Hispanics, and two others in the control group.

The average age of the experimental group was 15.4 years, ranging from twelve-years-old to eighteen-years-old. The average age of the control group was 14.6 years, ranging from eleven to eighteen years old.

Pre-testing of the kids began in February, 1978, and was completed in October, 1978. Post-testing began in May and was not completed until

---

[1] The results of the significance tests were as follows: sex (x^2 = .11; p = .74); race (x^2 = .32; p = .57); age (x^2 = .42; p < .50); and time lapse (x^2 = 6.75; p = .03).

November, 1978. The time lapse between the before and after testing ranged from one day for some juveniles to almost nine months for others. The reasons for this wide variation can be traced to some of the problems, administrative and others, already mentioned. Sponsoring agencies that had regularly scheduled tour days could visit the prison, and their subjects could be tested fairly quickly. Other agencies, on the other hand, were put on a two-month waiting list by the Lifers before they could visit. This resulted in different time gaps between pre- and post-testing. The longest lapses were for the two previously mentioned agencies that did not take their young people to the prison as scheduled. For example, the nine month gap was the result of one agency sponsor who was twice placed on the Lifers' two month waiting list. He failed both times to transport his charges to Rahway on the scheduled day. After I decided, with his agreement, that his kids should be used as controls, we were still unable to arrange a post-testing visit for several more months. It wasn't that he was hostile or uncooperative, he simply couldn't seem to get his kids organized for this purpose. In other cases, the gaps resulted from delays in trying to catch up with the juveniles to posttest them. Some were school kids who were first tested in the spring. Because of the school summer recess, which intervened, we were not able to test them again until the fall.

Because of this variation, I decided that time lapse should be treated as an independent factor possibly affecting outcomes. This meant that this factor would be analyzed to see if there were any decaying effects upon whatever attitude changes occurred. In order to do this, I broke down time lapse into three categories: less than one week, one to ten weeks, and eleven weeks or more. Most of the experimental group (54.3%) had a time lapse of one to ten weeks; but most of the control group (48.6%) had a time lapse of less than one week.

THE TESTS USED

Three different types of tests or scales were used to measure attitude changes. The first of these is something called the Attitude Toward Punishment of Criminals. This thirty-four item scale was originally developed by two researchers named Wang and Thurstone in 1931. The statements making up the scale are focused upon the purpose and appropriate use of punishment and upon whether or not to punish criminals at all. These purposes were deemed suitable to evaluate a program whose ostensible intent is to heighten awareness of punishment, as exemplified by a maximum security prison. In addition, there were other arguments in favor of using this particular instrument. First, of particular importance to researchers, the scale was deemed to be satisfactory with regard to both reliability and validity.[2] Second, the scale has a simplified children's or high school form which makes it appropriate for lower reading levels (but in fact, this simplified form was too difficult for some juveniles in the sample; and, each item had to be read to them individually). Finally, the Attitude Toward Punishment of Criminals scale was used by Brodsky in his study described in Chapter 3; thus, there would be a basis for comparing results.

The second set of measures are called Semantic Differential (SD) scales. "The semantic differential is a method of observing and measuring the psychological meaning of things, usually concepts."[3] It was invented by psychologist Charles Osgood.[4] The actual SD is made up of a number of scales, each consisting of a bipolar or opposite adjective pair such as fast-slow, sharp-dull, large-small, etc. These pairs of adjectives are used together with certain concepts that are considered to be relevant to what is to be measured, in this case attitudes about crime and punishment. Among the more than five-hundred concepts identified by Osgood and his colleagues are the following: crime, justice, law, policeman, prison, punishment, and I (myself). Given the content of the Lifers' sessions with the juveniles, which contain discussions, or actually presentations, on crime, on law enforcement, and the criminal justice system, on what it is like to be in prison and to be punished, and on the kids themselves, these particular concepts were considered relevant and appropriate.

In choosing scales or adjective pairs, one is supposed to consider the extent to which they are evaluative, indicating suitability for use as attitude measures; their relation to the concepts being tested; and their likelihood of being understood by the kids. This latter point is particularly important for use in a self-administered measure with subjects who may not read very well. The ten pairs of bipolar adjectives selected were: good-bad, beautiful-ugly, clean-dirty, kind-cruel, pleasant-unpleasant, happy-sad, nice-awful, honest-dishonest, fair-unfair, and valuable-worthless. These pairs have all been found useful in measuring attitudes. Each set of adjectives was used with each concept. The scales themselves can be found in Appendix A.

Semantic differential scales were chosen because they are sufficiently reliable and valid for many research purposes.[5] They are also flexible and

---

[2] Marvin E. Shaw and Jack M. Wright (eds.), *Scales for the Measurement of Attitudes* (New York: McGraw-Hill, 1967), p. 163.

[3] Fred N. Kerlinger, *Foundations of Behavioral Research* (New York: Holt, Rinehart and Winston, Inc., 1965), p. 564.

[4] C. Osgood, G. Suci, and P. Tannenbaum, *The Measurement of Meaning* (Urbana, Illinois: University of Illinois Press, 1957).

[5] Ibid., pp. 140–153, 192, 193.

adaptable, and quick and economical to administer and score. The latter was an important consideration.

The final measure is the Attitude Toward Obeying the Law test. This scale comes from a study published by H. Ashley Weeks entitled, *Youthful Offenders at Highfields: An Evaluation of the Effects of the Short-Term Treatment of Delinquent Boys.* Weeks was interested in learning whether delinquents participating in a residential treatment project called Highfields changed their attitudes toward, among other things, breaking the law.[6] The ATOL was one of eight scales constructed for that purpose. It was adopted for use here because of its simplicity (it contains only four items stated in the words of the boys in Weeks' study); its results can be compared to those found by Weeks; and, the nature of the items relate to the intended deterrent effect of the JAP. I considered it to be important and relevant to determine whether kids would express views more or less favorable to obeying the law after their participation in the program.

The entire test package of nine attitude measures and the Social Prediction Table (Appendix A) was pilot tested on a group of juveniles from Independence High School (an alternative school) in Newark, New Jersey. The results affirmed the feasibility and suitability of the measures with a comparable group of young people.

DID THE KIDS' ATTITUDES CHANGE?

Each of the nine measures is presented separately, beginning with the Attitude Toward Punishment of Criminals. In each case, it is the difference score between the before and after testing that is being compared.[7] When time lapse between the pre- and posttesting was introduced as a possible source of variation, it had no significant effect on any of the outcomes.

Attitude Toward Punishment of Criminals

The results from this test indicated that the juveniles in the experimental group who attended the project did not change their attitudes, at least as measured by this scale, *more* than did a comparable

[6] H. Ashley Weeks, *Youthful Offenders at Highfields* (Ann Arbor, Mich.: The University of Michigan Press, 1963), pp. 80–81.

[7] The results of the analysis of variance for difference between means on the pre- and post-tests were as follows: ATPC ($F = .068$; $p = .795$); CRIME ($F = 5.806$; $p = .018$); LAW ($F = .004$; $p = .95$); JUSTICE ($F = .157$; $p = .693$); I (MYSELF) ($F = .233$; $p = .63$); POLICEMAN ($F = .162$; $p = .688$); PRISON ($F = 1.421$; $p = .237$); PUNISHMENT ($F = .212$; $p = .646$); ATOL ($F = .383$; $p = .538$).

control group of juveniles who did not attend the project. There was a very slight but insignificant shift toward less punitive attitudes after the kids visited the Lifers' Project. This suggests that the visit stimulated some feelings of sympathy for the Lifers who had to endure the pains of the punishment that they described to the juveniles. The mean change for the visiting group was −0.67. This compares with Stanley Brodsky's finding of changes of −0.66 for forestry camp boys and −0.29 for high school predelinquents. The results are obviously very similar. The mean change for the control group was 0.28, a very small shift toward more punitive attitudes in the posttest. The kids who didn't go to Rahway obviously didn't become sympathetic to the plight of prison inmates.

Crime

There was a significant difference between experimentals and controls in their shifts in attitude toward crime. The juveniles visiting Rahway became significantly more negative in their outlook on crime than did the comparison group. The mean change for the experimental group was −4.21. In contrast, the control group mean change was in the opposite direction, increasing 1.83. This change is clearly of the kind hoped for by the sponsors and supporters of the Juvenile Awareness Project. It indicates that the Lifers' Group did change the attitudes of these young people toward crime. The kids had a greater tendency to see crime as being bad after their visit to the prison.

Furthermore, the significant difference between the visiting and nonvisiting groups remained when time lapse was introduced as a possible source of variation. This result added to the confidence in the conclusion about the effect of the project on this attitude. The fact that time lapse did not have a significant effect is important because it suggested that this attitude change may not be subject to decay, at least over the period of time studied.

Law

There was no difference in the change between the groups on their attitude toward law. Both groups became more negative the second time they were tested. The mean change for experimental kids was − 2.70; for controls it was −2.52. Law is perhaps a more esoteric and complex concept in the minds of the young people in this sample. As such, it is perhaps less likely than some of the other concepts to be subject to change through exposure to the Lifers' program. Because a negative shift occurred in both groups, it cannot be considered meaningful.

Justice

The result was no difference in the change between groups on their attitude toward justice. Both groups shifted in the negative direction, but the change was more pronounced for the controls (mean $= -2.03$) than for the experimentals (mean $= -0.67$). Justice is also a complex and multifaceted concept, probably not subject to simple manipulation. The fact that no significant changes occurred in attitudes toward law and justice is not surprising, given the nature of these concepts. They are relevant, but may simply be beyond the scope of the project's possible effects.

I (Myself)

One of the purposes of the evaluation was to determine whether or not the JAP had any effects upon the kids' self-perceptions. The concept I (Myself) was used in the Semantic Differential scales as a way to measure any such effects. The result indicated no difference between experimentals and controls on this factor. Mean change for the experimentals was only -0.04; for controls it was 1.63. The project seems to have no effect upon this measure of self-perception. Changing self-image, another complex notion, may also be beyond the scope of the project.

Policeman

There was no difference in the changes between the groups on their attitude toward the concept policeman. Although less esoteric a concept than law and justice, the ideas, which are conjured up by the word policeman, are somewhat removed from the direct influence of the Juvenile Awareness Project. Because of its symbolic meaning it is not an irrelevant concept; but, the results indicate that the existing attitude is not subject to change by the Lifers.

Prison

One of the major purposes of the Juvenile Awareness Project is to influence attitudes about prison. Although there was a shift among the attending juveniles in the direction of becoming more negative about prison, this shift was not significantly different from that of nonattenders. This result is complementary to that from the Attitude Toward Punishment of Criminals scale discussed earlier. The mean change for the juveniles visiting Rahway was -1.46. For the control group it was

1.83. This change also is in the direction desired by the sponsors and supporters, but it doesn't reach statistical significance. Whether or not it is socially or behaviorally important is a separate issue to be decided by others. Learning that prisons are bad may generate a group of prison reformers, but whether they will also be crime-free is another matter.

Punishment

Again, no significant changes appeared between the groups in their attitude toward punishment. Surprisingly, the overall change was in the direction of becoming slightly more positive toward punishment on the post-tests. The mean change for the experimental group was an almost imperceptible 0.04; for the control group it was 1.20.

Attitudes Toward Obeying the Law

As mentioned previously, the ATOL measure is a four-item scale employed to directly test the deterrent effects on perceptions resulting from participation in the Project. Each of the scale items was scored one to four, resulting in a range of possible scores for the entire scale of from one to sixteen. Low scores indicate more favorable attitudes toward obeying the law, and high scores indicate less favorable attitudes. The attending juveniles shifted very slightly (mean change = −0.06) toward more favorable attitudes after participation in the project. The control group change was in a similar direction, but of somewhat greater magnitude (mean change = −0.43). There was, however, no significant difference between the experimental group and the control or comparison group on this measure.

When this scale was used in the *Youthful Offenders at Highfields* study, posttest results classified into those for Highfields blacks and whites and Annandale (the reformatory) blacks and whites, indicated "a slight tendency for all but the Highfields Negroes to show a more favorable attitude toward obeying the law by the time the boys take their posttests, but the differences are very small. Examination of the internal shifts indicate that two-fifths or more of the boys change, and that relatively about as many boys change favorably as unfavorably."[8] Three of the four groups, Highfields whites being the exception, showed no significant change from the pretest to the posttest. The results from my administration of this test were not terribly dissimilar to these, that is, a slight tendency to be more inclined to obey the law.

The preliminary conclusions from all this were that the results were mixed. We did not, however, find any overriding reasons to reject

[8] Weeks, *Youthful Offenders at Highfields*, p. 81.

our hypothesis that the Juvenile Awareness Project has no effect on the attitudes of the juveniles attending.

That these results could be subject to a somewhat different interpretation was apparent from a letter to the editor of the Los Angeles Times prepared by the KTLA-TV publicity office. It should be recalled that KTLA first telecast Scared Straight! and is affiliated with the film makers. The letter read as follows:

> The results of the Rutgers University School of Criminal Justice evaluation of the Juvenile Awareness Program show a significant change in juvenile attitudes toward crime. The evaluation measured attitude changes of an experimental group who went through the program as compared to a control group who did not. Both groups were matched for age, sex, race and potential probability of becoming juvenile delinquents.
>
> The experimental groups showed a significant change in their attitude that crime was not desirable. This change did not occur in the control group. The obvious conclusion is that the Rahway Juvenile Awareness Program is successful in changing the attitudes of youngsters toward crime.
>
> Moreover, the evaluation shows the program is not affected by race or sex. The program is just as effective for whites as blacks, for females as males. Age did prove to be a variable factor: younger children were more affected by the program than older children. The age range of the children tested was 11 to 18.
>
> *None of the children suffered adverse emotional affects* as a result of going through the program.
>
> "One of the key results of the evaluation indicates sponsors should take more care in selecting high-risk, potential delinquents to go through the program," says Assistant Professor James Finckenauer, Rutgers School of Criminal Justice. There are available to any sponsor simple testing and scoring methods that give highly accurate juvenile delinquency potential measurements.
>
> The consensus is that a carefully structured and controlled Juvenile Awareness Program where sponsors carefully screen participating children is an inexpensive, effective deterrent to juvenile delinquency.

After these findings were reported to the New Jersey Department of Corrections and our first report became generally available, some who reviewed it criticized the data analysis and the results. A second analysis was therefore undertaken using the same technique employed with the behavior outcomes (multiple regression analysis). This technique permits a researcher to analyze the relationship between a dependent variable (in this case attitude change) and a set of independent variables (in this case delinquency probability, race, sex, age, time lapse, and experimental or control group). The characteristic making it most useful here is that it allows you to control for other confounding factors in order to look at the specific contribution of any one factor to the outcome. Among the few noteworthy results from that reanalysis was that delinquency probability, as predicted by the Glueck Table, was significantly correlated with changes in Attitudes Toward Punishment of Criminals. Experimental and control group differences in attitude toward crime were still significant, that is, didn't wash-out, when the other five factors were controlled. And, age was significantly correlated with differences in attitude toward justice, toward prison, and toward punishment. These results did not provide any reason to alter the main conclusion about the general absence of project effects upon attitudes.

A TRUNCATED ADDITIONAL SAMPLE

One of the original objectives of the study plan was to select and interview a random sample of approximately fifty juveniles who had participated in the project since its inception in September, 1976. Because our money was exhausted, these planned interviews had to be scrapped. However, I decided that at the least a records check of a random sample of previous attenders would provide informative before and after data on the effect of the Lifers' intervention. Since the original sample was smaller than expected (81 out of 100), and since checking court records is not terribly time nor resource consuming, I decided to increase the size of the projected random sample from 50 to 120.

This sample for before/after analysis of a new group of juveniles was obtained from the prison's roster of all juveniles who had attended the Juvenile Awareness Project. A random sample of sixty juveniles who attended the project during the first six months of 1977, and another sixty who attended during the first six months of 1979 was chosen. The 1977 sample was planned to represent the first six months of daily operation of the project, and would allow for a follow-up period of up to three years since their attendance. The 1979 sample would follow the considerable publicity which the project had received, the "Scared Straight!" documentary, and two evaluation reports, including my own, which was completed the previous December. There would be a six month to one year follow-up period for these latter juveniles. The 120 juveniles came from seventeen of the twenty-one counties in New Jersey.

But—a funny thing happened on the way to data collection! In November, 1979, I sent a letter to the juvenile court judges in the seventeen counties requesting access to any juvenile court records that existed on the sampled juveniles from their respective jurisdictions. I enclosed a copy of the permission letter which I had received from the New Jersey Administrative Office of the Courts in March, 1978. I did this in the belief that this sample was already included in the previously approved study plan since it was part of the original proposal as approved. However, on December 7, 1979 I received a letter from the AOC saying in part:

> My concern is that the 120 juveniles whose juvenile records you now wish to access represent a new and additional sample. If this is so, then you would need Supreme Court approval to access the records of this new sample.
>
> I would very much appreciate your advising me by letter as to whether or not my analysis of this situation is correct. Meanwhile, by copy of this letter I am recommending to the presiding judges that they hold off assisting your efforts until this matter is resolved.

Needless to say, I was not pleased with this new development. However, recognizing that you cannot successfully fight city hall, I engaged in a series of communiques—letters and telephone calls—with the AOC over the next six months. Finally, on May 13, 1980 I received the following letter from them:

> In recent letters to the AOC you requested permission to access certain juvenile court records with respect to your study of the Juvenile Awareness Project Help Program. Please be advised that the Administrative Director has determined that the potential benefits of your further research at this time do not justify further access to juvenile court records. We appreciate your recent efforts on this issue and anticipate continued mutual cooperation in the future.

I appealed this decision to the Administrative Director, but without success. C'est la vie!

Before the December 7 shutdown occurred, the judges in four counties had individually approved my access to their court records. I was thus able to check out thirty-four of the one hundred twenty juveniles in the random sample. These thirty-four juveniles did provide some interesting findings. First, seventy-one percent of them had no records of delinquency prior to attending the Lifers' Project. This rate of nondelinquency is even higher than that for the earlier sample. Their success rate (79 percent) was also higher than that of the control group. This figure has both a plus and a minus feature. The plus is that some of the thirty-four had a follow-up (exposure to risk) period of approximately two and one-half years. The minus is that most of them were not delinquent at the outset. Once again it is a situation in which nondelinquents remained nondelinquent.

Only twelve of these young people had any records, either before or after their visit. The offenses for these twelve are broken down by when they occurred as follows:

Before and After	5
Before Only	5
After Only	2

The recidivism rate (repeat offenders) is 50 percent. The failure rate (all subsequent offenders) among the delinquents is 58 percent. Neither of these is at all impressive, but the numbers are obviously very small.

Finally, in my discussion of the UDIS program in Chapter I, reference was made to an innovative method of assessing recidivism. This method employs what has been called a suppression effect criterion.[9] This simply means that if a treatment or other intervention is effective, delinquent behavior may not vanish, but it will occur to a lesser degree than was the case before intervention. In a rough approximation of this notion, I looked at the delinquency seriousness scores, both before and after, for the twelve juveniles in this sample who had records. The mean seriousness score for prior offenses was 5.7, for subsequent offenses 2.8, an average difference (decline) of 2.9. Admittedly the exposure to risk period in which offenses could have been committed was shorter after the visit than it was before. Despite this, the suppression effect from before to after is not significant ($t = 1.035$; $df = 11$). The conclusion is that the Juvenile Awareness Project does not seem to have had any notable effect upon these juveniles.

This truncated sample partially confirms the earlier results. It was an unfortunate blow to the search for knowledge about youth aversion programs that the New Jersey Administrative Office of the Courts determined that there were no "potential benefits" from "further research." Utilization of the suppression effect criterion with a considerably larger sample could have been extremely productive and informative.

CONCLUSIONS

As a result of these research findings, particularly the earlier ones, a number of observations have been made about the Juvenile Awareness Project. It seems to me that the success rate from the project falls

[9] Charles A. Murray and Louis A. Cox, Jr., *Beyond Probation: Juvenile Corrections and the Chronic Delinquent* (Beverly Hills: Sage Publications, 1979).

considerably short of the phenomenal 80–90 percent rate originally touted by its supporters and stressed in the "Scared Straight!" documentary. After the release of my findings, the Lifers' Group and others vigorously attacked the study. Among other things, the Lifers said that they had never claimed any particular success rate for their project. They said that any figures were collected and reported by others—presumably Judge George Nicola. However, I uncovered a letter to the "Helen help us!" column in the Newark Star-Ledger for August 28, 1978. This was before the release of either of my reports and before "Scared Straight!" The letter from the then secretary of the Lifers' Group said in part: "The Lifers' Group has been in existence since 1975. Our Juvenile Awareness Project was started in 1976. During this period, some 8,000 young people have participated—and we have been able to reduce their recidivism rate from 86.2 percent to 10.2 percent."

With a little arithmetic, the flipside of a 10.2 percent recidivism rate is an 89.8 percent success rate. It would seem that at least some Lifers did make the questionable claim. The Lifers and others have backed off from these figures since the initial release of my results. However, they have replaced them at various times with new claims: 59 percent success in the visiting group cannot be considered a failure; and further, if even one young person is helped that is sufficient reason to justify the project.

My response to these is to reiterate the substantially better performance, in all respects, of the nonattending control group, and the fact that a large number of the juveniles were already nondelinquents and thus already "successes." As to the helping only one young person rationale, one can decide for oneself whether it would all be worth it, and whether there would have been all the hoopla and panacea phenomenon effect if that had in fact been the case and was stated as such. I personally think not!

Zealous project supporters and "media Hype" specialists seem to have failed to take account of the complex nature of juvenile delinquency and of the overwhelming absence of success with most previous prevention and treatment efforts. Consequently, they raised unrealistic expectations and goals for the project by selling it as a cheap, easy, simple and effective cure-all.

I have also observed that the nature of the Lifers' Project is atypical when compared to other prevention and treatment programs. It is strictly a "one shot" effort for the most part, and does not engage its clients over any period of time. This characteristic both militates against its success and makes comparisons to other programs somewhat untenable.

The controversial *possibility* also exists that the project actually sets in motion a "delinquency fulfilling prophecy" in which it increases rather than decreases the chances of juvenile delinquency. This possibility cannot be dismissed in light of the finding (substantiated by the subsequent reanalysis of the data) that my experimental group juveniles, including the nondelinquents, did much worse than the control group juveniles in their follow-up behavior. There are several possible ways in which this could occur—and these need to be examined by further research on this project and others patterned after it. The project may romanticize the Lifers—and by extension other prison inmates—in young, impressionable minds. Or, the belittling, demeaning, intimidating, and scaring of particular youth may be seen as a challenge; a challenge to go out and prove to themselves, their peers, and others, that they were not scared.

In sum, my research strongly suggests that the Lifers' Project is not scaring kids straight. If nothing else, the findings challenge, and in my judgement, debunk any thoughts that this approach could be a panacea.

part four

The Aftermath

chapter nine

The National Response

Release of my second report, coming shortly after the national showing of "Scared Straight!" and its receipt of an Academy Award, stimulated an uproar—a storm of response. Beginning in the spring of 1979, the storm continued, with ebbs and flows, for more than a year. An integral component of at least part of this story is an organization called the National Center on Institutions and Alternatives. A private, non-profit Washington-based agency, NCIA was established in 1977 to increase the national awareness about institutions—particularly juvenile institutions—and to seek alternatives to institutionalization. Its president is Dr. Jerome G. Miller, a former social work professor, who at various times has headed youth corrections in Massachusetts, Illinois, and Pennsylvania. Jerry Miller's life's work has been trying to create alternative programs for delinquent youth and to reduce the populations of juvenile correctional institutions. His personal concerns about "Scared Straight!" stemmed from a belief that it could set back effective understanding and treatment of delinquency, and could serve to legitimate the continuance of inhumane prison conditions.

THE ROLE OF NCIA

Sometime in early 1979, Jerry Miller became aware of my study of the Juvenile Awareness Project. In March, he asked to meet with me.

We met and I briefed him on the study, including what some of the preliminary findings might look like. He was excited by the possibility of having something concrete to substantiate his vague fears concerning the project.

Miller asked if I would be willing to collaborate in an effort to disseminate my findings in order to raise the national consciousness about youth aversion programs in general, and about the Rahway project in particular. This was critically important, he said, because of the bandwagon effect which was rapidly developing. I indicated that the Department of Corrections should first receive what would be the second report and should have the opportunity to decide upon any dissemination that they wished to make. There had been no general dissemination of the first report, and in fact the Department had not actually acknowledged ever receiving it. I was, therefore, not optimistic that the second report would be handled much differently.

Another concern I had was to not jeopardize the possibilities for my own publication of the study in one or more professional criminal justice journals. This is the normal method for dissemination of research results in the academic community. Miller's response to this was to express dissatisfaction about the fact that such publication could probably not be realized for six months to a year after completion of the study; and, even then it would be targeted on a readership (largely academic researchers) which would be overly narrow for any practical purposes. He wanted to put my findings into the hands of a broad range of decisionmakers—public officials, concerned private citizens, corrections officials, relevant associations and organizations, inmate groups, etc.—in a timely and readable fashion. Otherwise, he said, decisions about developing "scared straight" type programs would proceed in a generally uninformed or misinformed manner. These views seemed very well-taken to me and consequently, I agreed to a collaborative effort with NCIA to get the study out.

I also agreed to go to Washington and to brief Miller and his staff on my results once they had been finalized. Between our two visits, Jerry Miller published a lengthy article in the NCIA investigative newsletter for March, 1979, parts of which were reproduced in Chapter 5. In addition to that commentary, Miller provided some information that supported the need for expediency. He said:

This week, in a move attributed to the showing of "Scared Straight," the Maryland House of Delegates passed a previously defunct piece of legislation. The bill allows juvenile judges to sentence youngsters as young as 14 to a county jail for up to 12 days in order to scare them straight.[1]

It was also about this time that a California State Senator introduced a bill which would mandate the busing of up to 15,000 southern California youngsters to northern California prisons, such as Folsom and San Quentin, to get the "cure."

During late March and through April, Miller and his staff carried out an investigation of the documentary "Scared Straight!" I had several contacts with them during this period, including the staff briefing mentioned earlier. In the interim, I turned in a copy of my finished report to the Department of Corrections. The April NCIA newsletter reported the findings of Miller's investigation:

Of the 17 youngsters shown in the film and variously portrayed as "hard core," "lifelong," or as one TV reviewer noted "offenders willing to continue their petty careers as muggers, rip-off artists, pickpockets, etc." . . . . 13 of the 17 were from one upper-middle class suburban bedroom community outside New York City. Not coincidently, these 13 are the white youngsters shown in the film.

The suburban town from which they came, is not now notable, nor has it ever been notable for any major delinquency problem. The filming of the kids on the street (a scene from the film) might have led the viewer to think these were ghetto street corners or city parks. However, one site for the interviews was a perfectly charming corner flower shop nestled in the middle of the three block main street. The other site was a kiddie park complete with merry-go-round and swings.

We wondered how these 13 youngsters portrayed in the film as serious delinquents had come to be picked. It turns out they volunteered. A group who hang around the park in the evenings, were approached and asked if they would care to be part of a film and to attend the Rahway program. Most agreed. Curiously, for some of them this was their second trip to the Rahway program. There was an earlier trip as part of a school program, and a later trip for filming.

We thought it might be interesting to look into the school program. We found an upper-middle-class high school of approx-

---

[1] National Center on Institutions and Alternatives, "Scared Straight: Columbo Meets the Young Frankenstein," *Investigative Newsletter on Institutions/Alternatives,* 11 (March 1979), 3.

imately 1200 students. As we looked around the parking lots and grounds, although we saw three or four hundred students, we could see no more than one or two blacks. The woman guidance counselor at the high school told us that originally the suggestion had been made that prisoners be brought to the high school to speak to students. . . . "I said absolutely not!" Later, she was taken to the program by a local policeman and "it was everything I had hoped for." When we asked her what this meant, she said that she was particularly impressed with the prisoners' use of the word, "M-F". "I am sure that some students had used that word around school. After going to the Lifers' group, they'll never use that word again."

And how many youngsters from the high school had been to the Rahway program? With a certain pride, she stated that 250 (out of 1200) had been to Rahway in the current school year. An additional 150 to 200 had been there previously. And how does one get into the program at Rahway? "We announce it on the loudspeaker . . we get the parents' permission. . . . we then choose those that we feel might be borderline. . . . though the majority that go to the program are not borderline." She described a "borderline" youngster as one who may have been involved in running away, bad language, etc. Speaking of the Rahway program, she said, "We haven't had more than two or three bad kids go to it."

The counselor here made the distinction between a "borderline" youngster and one who was "on the brink." The two or three "bad" kids were those who she described as "on the brink." When pushed further on the issue, she said that they were youngsters who had been sent away to "homes" . . . presumably to institutions.

So we found a high school in the suburbs with 1200 students, in which 300 to 400 had at one time or another been to the program at Rahway in order to get "scared straight." It appeared that a goal of the high school was to reach a point where most of the students in the school would have been sent to Rahway, unrelated to any putative history of delinquency or even "borderline" behavior.

The local juvenile police officer claims to have sent 407 kids to the Rahway program over the last 3 years. Not all of these were from the above-mentioned high school, since he feels able as well, to accept referrals from other counties and states.

He made a point of the fact that the youngsters who appeared in the film were the "worst kids in town." When asked how they were picked, he replied, "by coincidence." We took this to mean that the teenagers happened to be standing in the park on the night in which subjects for the film were being sought. The detective's comments regarding the "worst kids" piqued our interest.

We therefore sought out, and found the majority of those who had been in the film.

Virtually everyone we interviewed in the community knew of the "Scared Straight!" film, and a large percentage knew the youngsters who appeared in it. Most of the teenagers who we interviewed knew of the film, and of those who appeared in it. Here are some of their comments:

"I know a couple of kids in the movie . . . they weren't that bad . . . they made them look bad." When we asked one boy why the juveniles in the film seemed to be portrayed as having been in so much trouble, he commented, "They wanted it to sound that way . . . _____ _____ knew he didn't do any bad stuff." And why do you suppose they wanted it to sound so bad? "So people would be scared."

Or this comment from another high school student, "They made them sound like they were the biggest derelicts walking the streets." When we asked one juvenile why his friends would go on film and tell all the "crimes" they had committed? He replied, "They would be acting."

Although some students said that a few of those shown on the film had been in trouble, . . . they were viewed as not having been in much more trouble than anyone else.

This did not jibe with what we had been told by the policeman who had referred the youngsters to "Scared Straight." He indicated that virtually all of them had court records. When we asked how many, and what kind of record, he replied that it was "confidential". When we asked if he could give us a percentage of those who had been to court out of the 13, he said that was also confidential.

We had heard that one of the juveniles in the film had been involved in a breaking and entering. That seemed a real delinquency. . . . at least one that comes close to one of the "crimes" mentioned in the TV reviews alongside "mugging." And indeed we found that he had been involved at age 14 (two or more years before the film) along with six to ten other juveniles who went in and out of a candy store at night, stealing candy. But what about one of the other "stars" of the film, whose face appears tearful in a number of magazines, and who, as Peter Falk refers to juveniles involved in burglary, walks in front of the camera. This youngster, among those described as the "worst" by the policeman who chose them, was also involved in crime. His crime was setting off firecrackers on the 4th of July at age 14, (two years before the making of the film).

While surely there were others in the film who were hell-bent delinquents, there was another featured youngster whose crime was phoning in a bomb scare from the school. This appeared to be the most serious delinquent from among the group. He noted that although he may not have appeared to do much, that in fact, he never got caught. Since the film was made, he has appeared on numerous talk shows and has been offered a "screen test." As he understands it, he is to portray a "derelict" in a film set in the 1890's.

We did hear of one youngster who had been sent away to state schools before appearing on the film. Though he was listed as "scared straight," one source indicated that he had since been in other trouble.

Another source commented that the Rahway program did not appear to be suited to delinquents who had been institutionalized. "They thought it was a big joke."

There were also numerous allegations by a number of youngsters that certain juveniles were taken out of the room by inmates to another room where they were "roughed up," slapped, pinched, or otherwise physically intimidated.

In summary, we found a town which never has had a major delinquency problem, totally enthralled with sending a significant percentage of its teen-aged population to Rahway prison to keep them "straight." In 1975, the town had 140 formal complaints against juveniles, many of which did not go beyond initial police contact. In 1978 it had 126 complaints. In the last three years 3 or 4 juveniles from the town had been sent away to reform school. The statistics are not particularly alarming nor interesting. Why the hysterics? Why the unbelievable recidivism figures? Where did those figures come from?[2]

In a press release accompanying the Newsletter, NCIA called for a Congressional investigation of the Juvenile Awareness Project and of the promotional campaigns surrounding "Scared Straight!" Miller wanted Congressional action because of the large number of states rushing to create programs, and because of the public pressure on many correctional administrators to do the same. Miller said there should be "a cold hard look" into the whole matter before "the rush to carelessly replicate . . . does a disservice to thousands of adolescent youth and may do irreparable psychological harm to certain ill-chosen youngsters."

It is important to note that the NCIA investigation of Scared Straight! and my own study of JAP were separate and independent, although overlapping activities. Our agreed-upon collaborative venture resulted in the private publication in May of that year of a pamphlet entitled, "Scared Straight: A Second Look." Printed through a small grant from the Edna McConnell Clark Foundation, this pamphlet was

[2] National Center on Institutions and Alternatives, "Scared Straight" the Myth that Roared," *Investigative Newsletter on Institutions/Alternatives*, 11 (April 1979), 3-6.

disseminated by the thousands across the country. The pamphlet succinctly summarized and synthesized the research results from both parts of my study. Its purpose was stated in the preface as follows: "Rather than relying upon reported success rates, media accounts, and letters of commendation from parents or law enforcement people, it is our hope that legislators, judges, juvenile court officials, and anyone interested in the program will take the opportunity to read this report. . . ."

THE ROLE OF THE MEDIA

As has already been indicated, the media—particularly newspapers and of course television—had played a very big part in building up the "scared straight" phenomenon. The Lifers and the Juvenile Awareness Project had become a media event, familiar to millions of Americans and others in many parts of the world.

Sometime after becoming aware of my research, Jerry Miller and the NCIA decided that one of the only ways to defuse this media event— to bring the phenomenon back to reality—was to utilize the media itself. Consequently, overtures were made by Miller and his colleagues to representatives of *The New York Times* newspaper, *Time* and *Newsweek* magazines, and perhaps others. As a result, shortly after I had submitted the second report to the Department of Corrections, I was contacted about doing an interview by *The New York Times*.

The interview is important because it led to a *New York Times* story that sparked the beginning of a retreat from the heights which the Lifers' Juvenile Awareness Project and "Scared Straight!" had occupied. It is important also because it became the major basis for charges that I released my results to the news media in some unethical or unprofessional manner. Mr. Martin Waldron, a reporter on New Jersey news for *The New York Times,* was the interviewer. I distinctly recall being impressed at how well he had done his homework before the interview. For example, Waldron had already spoken with people from NCIA and the Department of Corrections, as well as others, and he had copies of various evaluation reports on the project. He asked me to describe my research and its findings, and to assess the implications. I did so within the limits of generalizability. Waldron's subsequent story appeared in *The New York Times* for Thursday, April 26, 1979, headlined: "Teen-Agers' Visits to Prisons Criticized." The story presented the initial data and findings reported in Chapter 7.

The reaction to the article was almost immediate. The wire services (AP and UPI) picked up the story and sent it across the country. The telephones began ringing. Thus began another media event of sorts—only this time it was going to run in reverse.

Over the following six month period—from late April through the end of October, 1979—I appeared on or was interviewed on twenty-five different radio and television programs around the country. Also included were interviews with the BBC in London, CBC Radio in Toronto, Canada, and one with an Australian radio station. This considerable media attention reflected the reach and power of television, and of the impact of the original airing of the documentary.

Numerous articles, editorials, and columns appeared in newspapers and magazines with such headlines as: "Criminologist flunks 'Scared Straight!,' "[3] "The Scary Lesson of 'Scared Straight!,' "[4] and "An 'I told you so' on lifers program."[5] At least three of these pieces hit upon the notion of the panacea phenomenon. New Jersey's *Trenton Times* published an editorial on April 30, 1979 which said in part:

The Overselling of "Scared Straight!"

A skillfully-done television program can easily oversell a particular answer or point of view. That's what happened to the Lifers Program at Rahway State Prison, whose tough talk to teenagers about prison life got national publicity in an Oscar-winning documentary, "Scared Straight!"

The reported "success" led some people to believe a magic panacea for juvenile crime had been found. Poor imitations sprang up in other correctional institutions. Entire school classes, including many children who were straight without being scared, were sent through similar sessions. . . .

Newsweek magazine for May 14, 1979 carried an article entitled, "Does 'Scaring' Work?" It said:

The "Scared Straight" uproar is far from over. Many Americans want to try anything that might moderate youth crime. "I don't think anybody but a fool would be interested only in statistics," says producer Shapiro. "Any kid who's been turned around is a life saved." But Diana R. Gordon, the vice president of the National Council on Crime and Delinquency, argues that authorities must face the "social forces behind serious delinquency—teen-age unemployment, the crumbling of the family, social and economic inequality"—before teen-age crime can be

---

[3] Stephen P. Morin, "Criminologist Flunks Scared Straight," *The Providence Journal* (April 17, 1979).

[4] *The New York Times*, Editorial (April 25, 1979).

[5] Diana Henriques, "An 'I Told You So' on Lifers Program," *Sunday Times Advertiser* (April 29, 1979), p. B7.

substantially reduced. At best, scaring youngsters might help, but there are no quick fixes for juvenile crime.

Shapiro seemed to be backing off from the movie's success claims, while at the same time downgrading the importance of "the statistics." In this article we also see the "one kid saved" rationale.

The *Milwaukee Journal* for June 25, 1979 published a column written by Mr. Sam Stellman of the University of Wisconsin. Entitling his article, "Juvenile Delinquency Too Complicated to be Solved by Easy Answers of 'Scared Straight,' " Stellman concluded:

> . . . it seemed too simple an answer. For convicts with the worst records to frighten crime out of juveniles in a single two hour session, using the worst kind of scare tactics, may make good television. It may win an Academy Award. It may receive plaudits from public hopefuls that delinquency can be curbed with a single, sure fire answer to diverting juveniles from criminal acts. But "Scared Straight" can hardly be, as some would have us believe, the instant answer to a widespread, nationwide problem that has overloaded our police departments, our courts, and our lockup institutions.

One of the more perceptive and comprehensive of the news articles during this period was done for *The Home News* of New Brunswick, New Jersey by Mr. Peter Genovese. It was entitled "Pros and cons of 'Scared Straight' stir controversy."[6] The following is some of what was included:

> The Rutgers University professor who authored a report critical of the nationally-acclaimed "Lifers" program at Rahway State Prison says his report doesn't prove the program causes crime, only that it does not act as a deterent [sic].
> But the president of the "Lifers" group says the program isn't even intended to deter crime, only to tell juveniles about the criminal justice system.
> The two men, Dr. James Finckenauer of Rutgers' School of Criminal Justice in Newark, and Robert Jones, a Rahway maximum-security prisoner who has been president of the "Lifers" group the past two years, are at the center of a growing national debate over the effectiveness of the so-called "scared straight" program at Rahway and the dozen or so programs in other states that have been copied from it. . . .
> Jones says Fickenauer's [sic] report was "unfair" to the Lifers program because its sample was not big enough. But the

[6] Peter Genovese, "Pros and Cons of 'Scared Straight' Stir Controversy," *The Home News* (May 13, 1979).

Rutgers professor says his study abided by all measures of statistical accuracy. . . .

Jones says his main objection to the study is not necessarily its conclusion, but that it assumes the program is meant to deter crime.

"We're not out to change attitudes. We can't change their (juvenile delinquents') problems. All we can do is highlight the pitfalls of engaging in criminal activity."

Jones says the program has actually been hurt by the nationwide publicity given it, especially in the wake of the Academy Award-winning documentary "Scared Straight!" . . .

. . . according to Jones, the program will undergo an image change. "We're trying to get away from the 'scared straight' label because we don't want to scare kids. We want them . . . to check out what we say. We want to teach them to respect authority, so they don't end up as we did," he says.

What is most interesting about Robert Jones' comments in this report is the point about the premise of the Juvenile Awareness Project. This point relates back to the issue of theoretical foundations discussed earlier. Jones says the project was not intended to deter crime. In other words, he seems to be saying, no one assumed that exposing the juveniles to the harsh realities of the prison system would cause a reduction in their future criminal behavior. This certainly runs contrary to almost everything that had previously been said, written, or portrayed about the project. That particular assumption was most definitely implied. Further, Jones' statement that the project is intended "only to tell juveniles about the criminal justice system," can also be questioned. Tell them about the criminal justice system for what purpose? To what end? If you are not trying to change the juveniles' attitudes or their behavior, what are you trying to do? But perhaps there are other potential purposes, and these will be discussed later in the text.

SOME OF THE PUBLIC RESPONSE

All the media attention paid to "Scared Straight!" and to my research stimulated some interesting responses from the public. Some of it was supportive, but much of it was not. An example is the following anonymous postcard mailed from Knoxville, Tennessee:

Sir—
If you knew anything except what you read in books you'd know Scared Straight is effective. If I could have seen something

like that I can assure you my life would have been a better life. With plain ordinary respect also comes fear—Or else we all wouldn't pay income tax. Think it over—

A criminal once.

A day treatment program coordinator in Pennsylvania had this to say:

Rahway State Prison may not be a cure all to our nation's delinquency problems, but it is certainly an aide [sic] to treatment. Your report is just as inconclusive and under-researched as the Rahway Prison success rates are.

.... I'd like to see you do a *good* report on what the effects of the program are and how it can be better utilized by referring agencies. Talking it down in a shoddy report does no one any good.

A juvenile court judge in Indiana said he was concerned ". . . that all apparent good things—from saccharin to charitable programs to inmate-helping projects—must be subjected to an unreasonable burden of proof as to their validity." The judge enclosed a copy of a letter to Golden West Television which said in part:

The Rutgers report and the ensuing criticism calls to my mind Walt Kelly's line in *Pogo*: "We have met the enemy, and it is us." I am convinced that if Jesus Christ appeared tomorrow, then certainly some professor or college institute or government bureaucrat would quickly release a study, complete with statistics, to clearly prove that what we knew to be true was false.

What comes across clearly in these particular reactions and was also evident at a number of the public appearances which I made, is that there is a certain air of anti-intellectualism or anti-academia among some people and some groups in the country. Because, in the words of a colleague, I had picked the wings off the butterfly, I became the target for this distrust of and perhaps dislike for what some see as "ivory tower" academics. These feelings are expressed in such time-honored comments as George Bernard Shaw's "Those who can, do; those who can't, teach!" And, this from Mark Twain: "There are lies; there are damn lies; and then there are statistics!"

Many people distrust and may even be intimidated by statistics, in part because they do not really understand them. Some of the people who reacted negatively to my research also felt that I was trying to defend the so-called professionals who had, by and large, failed in their efforts to combat delinquency. I was doing this, they said, by trying to shoot down a grassroots effort that might succeed where the professionals had failed.

All of this reflected the widespread and highly emotional response that the project and the documentary had stimulated. What was somewhat disappointing to me was the extent to which this arousal seemed to close the minds of some, including the aforementioned Indiana judge, who were in a position to know better. There may be lessons in these reactions, and in the others reported earlier, for program evaluators. Almost all programs, and delinquency prevention efforts are no exception, develop constituencies; these programs develop supporters with vested interests in seeing their programs praised and continued. Evaluators need to anticipate and prepare for the reactions that may ensue if these vested interests are undercut by negative results.

As Carol H. Weiss points out in her excellent book, *Evaluation Research,* ideological commitments to a particular set of values, and even to particular methods of doing things, may result in the rejection of anything that threatens these basic allegiances. She says that wherever strong ideological commitments are involved, even totally negative evaluation results may not lead to the abandonment of programs. Further, she says, criticism of the methodology is a common counterattack against an unfavorable evaluation.[7]

These thoughts about the role of ideology suggest perhaps another explanation for the panacea phenomenon. Delinquency prevention ideas that fit with our own preconceived notions about human behavior may fall on fertile ground. Thus, believers in deterrence, in the value of fear, and in behavior as a consequence of rational choice would be much more receptive to using aversive approaches. But the same might be true of those who have other ideological commitments. For example, educators and those who believe in the value of education would perhaps be more receptive to delinquency prevention programs which have education as their core; recreation specialists and the sports-minded believe in recreation and sports; group workers obviously believe in group techniques. Psychoanalysts believe that juvenile delinquency stems from inadequate development of the superego or conscience. Therefore to believers in psychoanalytic theory, psychoanalysis is the answer to delinquency; and the list could go on. The point is that any of these "answers" may be bought more readily—and doubted much less—if they are consistent with our preconceived notions.

[7] Carol H. Weiss, *Evaluation Research* (Englewood Cliffs, N.J.: Prentice-Hall, Inc., 1972), p. 7.

THE CONGRESSIONAL INVESTIGATION

A Congressional subcommittee, the House Subcommittee on Human Resources, decided to begin an inquiry into both the validity of the Lifers' Project as a deterrent to juvenile crime, and into the veracity of "Scared Straight!" The inquiry, undertaken at the request of the National Center on Institutions and Alternatives began in early May, 1979.

Day long hearings were held in Washington on June 4, 1979. Opening the hearings, Chairman Ike Andrews (Democrat of North Carolina) said:

As a Nation we are troubled by the problem of crime among our youth and, as reaction to this television film has indicated, we desperately seek ways to keep youngsters out of trouble and on the right side of the law. It is not surprising that this "Scared Straight" concept has struck a responsive chord among us.[8]

Andrews indicated that, "allegations have been raised about the film's veracity and concern voiced over whether the program's effectiveness in dealing with delinquent youth has been exaggerated." He said the purpose of the hearing was, "to provide an objective forum for both questions and responses." Its goal was, "to build on past efforts and to determine areas where caution might be advised." Andrews' statement reflected the purpose of the hearings and the reasons why a Congressional investigation was considered appropriate and necessary.

The subcommittee took testimony from a number of parties to the controversy, for example, Jerome Miller, New Jersey Corrections Commissioner William Fauver, Detective Sergeant Charles Martini, John Reynolds and Arnold Shapiro (Golden West Television), William McGuire (chairman of the Lifers' Advisory Group) and myself. Two parties, however, were not represented at the hearings. Not too surprisingly, because of security reasons, no inmates from the Lifers' Group were present, although a prepared statement was submitted. But, ex-Lifer Frank Bindhammer was present and did testify. He was at that time employed by Golden West. More surprising was the absence of Judge George Nicola. His name and his role in the project came up a number of times during the hearing. It was pointed out that Judge

[8] Statement to U.S. Congress, House, Subcommittee on Human Resources of the Committee on Education and Labor, *Hearings, Oversight on Scared Straight*, 96th Congress, 1st Sess., June 4, 1979, p. 1.

Nicola had been invited to testify, but had declined because of an illness or death in his family.

The hearing accomplished its purpose of airing all sides of the controversy, but whether it changed anyone's mind or resulted in other concrete action remains somewhat up in the air. Several days after the hearing, Chairman Andrews issued a statement that probably reflected the subcommittee's staff views, and perhaps those of other subcommittee members as well. Parts of the statement said:

> Within recent time my opinion has been sought as to whether it might be advisable to initiate some type of program in other prisons and jurisdictions whereby certain persons might be required or permitted to visit prisons in their State or area and be submitted to some type of program whereby certain of the inmates of the prison attempt to make the visitors aware of the life of the inmates in the prison. Some propose that our Subcommittee initiate legislation in furtherance of the development of such programs or to restrain their further use. Proponents seem to essentially say that each person, "particularly young persons," who has or seems to have a tendency toward crime or who has become engaged in a pattern of criminal behavior, should see where he or she may be likely to eventually become incarcerated and should be made aware of the fact that prison life is extremely rough and tough; that prisoners are not depicted by James Cagney and other "heroes" in some of the tough-guy movies. Instead, it is contended that the inmates can and will impress upon their visitors that life in prison can more accurately be described as lonesome and loathsome, fearful and frightening, virtually hopeless and helpless. They might suggest that one of the most persuasive statements made by one of the inmate participants in the "Scared Straight" film to the 17 juveniles in the audience was to the effect that, "There are some 1500 of us in this hole, and the number one desire of every one of us is to get out, and yet you damn dumb————seem to be determined to break in."
>
> I have also within recent weeks had the opportunity to secure certain information and talk with people involved in prison programs other than at the Rahway Prison wherein juveniles are caused to visit such other prisons and to engage in a confrontation with inmates in a setting quite different from the Juvenile Awareness Project at the Rahway Prison. These other programs tend to omit or at least substantially decrease the injection of fear, pretended violence, exaggeration, and vulgar and crude language. Most of these other programs permit and even encourage the visiting juveniles to participate in two-way conversations with the inmates. People who support these latter programs and with whom I have talked, and some of whom are involved in them, seem to

consider themselves as opposed to the Rahway type approach. During the program at Rahway Prison, the visiting juveniles are required to remain mute and are only the subject of a rather bizarre act which is staged for them and in which they are somewhat forced to participate only in the form of stooges (audience or even objects). . . .

I have arrived at some opinions with respect to this matter. It is my opinion that all persons should be encouraged to visit prisons and other facilities occupied by people within the criminal justice system. This includes courtrooms, jails, various types of correctional facilities including those which house juvenile offenders. I think it to be especially advantageous for our young people to visit all of such facilities and to become well acquainted with our criminal laws and with the people who are involved in the criminal justice system. For one thing, this should enlist more much needed understanding and support for this most important aspect of our government and society. I think that these visits should include conversations with inmates within the prisons.

I am less certain that any citizen should be *required* to visit a prison and the answer to this becomes somewhat a matter of degree. It now seems generally agreed that it was a mistake to subject children as young as 8 to 10 years of age to the rather extreme Juvenile Awareness Project at the Rahway Prison. If juveniles are to be required to attend programs that even approach the intensity of this program, then considerable screening should be used to determine which juveniles should or should not participate in the program. Certainly parental consent should be obtained unless the juvenile actually has been convicted of a rather serious crime, in which case I am of the opinion that a proper court should have the authority to require such a juvenile to attend the program if the court has first determined that such a child is not suffering from instability or disability that might be worsened by such an experience. I should think that such a judge would consult the parent of the juvenile as well as other presumably qualified people who are available to the court for advice and assistance with respect to the care and treatment of juvenile delinquents.

It is my further opinion that the intensity of the program on the part of the inmates should be varied somewhat in a effort to better conform to the total circumstances of the members of various groups of juveniles who participate in the program. I think that the intensity, the rawness, of the project at Rahway Prison is justified for the "hard-core" kids such as those who are as some of those depicted in the film.

The Lifers who "run" the program at the Rahway Prison insist that their program cannot be of maximum effect and consequence unless they alone determine which inmates will be permitted to participate in the program and exactly what such a participant should be permitted to say and do. The vocabulary which they employ includes some of the most base language I have ever heard. Such words are repeated over and over—in literal streams of repetition. The innuendo of and even potential for homosexual rape within prisons is forcefully and repeatedly injected into their presentations. All who testified before our Subcommittee seemed to concede that the "horrors" of prison life as portrayed in the program were exaggerated. One of our witnesses was an inmate at the Rahway Prison before and during the time that the project was initiated and represented himself to be one of the founders of the program. He acknowledged the exaggeration but contended that he and the other Lifers felt it necessary to use everything possible to accomplish their presentations of "scaring those kids right out of that prison with the determination never to participate in anything to cause them to enter it again." And he contended that homosexual rapes probably do occur in some prisons, and the young people should be apprised of this.

Numerous of our witnesses and some of our Subcommittee members expressed the opinion that no one can be motivated by fear—that such an effect is a negative one and therefore uneffective [sic] and undesirable. I do not agree with this contention, and I do not believe that society does now or ever has agreed with it. Certainly all major religions of the Western World, including Christianity, Judism [sic], and Islam teach of "another life" which will be spent in the equivalency of a Heaven or Hell. In other words, there is both a reward for right and a punishment for wrong. We are all aware of the first teachings of the Bible to the effect that our earliest ancestors, Adam and Eve, were instructed not to eat of the forbidden fruit or punishment would ensue. I think that our juvenile justice system should offer the possibility of either or both reward and punishment in appropriate circumstances to all who are properly charged with violation of our criminal statutes.

At the same time, however, I think that it is of the essence of importance that anyone who seeks to evaluate the prison visitation experience for juveniles should be aware that virtually no one contends that any such experience can in any way substitute for a host of other things which need to be done in our overall effort to prevent or deter juvenile delinquency and crime. The Lifers' Group at Rahway Prison certainly does not contend that their program is a panacea, a cure-all or a substitute for parents, schools, courts, trained professionals, and many other people who are needed in every community to work for and with the young people of that community and particularly with those who engage in or have a tendency to engage in promiscuous or criminal activities. These young people desparately [sic] need the best assistance that can be afforded them in their homes, schools, local juvenile justice systems, and by all of us. I simply have become convinced that certain selected juveniles can be assisted substantially by being temporarily subjected to a prison setting and by being confronted with inmates who have spent a long time in the prisons and who have no expectation of being permitted to leave for yet years to come. I think these carefully screened young people can profit from getting some feeling—as distinguished from a verbal description—of the possible end of the road on which they may be traveling or tempted to travel. I think it is simply unjust of us not to show them this reality. Its benefits can be substantial, and its cost should be minimal.

Such a program, I believe, can also be of tremendous importance to the inmates and prison authorities as well. Some of the prisoners, who talk and act in the very roughest manner to the young people before them and who literally seem to go through tirades to the point of extreme perspiration, tension, and trauma, leave the presence of the young people and break down in tears. The kids tell me and I believe that they perceive these inmates as not only being tough. They can obviously ascertain that the inmates are desparately [sic] trying to instill a high degree of fear, and yet these kids can also perceive that the real motivation of the inmates is an uncommon degree of care and concern for them. The inmates are really saying not only "get the Hell out of here and stay out" but they are also saying "Get back in school, get as much education and training as you possibly can, 'mind' and get along with and be helpful to parents and others in positions of authority. Make something of your lives. We have failed to do this, and look where it has brought us." The young people know that these inmates are not just pursuing a profession, a role that has been assigned by "the system;" they are in fact not a part of the system; and they are not being paid. "They are for real, Man."

It also occurs to me that probably many of the kids who go through the program are never confronted with people they conceive as being quite as honest and selflessly motivated—and perhaps as highly motivated—as those truly tough guys who have fought the system and lost—lost so much—and now care so deeply that their loss has no gain except if it might help the kid each somewhat sees as himself at the crossroad—help keep *"you"* kid from coming *here*—"NOWHERE, MAN."[9]

While coming down neither wholly for nor against the project, the statement provided considerable food for thought for the Juvenile Awareness Project and others like it. The stress on the potential educational aspects of prison visits, as opposed to the stress on deterrence, was a subject that had been discussed at the hearing. Also discussed was the importance of selection and screening.

[9] Ibid., pp. 140–42.

SOME PROFESSIONAL RESPONSE

Professionals in the criminal justice and juvenile justice fields also responded to the project, and to the film and the study. These responses were supportive of the research, doubtful and questioning about the project, but almost uniformly negative toward the documentary. What follows is a sampling of these responses.

- From John J. Buckley, Sheriff of Middlesex County, Massachusetts:

"Scared Straight!," the Oscar-winning documentary narrated by Peter Falk, has racked up high television ratings and grabbed media headlines; it's been a critical and commercial success. But viewed from a criminal justice standpoint, it is nothing more than a super con-job—a slick, seductive, simple-minded approach to juvenile crime, and one which threatens to become a dangerous model throughout the nation.[10]

- From Christians United in Mission, Inc. in Albany, New York:

Since crime, particularly youth crime, dominates much of our news and is of great concern to all of us, it is understandable that the quick solution offered by the TV documentary "Scared Straight!" was embraced with such enthusiasm. . . .
We understand people's frustration and desire for an answer. We too wish there was an instant solution. "Scared Straight" is not it. There is no simple easy cure for such complex social problems. Scaring further alienates those we should help.[11]

- From the American Correctional Association:

Our goal should be to eliminate violence in prison, not to build programs around it . . .
A deeply rooted social dilemma such as juvenile delinquency cannot be contained simply by verbally abusing youths for two hours, particularly in a program with uncertain validity and reliability.[12]

[10] Sheriff John J. Buckley, "Jail Show: a Super Con-Job," *The Boston Globe* (June 14, 1979).
[11] Christians United in Mission, Inc., "Scared Straight—This Year's Panacea," 3 (June, 1979).
[12] American Correctional Association, "Scared Straight—Rapped Again," *The Trentonian* (August 25, 1979), p. 3.

• From the National Council on Crime and Delinquency:

> Contrary to what the makers of "Scared Straight!" and other supporters of the Rahway Lifers' Group say, there are no simple, fast, foolproof cures for any problem as complex as juvenile delinquency.
>
> It is extremely shortsighted to believe that the fear created by a few hours of haranguing of youthful offenders can miraculously cause them to cease their anti-social behavior. Simply trying to scare kids straight does nothing to address the underlying social and economic problems—racism, poverty, unemployment, and disintegrating families—associated with many delinquent acts.
>
> Inmate programs cannot substitute for the supportive love and help every young person needs while growing up. Such programs can too easily become dumping grounds that would be used by police departments and courts frustrated by juvenile crime and by parents who think their stubborn children need to be taught a lesson.
>
> From a reform perspective, perhaps the worst aspect of the "Scared Straight!" approach is its implied support for the modern-day American penal system. The lifers have vividly demonstrated that our prisons are inhumane and dehumanizing places. The efforts by law and order advocates to hail Rahway-type programs as an innovative and virtually foolproof way to stop juvenile delinquency suggests that such destructive incarceration is a useful deterrent to crime.[13]

• From the National Advisory Committee for Juvenile Justice and Delinquency Prevention:

> The NAC adopted a position opposing any immediate legislative or programmatic replication of the highly publicized program dramatized on TV in the film "Scared Straight!" because of the urgency and great public interest generated in the TV film and fully recognizing the merit and value of many time-tested offender and ex-offender prevention and treatment programs for children and youth.
>
> Preliminary research findings questioning the validity and reputed success of this program, raises sufficient doubts as to require the NAC to adopt a position opposing the immediate development of replications of specific programs depicted in "Scared Straight!," pending further information and inquiry regarding the

---

[13] National Council on Crime and Delinquency, "Scaring is Not the Answer," *Youth Forum*, 3 (Summer 1979), 2.

violation of juvenile rights, possible psychological abuse and due process issues raised by this program.[14]

• From the Center for Responsive Psychology at Brooklyn College in New York:

In spite of the criticisms of the film "Scared Straight!" and the program itself, many other states have indicated that they are considering adopting the program in their own prisons. Will this lead to a degree of coercion from prison officials on their own prisoners to put up such a program in order to gain some favorable publicity? Will the program itself spread to school? We hope not. We hope that carefully conducted research on properly chosen delinquents and matching control subjects be tested to see if the program does any good at all. Indiscriminate application of what may be a bad idea will be even worse—raising the possibility of damaging people and offering very little hope for dealing with the problem of juvenile delinquency in the United States.[15]

• From *Corrections Magazine:*

Why have people so readily accepted the Scared Straight model as a major deterrent to juvenile crime? Like a McDonald's hamburger stand, it has apparently come into view at a bend in the road where solution-hungry citizens are on the lookout for something fast, uncomplicated and cheap. "Juvenile corrections has gotten a reputation of futility. People feel we have nothing to give kids, so they are ready to pounce on anything," said Albert Elias [Assistant Commissioner of the New Jersey Department of Corrections].[16]

Several points recur again and again in these commentaries. One is that the project has been literally sold as a simplistic panacea, in much the same way that miracle cleaning detergents, or miracle headache remedies, or designer jeans are sold. Another is that the maintenance of brutal and brutalizing prisons as examples of the hell and damnation which awaits youthful sinners may be appealing to hardnosed "law and order" types who are true believers in the free will philosophy of human behavior which says that individuals consciously choose to engage in

---

[14] U.S. Department of Justice, National Advisory Committee For Juvenile Justice and Delinquency Prevention, "Memorandum" (July 23, 1979), p. 3.

[15] Reprinted by permission from "Rahway," by Mark Greenwald, *Social Action and the Law,* 1979, Vol. 5, pp. 25–26. Copyright 1979 by The Center for Responsive Psychology, Brooklyn College, C.U.N.Y.

[16] Kevin Krajick, "Scared Silly," *Corrections Magazine* (June, 1979), p. 20.

crime and delinquency. According to this philosophy, criminal behavior is rooted in defects in people themselves. It is something that government, for example, can do little about, except try to deter. Failing that, the government (the criminal and juvenile justice systems) can only arrest, convict, and imprison or perhaps execute the offender. For those believing in this approach, this is an example of receptivity being enhanced by ideology. Last, there is a concern that the spotlight on the "scared straight" bandwagon may draw needed attention and money away from other prevention initiatives that have far less sex appeal, are more complex and expensive, but perhaps hold greater promise of future success.

It is far easier to criticize and denigrate the efforts of others than it is to conceive and activate ideas of one's own. It may also be true that some professionals in the juvenile delinquency field were only defending their turf in criticizing the Lifers' Project. However, I personally believe that most were behaving responsibly, were as properly skeptical of this approach as they should be of any other, and that they were only fulfilling their appropriate role of trying to inform and educate.

It is no surprise that all of the controversy and publicity had major repercussions for the Lifers and the Juvenile Awareness Project. These repercussions and the results of some subsequent studies of the project and others like it are the subjects of the next chapter.

chapter ten

The Juvenile Awareness Project and Scared Straight Revisited

Within a day of the release of my report in April, 1979, New Jersey Corrections Commissioner William H. Fauver announced that the Rahway State Prison superintendent, Robert S. Hatrak, was being removed and reassigned. The reasons given for this action were a report received from the State Attorney General's office on Hatrak's business dealings, and a department probe of prison escapes. However, there were strong implications that there was a connection between the superintendent's removal and the developing controversy over the Juvenile Awareness Project. For example, Fauver was quoted as saying, "Not enough attention was being paid to running the jail. You have to run it like a jail, not a Hollywood studio." Hatrak and other officials at Rahway were accused of becoming too interested—too engrossed—in the national publicity surrounding the project. Hatrak ultimately left the state and assumed a corrections position in Oregon.

The Corrections department also made a series of changes in the admissions criteria of the project. These included denying admission to any youngsters who are not "certified" juvenile delinquents. Although the meaning of this requirement is somewhat unclear, ostensibly it means that only juvenile justice agencies—the police, courts, probation, etc.— can refer juveniles who have known records of delinquency. This particular requirement was criticized by the Lifers and others on the grounds that the project was intended to reach youngsters before they became delinquent; it was, they said, supposed to be a delinquency prevention project.

Delinquency prevention generally operates at two levels. One level is before the fact of delinquency; the other is after the fact. There is what is called primary prevention, which tries to reach any and all youngsters, whether or not they are delinquent or show even any predisposition to delinquency. Efforts to work with very young children and their families, or school-based programs are typical examples of primary prevention. These programs try to prevent delinquency before youths become involved with law enforcement and the juvenile justice system. Secondary prevention, on the other hand, focuses upon those who have already been in trouble with the law. Secondary prevention programs are often diversion programs that offer alternatives to young people referred as a result of delinquent behavior. From our earlier discussion, the Cambridge-Somerville project and Mobilization for Youth are examples of primary prevention efforts. The California Treatment Project and UDIS, were secondary prevention projects. The new Corrections department admissions requirement effectively changed the focus of the Lifers' Project from primary and secondary prevention to secondary prevention only.

Other changes in the admissions criteria included precluding attendance by youngsters under twelve-years-old, and also by girls. The latter exclusion was justified on the grounds that the women's prison in Clinton, New Jersey had a similar awareness project, and that it would be more appropriate for girls to visit there. The Lifers disagreed with these changes as well.

The first major public response to my research came in May, 1979, at a press conference held at New York's famous 21 Club. Called by Golden West Broadcasters, the conference was attended by a range of project supporters. All the speakers vigorously defended the project and attacked both my methodology and my conclusions. The consensus at the conference was that there was need for a major, comprehensive, and independent study, perhaps by the U.S. Congress. The Congressional investigation described in the previous chapter was in part a response to this call.

About this same time (May, 1979), some more research findings jolted the project. The Mercer County (NJ) Criminal Justice Planning Unit conducted a survey of that county's agencies that had been referring juveniles to Rahway. This survey disclosed an 80–90 percent failure rate among the participants. Among a group of sixty-seven youths referred by Mercer County agencies and the Trenton Police Department during 1977 and 1978, fifty-one (76 percent) were subsequently rearrested. The reason offered for these poor results was that these particular juveniles had lengthy records (were "Uglies") and were thus not good bets for deterrence. This survery received some coverage by the local media.

One of the immediate effects of the adverse publicity and controversy was a sharp decline in the number of youngsters attending the Lifers' sessions. The number of sessions declined from ten a week to about two per week; participation from two-hundred juveniles a week to about twenty-five. In January 1980, for example, only 134 juveniles visited the prison as opposed to more than eight-hundred a month during the project's heyday. The reasons for this decline are not hard to discern: the negative evaluation results, the lawsuit involving "Scared Straight!," and the tightened admissions criteria that cut off the largest pool of potential attendees.

During the period after my study was released, I had a number of telephone contacts with the Lifers. At first they were somewhat hostile and defensive. Later contacts, however, after their decline set in, reflected more sadness and frustration than anger. At times they indicated that they might scrap the project. They felt that some of the things that I had criticized, for example, the absence of a selection procedure, the absence of any formally structured follow-up programs in the community, the exorbitant success claims, etc., were all things over which they had no control. The Lifers felt they had been exploited and abandoned by just about everyone. Their proposal to the Department of Corrections for a follow-up program in which the Lifers would be permitted to leave the prison to meet with youngsters and their parents was not approved. "Scared Straight!" seems to have become the worst thing that could happen to the Juvenile Awareness Project. However, despite all the adversity, the project survives. The Lifers celebrated its fourth anniversary in September, 1980.

THE LANGER STUDY

In October, 1979, Dr. Sidney Langer, a sociology instructor at Kean College of New Jersey, released a study entitled, "The Rahway State Prison Lifers' Group: A Critical Analysis."[1] This paper has received some media and professional attention, and it has seemed to fuel the controversy about the project. Because Langer's study has been said to revive interest in "scared straight" programs, including the Juvenile Awareness Project, and because it has added to the confusion about whether this approach works or not, I will describe the study and then attempt to analyze and critique it at some length.

[1] Sidney Langer, *The Rahway State Prison Lifers' Group: A Critical Analysis* (N.J.: Kean College Department of Sociology, October, 1979).

Langer says at the outset of his report, ". . . the main focus of my study is an evaluation of the effectiveness of the program in the deterrence of delinquency . . ."[2] Thus, Professor Langer too made an after the fact causal assumption that deterrence is the basic underlying premise of the project. His outcome criterion (measure of success) was "change in officially recorded rates of delinquency as represented in police files."[3] Professor Langer describes his study's approach as follows:

The research design involves an examination of the aggregate *number* of and *nature* of encounters with the police of a sample number of juvenile offenders, prior to and after their participation in the Lifers' Program. The experimental group of participants was compared with a control group of delinquents who had similar encounters with the police but did not attend the Lifers' Program. An encounter with the police, for purposes of this study, is defined as any offense officially recorded on a youth's juvenile police file regardless of the ultimate disposition of the case in question. . . .

The hypothesis of the study is that the juveniles' contact with the Lifers' Program is both sufficient and salient to make a significant contribution toward the deterrence of further delinquency.

Because of the restrictions in access to data, the experimental group of delinquents was not randomly assigned but rather is a select sample of juveniles who were referred to the Lifers' Program by the police departments of Plainfield and Rahway, New Jersey. The total Number [sic] for the experimental group is sixty-six. Two criteria were established for inclusion of the subjects in the experimental and control groups. One, the youths had to have committed one or more recorded offenses prior to the date of participation in the Lifers' Program for the experimental group and pre-test period for the control group. Two, in order to evaluate the sample over a significant period of time after participation in the Lifers' Program, ten months of exposure time became the minimum and 31.5 months the maximum time span for any youth who was included in the experimental group. Exposure time is defined as the amount of time from the date of participation in the Lifers' Program until the date when evaluation of the records was completed.

The selection of the control group was accomplished in the following manner. I asked the police officials and/or juvenile counselors assigned to the Juvenile Aid Bureau of the police department to randomly select from the files juveniles who could be considered comparable to the youths in the experimental group. The comparability of the youths was to be based on the following independent variables: age, race, sex, aggregate number of and

[2] Ibid., p. 3.
[3] Ibid., p. 4.

seriousness of offenses. The total number for the control group is sixty-five.[4]

Langer compared his experimental and control groups on age, race, sex, and number and seriousness of prior offenses. He found that there were no statistically significant differences between them.

His primary finding was that after a twenty-two-month exposure (follow-up) period, there was a significant difference between his two groups in the seriousness of their subsequent delinquency. Specifically, delinquency seriousness increased for only 52 percent of the experimentals as compared to 74 percent of the controls.[5] Conversely, 47 percent of the experimentals had less serious delinquency during the follow-up periods, as compared to only 25 percent of the nonparticipant controls.[6] Thus, although the delinquent activity of both groups increased during the follow-up period, Langer concludes: "In essence, the experimentals' delinquent activity was held relatively constant after their participation in the Lifers' Group while the controls' delinquent activity increased substantially during the same period."[7]

Langer also looked at a shorter (ten month) follow-up period for the same subjects. He found, "that there is no significant difference between the experimentals and controls at the end of the ten-month period."[8] During this shorter period, both groups became significantly more delinquent, but the participating experimental juveniles did not become as bad as the nonparticipants.

Before I examine these findings in some detail, I think it is important to discuss briefly what seem to me to be two noteworthy contributions to our knowledge about juvenile delinquency which Professor Langer's study makes.

The first of these contributions is on the subject of what might be termed maturation effect. Maturation refers to changes (in attitudes and behavior, for example) occurring in children as they mature. We know that maturity has several dimensions; and, we know that among these dimensions are social maturity and physical maturity. Social and physical maturity—with the latter measured by chronological age—are not identical. Some younger children may be socially mature beyond their years, and vice versa. However, there is a strong association between maturity and age in that older children tend to be more socially mature.

[4] Ibid., p. 5, 7-8.
[5] Ibid., p. 20.
[6] Ibid., p. 20
[7] Ibid., p. 20.
[8] Ibid., p. 28.

There is a considerable amount of research that suggests that delinquent behavior is a function of age. That is, the earliest onset of delinquency is usually around age seven or eight; it inclines sharply to a peak at about age fifteen; then it begins to decline between ages sixteen and eighteen. An example of this pattern is found in some data collected by the Vera Institute Violent Delinquent Study.[9] Among a sample of 494 juveniles against whom delinquency petitions had been filed in court, the age distribution in percent was as follows:

Age	Percent
10 or under	2.6%
11–12	9.1
13	9.5
14	25.7
15	34.2
16 or over	18.8

The distribution of delinquency by age, shown above, clearly implies that maturation effect is really two effects. The first—between ages seven and fifteen—is an increase in delinquent behavior. This is a period during which the young person is growing in many ways, is becoming more independent, and is usually becoming more peer-oriented. The second effect—between ages sixteen and eighteen—is a decrease in delinquency. This is the period when the adolescent is approaching and entering adulthood, with all that that entails.

There is a factor besides maturation which contributes to this age and delinquency profile and which must be considered in interpreting its meaning. That factor is the definition of who can be legally considered a juvenile delinquent. Our common law tradition presumes that children younger than seven are incompetent to commit crimes, and therefore cannot be held criminally responsible for their behavior. At the other end of the age spectrum, young people aged sixteen to eighteen can and are legally handled as adults in some jurisdictions. Almost all legal jurisdictions treat those eighteen-years-old or older as adults.

Our knowledge about the relationship between age and juvenile delinquency, which is heavily dependent upon official records, may be biased by these legal age parameters—biased in the sense that the records are indicators of system responses to delinquency, rather than being true indicators of the actual age/delinquency profile. Fortunately,

[9] Paul A. Strasburg, *Violent Delinquents—A Report to the Ford Foundation* (New York: Vera Institute of Justice, 1978), p. 51.

the age factor has been examined in some self-report studies of the type referred to earlier. For example, Jay R. Williams and Martin Gold discovered from their self-report data, "that older teenagers are more frequently and seriously delinquent than younger ones."[10] However, they also discovered the fact that more older teenagers have police records than younger ones "is not due solely to the greater frequency and seriousness of the older teenagers' delinquent behavior."[11] Instead, said Williams and Gold, it was because, "police make a record on a higher proportion of those older teenagers whom they apprehend. The differential decision to make a record amplifies the relationship of age to delinquency."[12] Fewer of the younger children who come into contact with the police are officially labeled delinquent, and therefore it appears that there are relatively fewer of them than may actually be the case. So, although delinquency is a function of age, this function is "amplified" by official actions.

Professor Langer posed this concept of maturation effect (borrowing from David Matza, what he terms "maturational reform") as a speculative explanation for his findings. He says that since the average age of his experimentals at the outset was 13.62 years and of the controls 13.55 years, the twenty-two month follow-up period could be expected to be a time of increasing delinquent activity. At the end of the period, the average age of both groups was approximately fifteen. This would normally be the peak age of delinquency. Langer found, however, that only the control group delinquency increased significantly. He explains this result by suggesting ". . . that the participation in the Lifers' Group 'accelerated' this process of decline in delinquent activity for the experimental group," because he says, ". . . the experience of the youths at Rahway becomes more relevant in their lives as they approach the age of adulthood."[13]

This speculation raises an interesting hypothesis which deserves testing. Its plausibility as a valid hypothesis generated by his data is very much dependent upon the degree of similarity and comparability between Langer's experimental and control groups—a subject to which we shall return shortly. Suffice it to say here that there is an implied assumption that other influences which entered these young people's lives over this nearly two-year period have been controlled or at least accounted for. Some of these other influences may be positive and some negative, but certainly the Rahway visit alone did not affect their

[10] Jay R. Williams and Martin Gold, "From Delinquent Behavior to Official Delinquency," in, *The Children of Ishmael*, by Barry Krisberg and James Austin (Mayfield Publishing Co., 1978), p. 314.

[11] Ibid., p. 323.

[12] Ibid., p. 323.

[13] Langer, *The Rahway State Prison*, p. 37.

maturational reform. In addition, it is reasonable to expect that different kids, whether they be experimentals or controls, have different growing up experiences. These differences would need to be examined and explained in order to really test Langer's hypothesis. Still, the idea is an intriguing one.

The second contribution which Dr. Langer's study makes is in the area of seriousness scaling of delinquent offenses. Weighting offenses according to seriousness is an effort to identify them by the amount of harm inflicted on the community. For example, is a robbery of $1,000 more serious than an assault resulting in hospitalization? Is a burglary of $250 more serious than an auto theft? In order to answer these questions, a scale is needed that reflects which crimes are serious and which are not. The scale itself, which is derived from the public's perceived amount of harm that various offenses inflict, can be used to assign seriousness weights to each crime. According to the widely used Sellin-Wolfgang Index, the $1,000 robbery mentioned receives a score of 5 (if no weapon is used); the assault, on the other hand, receives a score of 7. This indicates the assault is perceived to be more serious. Likewise, the burglary receives a score of 3 and the auto theft a score of 2.

The idea of judging and scaling crimes according to their seriousness has a history stretching back more than fifty years. Some of the most extensive and careful work in this area to date has been that done by Thorsten Sellin and Marvin Wolfgang and their colleagues at the University of Pennsylvania. They created the aforementioned Sellin-Wolfgang Index.

The ability to scale offenses for seriousness has obvious value for understanding and explaining the decision-making processes in the juvenile justice system. For example, do the police respond differently to offenses of different seriousness? How do the police judge seriousness? How do judges consider offense seriousness and with what effect on their decisions? There is also merit in being able to evaluate the nature and extent of the public's perceived social harm from particular offenses, and its consequent fear and anxiety. Finally, there is great value in the use of seriousness scaling for evaluating treatment programs.

The use of offense seriousness scaling in evaluations enables the evaluator to move beyond the traditional all or nothing recidivism measure. It permits the evaluator to determine whether there is a decline in subsequent offense seriousness after some programmatic intervention such as the Juvenile Awareness Project. It is in precisely this way that Professor Langer used the National Crime Severity Scale (a successor to the Sellin-Wolfgang Index) developed by the same University of Pennsylvania researchers.[14]

[14] Ibid., p. 13.

Langer assigned a National Severity Scale score to each offense recorded in his juveniles' records. He then added all these scores for both the experimental and control groups in order to obtain an aggregate seriousness score for each juvenile. One score was obtained for the prior to participation period, and one for the postparticipation or follow-up period, again for each group. These two sets of pre and post scores were then compared. It was this process and comparison that resulted in his findings and conclusions reported earlier.

Professor Langer's seriousness scaling is much more complex and sophisticated than the simple technique that I employed in my own research (See Chapter 7). He is correct in his assessment of my study when he says, "This system [mine] of weighting offenses does not adequately take into consideration the qualitative scope of juvenile delinquency offenses."[15] Langer's use of the scaling technique is both innovative and informative.

In viewing Langer's findings, I do not think that Langer's results refute mine and establish that the Lifers' Project has so-called therapeutic value. I offer my criticisms of Langer's study because there is confusion about our conflicting conclusions. Those who must make judgments about this kind of program deserve to be fully informed. I think a careful look at the Langer study can have the same educational value that analyzing my own study has had.

A close reading of the Langer report discloses that fifty-six of the sixty-six juveniles in his experimental group (85 percent) engaged in delinquent offenses after visiting the prison. Not withstanding declines in subsequent delinquency seriousness, this recidivism rate by itself is obviously not a very impressive result. It is unlikely, for example, that the Scared Straight! phenomenon would have sold as well if it had been reported that it had an 85 percent failure rate.

Because of this result, Langer's findings can be considered to show that the project is truly valuable *only* if the experimental group does relatively better than does the "untreated" control group. This relates back to our earlier discussion of experimental design and its use of experimental and control groups. In Professor Langer's study, the control group is critical; it is the linchpin that holds the entire study together. And, it is with exactly this element that the greatest problems exist.

Dr. Langer did not employ a random assignment procedure to select his experimental and control groups. But worse than that, the selection of the control group seems to have been almost entirely out of his hands. This was because he could not gain court permission to have personal access to the police records for either group. Consequently, the

[15] Ibid., p. 38.

actual selection was done by police officers in the two departments studied. Langer says that the officers were asked to "randomly" select from police files juveniles "comparable" to those in the experimental group. However, what is to deny that these officers, perhaps with the best of intentions, but simply wanting to make the Lifers' Project look good, purposely selected juveniles for controls who were comparable in every respect except that they had worse records during the follow-up period? After all, the fact that these two departments made referrals to Rahway seems to indicate that they believed in the Lifers. Might they not want to try to insure that the evaluation came up with positive results? I am not saying that this happened because I do not know that it happened, but neither do we know that it did not. Because randomization was not used, it is not possible to assume that Langer's groups are equal, and it could be that it is this inequality that accounts for the differences in outcomes that he found.

A further problem rests in his use of what is known as an ex post facto study design. This means that he was forced to work backward in time and could not control the "treatment" relative to the subjects in his sample. The experimental kids had all gone to the prison before Langer came on the scene. Also, the outcomes for both groups were already known. It is this ex post facto characteristic that accounts for his more lengthy follow-up period.

A further question that can be asked about the control group is why, if they met the criteria, were they not taken to the Juvenile Awareness Project in the first place. Langer's use of only police department records in the two cities studied precluded his determining whether or not his kids got into trouble elsewhere. His information about subsequent offenses could have been severely limited by this constraint. Finally, neither experimentals nor controls are representative of the range of Lifers' clients since they come from only two police departments in the same area. As we have seen, the Lifers received referrals from a whole host of agencies across the state and elsewhere, and importantly, most of the referrals were nondelinquent.

In sum, I think there are major limitations with Langer's research which seriously bias the conclusions that can be based upon it. This criticism is echoed by the National Juvenile Justice System Assessment Center that said of the absence of randomization, ". . . it is so basic a deficiency as to effect the credibility and interpretation of the findings."[16] Use of these findings for purposes of making decisions about aversive programs should be done if at all, only with extreme caution. I

---

[16] David J. Berkman and Steve R. Pearson, *Juvenile Aversion Programs: A Status Report* (Sacramento, CA: American Justice Institute, August 15, 1980).

can, however, concur whole-heartedly with Dr. Langer's own concluding remarks, which said in part:

> Prior to the publication of the above mentioned empirical evaluations, the Lifers' Group had been presented to the public as a panacea for the problem of juvenile delinquency. It is clear that, given our knowledge of the complexities of the problem, it would be unrealistic and unfair to expect that the program could provide that "cure all." It is therefore necessary to place the Lifers' Program in perspective and more clearly define what contributions this and/or similar projects can make. . . .[17]

THE LIFERS AND "SCARED STRAIGHT!:" YET ANOTHER LOOK

Nearly a year after the onset of the controversy, a Langer colleague at Kean College, Dr. Michael Israel, wrote about the Lifers' Project, the film, and our two studies.[18] Professor Israel is a member of the Lifers' Group Advisory Committee. The premise in his paper was that, ". . . a chain of circumstances and misunderstandings . . . have led to tragic consequences for this group, and perhaps to a great loss for the entire criminal justice community." He said, "everyone interested in innovative and experimental self-help type programs within prisons, or any criminal justice agency, should take heed of what happened to the Lifers, and try to take steps to see to it that . . . [it] will not happen again." Israel said the demise of the Lifers, ". . . relates to the broader issue of how the criminal justice system is vulnerable to self-serving interests in the entire American system, its politics, its economics, and unfortunately, its academic community."

Professor Israel had both negative and some positive reactions to my own research. He said that my paper "offered little explanation for his results. He [meaning me] recited literature that showed virtually nothing deterred crime, so why should this program. . . . It was clear, however, that his hypothesis was straight deterrence theory, as articulated by Scared Straight." Israel said, "There is some question, at least in my mind, of what was the source of his hypothesis. An experimental design can be no better than the model it tests. Finckenauer studied a movie, not a real program." Israel's criticism of my deterrence

[17] Langer, *The Rahway State Prison,* p. 39.

[18] Michael Israel, *The Rahway Lifers' Group: The Politics of Being My Brother's Keeper* (N.J.: Kean College, March, 1980).

premise seems a little incongruous with another statement in his paper: "The initial idea of this inmate self-help program was simple: prison can not *deter* [italics mine] unless potential criminals are aware of them, and can see what the consequences of criminal behavior will be."

On the other hand, Israel said:

The Finckenauer Report was a scholarly paper, with appropriate scholarly caution and qualifications that were missed in the public debate. Much of the language of the paper was positive, ironically. He wrote that with proper follow-up by professionals the Lifers' Group could be an effective beginning to successful treatment, and going into prisons was an important awareness and educational experience for young people. This is precisely what the more professional supporters of the program had been saying, as well as the Lifers themselves (sometimes), but this part of the paper was lost in what I would call the hysterical public reaction.[19]

Professor Israel's generally supportive commentary about his colleague's study said:

Langer's findings are pretty much in the main stream of contemporary sociological theory about the effect of deterrence on juvenile delinquency, namely, that a profound awareness experience like the Lifers, only if associated with other factors of positive reinforcement, or other factors of community or family support, can contribute significantly to the growth and maturity, and hence the decline in delinquency, of some juvenile offenders. These findings do not fit in quite so well in a public debate, however, and even many Lifers' supporters have misinterpreted them. My distinct impression is that the Lifers themselves do not understand Langer's study and consider it irrelevant.[20]

In the end, Dr. Israel makes the following broad and sweeping assessment of the whole Lifers' story:

What can we make of all this? A combination of bad luck and betrayal appears to have done in the Lifers' Group, but some thought should be given to the proper role of the academic community in a controversial and scrutinized criminal justice program such as this. This was an intolerable situation for the criminal

[19] Ibid., p. 10.
[20] Ibid., p. 15.

justice discipline to be in, but there was no available alternative. Finckenauer saw his research exaggerated and exploited. Langer was under-interpreted, and for months was in the uncomfortable position for a scholar of rushing to finish while the press and supporters await. Furthermore, all three professors involved, including myself, have a bias. There are no disinterested observers.

Scholars cannot work in the hostile and suspicious environment that the Lifers' controversy created. Both Finckenauer and Langer had enormous difficulties securing the cooperation of Juvenile Court Judges to make files available to them, even on a confidential basis, and before "Scared Straight!" Some Juvenile Judges who publicly supported the Program would not let either of these scholars see files with data on juvenile criminality. A climate of "whose side are you on" prevailed.

There are ethical questions whenever scholars involve themselves in current community issues, and using our office to promote a point of view is questionable at best. Having data, which is presumably value free, has been our rationalization, perhaps our crutch, and at times our saving grace. We do not take sides, goes the myth, we just present data. This experience with the Lifers' Group has suggested the possible consequences of research being introduced into a volatile public realm. It is a tragedy and a failure of the criminal justice academic community that the Rahway Prison Lifers' Group has apparently declined. Our work should not be used for that purpose—either killing or saving the program—for that is a moral question, not an empirical one.

There is no data that can answer the question if adult offenders in prison should confront youthful offenders, or anyone else for that matter, about their own feelings of why they are there and what they see as the consequences of their actions as younger men. If we ask the question, does this "work", we are asking the wrong question. The relevant policy question is whether this is an intrinsically valuable experience. If it is, and that is my view, then we should support programs like the Lifers. Research—especially only two studies—can not make that decision for us, but at best can only contribute to it. Even extensive research (and we have precious little of that) is only as good as its premises and definitions. The incident described here is of a great controversy over whether a program works, without a consensus on what *works* means.

Juvenile delinquents are often treated with a double standard, a higher standard than the rest of society. No treatment they undergo is worthwhile unless it deters them from crime. All other young people in American society are allowed to have intrinsically valuable educational experiences that will not lead necessarily to any particular measurable behavioral change, like studying academic subjects in school, for example, but not delinquents. I suggest we turn our attention away from deterrence as a model for evaluating juvenile programs, and look instead for such characteristics that we admire in someone in the so-called outside world. If we admire honesty and selflessness—and that is what I have seen in my observations of the Lifers' Group—then we should support programs where those values are found.

 A maturation process may spark crime in the short run, for there are always risks whenever there is change in people. There are times when the academic community must take some leadership to encourage a climate of opinion that is willing to take some risks. Of course the Lifers were motivated partly by self interest, such as early release or status within the institution, but that does not detract from this magnificent program. To see it ruined by a control group of 35 juveniles, with a failure net of four, is a violation of the sacred values of our discipline, and the social responsibility that should accompany our influence.[21]

There are a number of statements in this assessment with which I can easily agree. For example, it is true that research in criminal and juvenile justice is difficult, as I have tried to illustrate. It is also true that we all have biases and cannot be totally objective. However, there are a number of points here that are at least debatable. Why should juvenile justice program decisions necessarily be "moral" questions? And, just what does that mean? Why is asking if a program "works," the wrong question? And, why is deterrence not a useful model for evaluating some juvenile programs?

On one point about the Juvenile Awareness Project there seems to be little disagreement, either by me, by Mike Israel, by Sid Langer, by the Department of Corrections, by the criminal justice community, and even by the Lifers themselves: this entire episode has been a classic example of the panacea phenomenon. Was the Lifers' Project promoted as a cure-all? Was it sold as being appropriate for all kids? Was it "hyped"? Were unrealistic expectations raised by the sales pitch? Did frustration ensue? The answer to all these questions is a definite yes! Did this end our foolish search for the elusive panacea? What do you think?

THE PHENOMENON SPREADS

The poststudy history of "scared straight" programs is a rich and continuing one. The evidence for the existence of a panacea phenomenon effect seems overwhelming. There is little doubt that this

[21] Ibid., p. 16-18.

approach is better known, has been more widely adopted, and is perhaps more controversial than almost anything in the previous history of juvenile justice and delinquency prevention.

Here I will update this poststudy history. To do so, I draw upon two assessments of so-called juvenile aversion programs compiled by the American Justice Institute's National Juvenile Justice System Assessment Center for the National Institute for Juvenile Justice and Delinquency Prevention. I will briefly describe a number of such programs operating both in this country and in Canada. Finally, I will present some findings from three other aversion programs that have been studied.

The American Justice Institute Analyses

In late 1979 the American Justice Institute's Juvenile Justice Assessment Center prepared a survey report at the request of the federal government's primary juvenile justice research agency.[22] This report was admittedly only preliminary, and its focus was on only selected programs. The survey was updated in August, 1980.[23] Because of their potential effects upon national policy in this area, I think the reports are important and useful.

The surveys concentrated upon seven programs, including the one at Rahway, and provided a simple listing of fifteen other programs. The descriptions, discussion, and conclusions are of considerable interest.

AJI indicated in its first report that the major goal of these "scared straight" programs was "the deterrence of future criminal behavior."[24] However, it pointed out that the absence of "specific and measurable goals is a major weakness of all the programs."[25] Whether a program's goal is to improve a juvenile's amenability and accessibility to treatment (as was recommended in the AJI report) or to deter him or her from crime, is obviously an important distinction. Not only does the failure to make this distinction create difficulties for program evaluation, but more broadly it relates back to the absence of causal assumptions problem that I described much earlier. The first report said that the general goal of deterrence was "too broad," was "generally undefined," and was "too simplistic." It concluded that, "none of the programs reviewed utilized the institution exposure as part of a comprehensive approach to delin-

---

[22] David J. Berkman and Charles P. Smith, *A Preliminary Comparative Analysis of Selected Juvenile Aversion Programs* (Sacramento, CA: American Justice Institute, October 31, 1979).

[23] Berkman and Pearson, *Juvenile Aversion Programs.*

[24] Berkman and Smith, *A Preliminary Analysis,* p. 2.

[25] Ibid., pp. 2-3.

quency prevention or reduction."[26] AJI proposed that an expectation of breaking the juvenile's protective shell and facilitating accessibility and interaction might be more realistic than the expectation of reducing delinquent behavior.

The report suggested that "perhaps the goals of the juvenile aversion programs need to be scaled down to a more reasonable level."[27] This is a position with which I obviously concur, since it is consistent with my point about unrealistic expectations being part of the panacea phenomenon. I would only add that this same advice could be well-taken by most other delinquency prevention programs as well.

Commenting upon the limited evaluation results available at the time, AJI concluded that, "the evaluations . . . provide a mixed picture of success."[28] Expanding upon this conclusion, the report said:

> In contrast to the overwhelmingly positive portrayal of these programs by the media, the public, and some personnel from the criminal justice community, the few evaluations available indicate that juvenile aversion programs are far less an answer to delinquency prevention or deterrence. . . . Based upon the limited evaluation results to date, juvenile aversion programs as they are currently operated may offer very little as deterrent programs; however, coupled with other programs which use traditional forms of counseling and community supports, they may be able to contribute to the overall efforts for certain juveniles at a specific stage in the rehabilitation process. Prior to the initiation of such programs on a wide scale, more careful evaluation of existing programs should be undertaken.[29]

The first report raised other issues relative to most juvenile aversion programs. These included the fact that there was little or no pre-entry orientation for the juveniles; that there was no psychiatric or health screening of participants; that there was no involvement of parents or counselors; and, that there was no follow-up counseling.[30] The issues of screening and follow-up are issues I had raised earlier about the Lifers' Juvenile Awareness Project. Further, said the report, we have only limited knowledge about deterrence anyway.[31] Finally, the report made the important observation that, "the reactions of the public, legislators, and

[26] Ibid., p. 3.
[27] Ibid., p. 3.
[28] Ibid., p. 6.
[29] Ibid., p. 6.
[30] Ibid., p. 7
[31] Ibid., p. 7.

criminal and juvenile justice personnel to the publicity surrounding these programs is a significant issue worthy of further consideration. Aversion programs, especially those that may appear cruel or harsh, raise important ethical and moral issues."[32]

The ethical and moral issues seem to me to include such questions as: Where is the balance between crime control and humane treatment? Do the ends justify any means? If not, which means are justified and which are not? Then again, are aversive techniques of this kind necessarily inhumane and thus unjustified? AJI asked this question about the use of aversive techniques to modify juvenile behavior—"Just how far is society willing to go in the use of physical or psychological pain to change attitudes and behavior?"[33] The report offered one possible answer. "Evidence from the public's reaction to the 'Scared Straight!' film suggests that, probably out of desperation, many parents, legislators, and justice personnel would be willing to subject juveniles to a psychologically painful experience if it could prevent or change delinquent behavior."[34] I contend that that desperation is borne, at least in part, from past failures and frustrations, and from a generalized fear of juvenile crime and violence.

The American Justice Institute concluded its first analysis with the following statement:

> While the two major questions most often asked regarding juvenile aversion programs (e.g., does it work, and is it harmful to juveniles) are discussed extensively, many questions have not been even raised. The answer to the first question—does it work— cannot be adequately answered yet, due to the incompleteness of the evaluations done so far. The second question can be answered by conjecture in that juvenile aversion programs could be harmful if the wrong juveniles are exposed and that exposure is too severe. Beyond these questions, the territory is relatively unexplored.
>
> It is the unexplored nature of these programs (e.g., experimenting with program modifications; more complete evaluations which are able to relate to an accumulated body of knowledge and theory of delinquency causation, prevention, and deterrence; and their operation within a more comprehensive educational and counseling program) which could make a valuable contribution. To merely dismiss these programs as simplistic or as misdirected efforts, and hope that they will go away, would be a loss of a potentially significant opportunity to learn more about juvenile delin-

---

[32] Ibid., p. 8.

[33] Ibid., p. 8.

[34] Ibid., p. 8.

quency, counseling techniques, and community efforts to do something about juvenile crime. . . . considering all the potentially useful aspects of these programs, further careful experimentation, research, and evaluations should be undertaken.[35]

The second AJI report provided a summary of more recent major program developments. These included the following:

- There is a more cautious approach toward publicity and visibility.
- A significant trend has evolved de-emphasizing direct confrontation in the program approach.
- There is a decrease in client volume and funding.
- Evaluations of programs have been inconclusive.
- Aversion programs have not exhibited significant growth and development.

The Institute also identified the following needs and recommendations.

- Need for a clarification of program goals and objectives.
- Need for realistic expectations.
- Need for a definition and control of abusive treatment.
- Need for better networking and coordination between programs.
- Need for better utilization of program potential.
- Need for well-defined client and inmate participation criteria.[36]

A SAMPLE OF "SCARED STRAIGHT" PROGRAMS

Over the past five years or so a vast array of programs patterned after the Rahway model have sprung up. What follows are brief illustrative descriptions of some of these programs. These examples have not been selected in accordance with any particular rationale or criteria, but are simply a sampling of programs on which I have been able to obtain information. Any of these projects may or may not be operating at a particular point in time, since most of them seem to suffer from the characteristic of being transient, of being here today and gone tomorrow.

Juvenile Intervention and Enlightment Program
Queensboro Correctional Facility
Long Island, New York

[35] Ibid., pp. 10–11.
[36] Berkman and Pearson, *Juvenile Aversion Programs,* pp. 11–12, 17–18.

JIEP operated in a medium-security adult correctional institution in New York City. Started in April, 1977, it was said to be a "toned down" copy of the Rahway program. The toning down occurred because, according to the inmate executive director, the intimidation element seemed to "turn off" the youths. The objective was said to be the education of juveniles—to get their attention, but not to scare them. The reported number of juveniles visiting was approximately 4,800 annually.

JIEP was publicized by *The New York Times,* which concluded in an editorial that such programs should not become a standard feature of innercity school curriculums without much more being known about their effects. The American Justice Institute reported the eligibility criteria for JIEP as limiting it to sixteen to eighteen year old males and females, both offenders and nonoffenders; but, when *The New York Times* reporter visited the program, a session involving fifth-graders was observed. The AJI August, 1980 update found that the program had been terminated because of a lack of interest on the part of the inmate participants.

> *Youth Assistance Program*
> Fishkill Correctional Facility
> Fishkill, New York

YAP started in March, 1977. The prison inmates experimented with a variety of approaches before deciding upon three different types of "seminars"—one for nondelinquent high school students, one for predelinquent status offenders and minor offenders, and one for adjudicated and institutionalized delinquents. The YAP inmates also claimed they simply want to inform youths about prison life, without using scare tactics. Their stated purpose: "to educate, not intimidate." Tom Wicker of *The New York Times* reported that upwards of one-thousand young people had received the "grim message" in "tough, profane, frightening, frequently moving 'rap sessions.' " The Fishkill inmates have also operated a program in Bridgeport, Connecticut, called Juvenile Awareness Program of Connecticut.

> *Youth Aversion Project*
> Dead End Center Project
> California Correctional Center
> Susanville, California

Susanville is a medium-security adult facility. The Youth Aversion Project started in February, 1978 and has had an annual volume of 240 participants. Its major goal was deterrence; eligibility criteria included fourteen to nineteen year old male offenders and nonoffenders. In a personal communication, I was informed that a preliminary evaluation had turned up only eight "reoffenders" from among eighty-seven attenders over a nine month period. The letter from an inmate associated with the program said:

> We do not employ nor share the methods and concepts of "Scared Straight!" and for the past several months we are bombarded with publicity we do not want. We have tried to state our differences but the wave of the publicity due to the film seems to have deafened all to the very important difference between our program and "Scared Straight."
>
> As a result of the film we are also faced with a Senator who has discovered a political bandwagon and is attempting to have legislation passed in California so the Prison system here will be forced to implement "Scared Straight" programs throughout the system. We feel this would only attract the kind of convict who is looking for "good-time" credit or publicity, etc.

The AJI update reported a 50 percent decline in volume, and adoption of a much "softer" approach than that used originally.

The Insider's Group
Virginia State Penitentiary
Richmond, Virginia

The Insider's Group started in Virginia's adult maximum-security prison in September, 1978. Its annual volume was originally reported to be 9,600 participants—males and females, thirteen to eighteen years old, with some type of court contact and a required psychiatric evaluation. This program was said to be "unabashedly patterned" after the Lifers' Project at Rahway. The American Justice Institute's August, 1980 survey found that volume had declined to only twenty juveniles per month. Their report said: "No programs have been scheduled for several months . . . nor are any planned. Therefore, the project is in 'limbo' at present. . . . There appears to be little staff support for present concept and program claims to have been initiated by public pressure. It has rated its effectiveness as 'little if any.' "[37]

STYNG (Save the Youth Now Group)
Millhaven Penitentiary
Ontario, Canada

[37] Ibid., p. 37.

STYNG was started in September, 1979. The original plan, beginning in the fall of 1979, was to conduct a year-long experiment involving one-hundred juvenile offenders from two training schools in Ontario. The juvenile participants were to be all boys, aged fourteen to sixteen. STYNG was to have several aspects—an adult program, an educational tour for high school students, a "soft core" treatment and a "hard core" treatment (presumably determined by the delinquency classification of the juvenile attenders). The results of the planned evaluation of the experiment have not been released.

Project Inform
Indiana State Prison
Michigan City, Indiana

Started in 1979, this Indiana program was also patterned after the Rahway Project. Project Inform and two other Indiana programs— Project Encounter and Project Think (for girls)—had minimum age limits (fourteen for boys and fifteen for girls); referrals had to come from a juvenile court; and the youth must have had two prior felony convictions. Again, the more abusive elements of the Rahway-type confrontation with the inmates were said to be toned down. Project Inform received early positive feedback from both escorting probation officers and juvenile participants.

JAIL (Juvenile Awareness of Institutional Life)
Idaho State Penitentiary
Idaho

The director of rehabilitation at the Idaho State Penitentiary stressed that JAIL was not a Rahway type of program. He said: "This program was developed using bits and pieces from other programs we studied. . . . Our approach is to present the way life is at an institution. Rahway uses shock therapy. We use reality therapy." All referrals were to be made by juvenile court judges, and parental permission was required. Part of the so-called reality therapy was to process the participating youths as if they were incoming inmates. A preliminary look at JAIL's success (undefined) disclosed nineteen successes and eighteen failures among an initial group of thirty-seven attenders.

And the list could go on. Other similar projects include:

The Glimmer of Hope Juvenile Counseling Program
Lifers, Inc.
Missouri State Penitentiary
Jefferson City, Missouri

The Juvenile Education Program
Lifers Group
Kansas State Prison
Lansing, Kansas

Y.O.U. (Your Opportunities are Unlimited)
Federal Penitentiary
Leavenworth, Kansas

Project Conway
Rochester, New York
Coordinating agency for programs at Albion Correctional Institute,
Auburn Correctional Institute, Elmira Correctional Institute, and
Attica Correctional Institute

Community Involvement Group (CIG)
James River Correctional Center
State Farm, Virginia

Inner Voices
Lorton Institution
Washington, D.C.

JAIL Program (Juveniles Avoiding Institutional Lock-Up)
Southern Ohio Correctional Institution
Lucasville, Ohio

Youthful Offenders Visiting Program
Birmingham, Alabama

Juvenile Awareness Program
Raiford State Prison, Florida

Eddyville State Penitentiary Program
Eddyville State Penitentiary
Paducah, Kentucky

Project Teen-Alert
West Virginia Penitentiary
Moudsville, West Virginia
(Operated by Convicts Against Delinquents in Society)

Juvenile Delinquency Prevention Program
New York City Correctional Facility (Tombs)

Juvenile Awareness Project
Chester County Farms Prison
West Chester, Pennsylvania

Day in Jackson Program
Jackson State Prison
Jackson, Michigan

The Knights of Henri Christophe
State Correctional Institution at Graterford
Graterford, Pennsylvania

Shock Probation
Reidsville Maximum Security Prison
Reidsville, Georgia

Face-To-Face Program
Dallas County Juvenile Department
Dallas, Texas

Project Aware
Waupan, Green Bay, Kettle Moraine and Taycheedah
Correctional Institutions
Wisconsin

Living In a Freedomless Environment (LIFE)
10th Judicial District
North Carolina

Young Offenders Correctional Centre Visitation Program
Alberta Correctional Services
Alberta, Canada

Reach 'em
Florida State Prison
Starke, Florida

THREE PROGRAM EVALUATIONS

Three other juvenile aversion programs have undergone fairly detailed and comprehensive study since my Rahway evaluation. The first of these programs is one referred to earlier in Chapter 3—the SQUIRES program at California's San Quentin State Prison.

Squires

The purpose of the first of two planned studies of the SQUIRES program was to determine the effect of the visitation on the attitudes of the juvenile participants. In the Spring of 1979, experimental subjects from Los Angeles and Contra Costa counties visited San Quentin on three consecutive Saturdays. All the juveniles in the study were on probation; all were males; and, all were randomly assigned to either an experimental or control group. There were thirty-four experimentals and thirty-five controls determined to be similar in background and on certain pretests.

The subjective impressions of both program participants and staff suggested that the visits made a vivid impression on nearly all participants. Participants (experimentals) also showed more positive change in attitudes than did their controls. The report says: "Given the strong findings on Attitudes-toward-Crime and on the Composite (Delinquency) Index, and given the mixed findings on other measures, we can be cautiously optimistic regarding the existence of relevant attitude-change among program participants—that is, of more positive change than among nonparticipants."[38]

A Youth Evaluation Questionnaire indicated that the participants had a positive view of the program. The effects of these attitudes and views on behavior change—the number and rate of official arrests—were still to be determined.

The preliminary report pinpoints three issues emerging from the evaluation. First is the issue of determining which type of youth might benefit most from these youth aversion programs. Second, the report questions the underlying assumption that the visits must be unpleasant or frightening in order to be effective deterrents. The report says: ". . . while a youth may indeed come to view prison in a more negative light than before, he may simultaneously obtain a positive impression of the program itself, and/or of the inmates involved in the program."[39] Third, the evaluators admit that their positive results may have been confounded or biased because experimental kids received additional input (about prison) from the staff. This was input that the control kids did not receive. How this additional discussion influenced the participants' attitudes is unknown.

JOLT

The Juvenile Offenders Learn Truth program has been in operation at the State Prison of Southern Michigan at Jackson since May, 1978. The idea underlying JOLT is familiar, that is, to show juveniles who have been in serious trouble with the law what life in prison can be like. The requirements were that JOLT participants (juveniles) be male, have had an arrest or petition for an offense that would be a crime if committed by an adult, and that they be accompanied by a parent or legal guardian. While "street" language was used in the JOLT sessions, they allegedly did not contain "extreme obscenities" and "gross verbal intimidation." Usually four to six juveniles at a time toured the prison twice a week. During the

---

[38] Department of the Youth Authority, *The Squires of San Quentin: Preliminary Findings of an Experimental Study of Juvenile Visitation at San Quentin* (California: Department of Youth Authority, November, 1979), p. ii.

[39] Ibid., p. 82.

tours, the juveniles were finger-printed, searched, and locked in a cell for a short period.

JOLT was evaluated in 1979 by the Michigan Department of Corrections.[40] A total of 227 juveniles (randomly assigned experimentals and controls) were followed for three or six months after visitation. The study's conclusion was: "Few significant differences were found between the groups, and those which were discovered tend to reflect the influence of living in an intact family situation and involvement in usual education and employment roles, rather than JOLT."[41] The evaluation report said the program was not successful in reducing criminal offenses and that there was "no measurable benefit for those juveniles who toured the prison." Interestingly, the experimentals did somewhat worse than the controls during the follow-up period, although the difference (only 2 percent in the recidivism rate) was not statistically significant.

The Michigan Corrections Commission suspended JOLT for sixty days in July, 1979, while these research results were reviewed. After the suspension, the Commission voted to allow the program to continue, but with stipulations. The stipulations were: there must be follow-up services; no juveniles under fifteen may participate; there can be no verbal intimidation or abuse; and, juveniles must be accompanied by parents or guardians throughout their visit. There was also stipulation that there would be another evaluation in six months.

Menard Correctional Center Juvenile Tours

Beginning in January, 1978, six tours of youths visited the Menard Correctional Center in southeastern Illinois.[42] The tours consisted of "dialogues" with Menard's Lifers Group and visits to various sections of the Correctional Center. The study population consisted of 161 adolescent boys, aged thirteen to eighteen years. This population was subdivided into youths who had been petitioned to juvenile court; youths having police contact but not referred to court; and, youths who had had no previous contact with the police. A total of ninety-four boys were in the tour (experimental) group, and sixty-seven were in the control group.

Both groups were followed for five to fifteen months after the tours. Using subsequent police contact as the outcome measure, the researchers found that 17 percent of the experimentals had subsequent contacts,

[40] James C. Yarborough, *Evaluation of Jolt as a Deterrence Program* (Lansing, Mich.: Department of Corrections, July 18, 1979).

[41] Ibid., p. ii.

[42] Greater Egypt Regional Planning and Development Commission, *Menard Correctional Center Juvenile Tours Impact Study* (Carbondale, Ill., August, 1979).

whereas only 12 percent of the controls did. Their conclusions and recommendations were:

> Based on all available findings one would be ill advised to recommend continuation or expansion of the juvenile-prison tours. All empirical findings indicate little positive outcome, indeed, they may actually indicate negative effects.
>
> Why would a tour of a dreary prison and diaglogue [sic] with inmates outlining horrors of prison life prompt some adolescents towards negative behavior? Many delinquent youth feel alienated and cut off from interaction with others and are often unable to verbalize thoughts or feelings. Perhaps some of the more extreme delinquents view a prison as a place where they can have "friends" and a community now lacking in their lives. For some the world is too large and threatening. Four walls and bars may, in some way, offer security and a sense of belonging. It is interesting that most of those recontacted by police following the tours had more serious criminal involvement previous to the tours. These youths are probably feeling most alienated and exhibit minimal impulse control. . . .
>
> The prison tours and dialogues with inmates as now conceived do not affect desirable change in juveniles. Based on these findings the tours, as they were conducted, should be discontinued. . . .
>
> There may be benefits to be derived from the tours as *part* of an overall treatment; but not as an isolated event in an adolescent's life.[43]

All these findings speak for themselves. They seem to add to the chastening effect upon this particular phenomenon. The potential for a boomerang (negative) effect receives support from two of the studies—evidence that mine may not have been an isolated and unique finding.

---

[43] Ibid., pp. 19–20.

chapter eleven

Future Implications: Does Anything "Work"?

This concluding chapter outlines issues of concern for those planning, operating, or studying delinquency prevention programs. I will describe some successful projects and programs that might serve as models. And, I will try to draw implications for delinquency prevention from the panacea phenomenon.

Let us begin with a description of an intriguing community awareness program idea, which I had some small part in helping to develop, and which is being pilot tested by ex-Rahway Lifer Frank Bindhammer in Tyler, Texas.

A COMMUNITY AWARENESS PROGRAM

Frank Bindhammer's community-based awareness program is derived in part from some of the same theories and concepts that provide the foundation for prison-based awareness (as opposed to aversion) programs. For example, its goals include educating young people about the realities of crime and institutional life; and educating parents about the particular roles and responsibilities of parents in preventing delinquency. It is different, however, from most of the prison-based approaches in an important way. The Tyler program has explicitly adopted the additional goal of trying to increase the effectiveness of existing youth-serving programs by helping their young clients to become more amenable and receptive to the efforts of those who are attempting to assist them. It is built around principles of personal one-on-one counseling (including a twenty-four-hour hotline service) and group interaction. It utilizes volunteer exoffenders, as well as suitable educational films, in an atmosphere of positive peer pressure oriented toward prosocial behavior. All activities are conducted in a community facility.

The evaluation design for this community awareness program clearly reflects its different intent and its considerably more modest and realistic expectations. The objectives are to increase awareness, to increase amenability to treatment, and to improve agency outcomes. The first of these objectives is to be assessed by testing for changes in attitudes (before vs after); by measuring increases in knowledge about the criminal and juvenile justice systems; and, by measuring changes in the estimation of probabilities of arrest, conviction, and incarceration. The latter will provide an indicator of the possible deterrent effects of the program.

Achievement of the second objective will be determined by having representatives from all referral agencies provide information about their clients' amenability to treatment (receptivity to counseling, compliance with referrals to community services, obeying parents, attending school, etc.) before and after program participation. Participating juveniles will be compared with a control group of nonparticipating juveniles from each agency on this dimension.

Third, outcome measures normally employed by each referral agency will be identified. These might include recidivism, for example, rearrests, or they might include attendance, drug-free days, a training or educational achievement, etc. Using these indicators as baseline measures, data will be collected to determine whether participation in the Tyler awareness program produces an improvement in agency outcomes. Are fewer juveniles arrested? Does attendance at school or elsewhere improve? Are there more drug-free days? Do more juveniles complete training or education? Collection of these data before and after, and use of a randomized experimental design, will provide the most definitive indicator of the effect of the community-based awareness program.

The pilot for this approach began in Tyler, Texas in June, 1980. The Junior League in Tyler originally agreed to sponsor Frank Bindhammer and to activate his idea. However, for reasons that are not entirely clear, this support was later withdrawn. But that was only a temporary letdown or roadblock. The former president of the Tyler Junior League, and her husband—believing in Bindhammer and his proposal, believing that a commitment had been made and an obligation incurred, and that such a community program was needed in Tyler—decided to support this experiment with their own resources. A board of directors was formed, an office setup, and the program activated and began receiving referrals. Only time will tell what its ultimate success will be.

SOME SUCCESS STORIES

As noted in the first chapter, the history of delinquency prevention has been largely characterized by failure. I have tried to develop an explanation for that failure—the whole notion of the panacea phenomenon. Although I believe that the pessimistic characterization is correct, and that the panacea phenomenon definitely exists, it would be wrong to conclude that "everything" has failed and that "nothing" works.

For example, turning to other approaches for dealing with juvenile delinquency, one need only review carefully the aforementioned work of Robert Martinson and his colleagues to discover that the assertion that nothing works with juvenile offenders is not necessarily a fact. Among other things, Martinson and his colleagues found that "individual psychotherapy administered to young offenders in the community can be effective in reducing recidivism when it is focused on immediate, day-to-day problems rather than being psychodynamically oriented."[1] They found from a study of the Outward Bound program for adolescent male offenders that "the program did indeed work in reducing recidivism rates."[2] Finally, after reviewing a group of studies with adolescent male probationers they discovered that "by and large, intensive supervision does work—that the specially treated youngsters do better according to some measure of recidivism."[3]

In his similar survey of evaluations extending through 1975, David Greenberg also found some successes. For example, "in Lincoln and Lancaster, Nebraska, high-risk misdemeanant youths (ages sixteen to twenty-five) were randomly assigned to routine probation or to volunteer probation counselors. As measured by rearrests for nontraffic offenses, experimental youths had a very substantial reduction in the frequency and severity of recidivism and the number of offenses per recidivist. A

---

[1] D. Lipton, R. Martinson, and J. Wilks, *The Effectiveness of Correctional Treatment* (New York: Praeger, 1975), p. 213.

[2] Robert Martinson, "What Works? Questions and Answers About Prison Reform," reprinted in *Rehabilitation, Recidivism, and Research* (Hackensack, N.J.: National Council on Crime and Delinquency, 1976), p. 23.

[3] Ibid., p. 27.

comparison of arrests before and during the program was also highly favorable to the experimental program."[4] Homeward Bound, a program involved in sending delinquent boys to camp, also has proved to be an effective alternative to the training school, according to Greenberg.

Five years after his first controversial publication (discussed in Chapter 1), Robert Martinson reversed his opinion. Rejecting his original conclusion that treatment programs have had no appreciable effect on recidivism, his new conclusion was that ". . . treatments will be found to be 'impotent' under certain conditions, beneficial under others, and detrimental under still others."[5]

Martinson said in his 1979 recantation:

> The most interesting general conclusion is that no treatment program now used in criminal justice is inherently either substantially helpful or harmful. The critical fact seems to be the conditions under which the program is delivered. For example, our results indicate that a widely-used program, such as formal education, is detrimental when given to juvenile sentenced offenders in a group home, but is beneficial . . . when given to juveniles in juvenile prisons.[6]

Beneficial, according to Martinson, means that the "reprocessing rate" is lower than the standard rate with which it is compared. Detrimental means that it is higher. Reprocessing rate (Martinson's term for recidivism) refers to the rate at which offenders are subject to further arrest, conviction, or imprisonment.

Martinson examined fourteen different treatment conditions with juvenile sentenced offenders in three settings—group homes, so-called juvenile prisons, and shock probation (a brief period of confinement followed by standard probation). He found that all but two of the treatments (job placement and benign custody) "have beneficial effects when given in prison . . ."[7] "On the other hand," he said, "all but one of the treatments have detrimental effects when given in the group home condition. One treatment, job training, is beneficial under both conditions."[8] All four treatment effects analyzed for shock probation (benign custody, volunteer/help, psychotherapy, and intensive supervision) were beneficial.

---

[4] David F. Greenberg, *Corrections and Punishment* (Beverly Hills, Sage Publications, 1977), p. 118.

[5] Robert Martinson, "Symposium on Sentencing, Part II," *Hofstra Law Review,* 7 (1979), 254.

[6] Ibid., pp. 254–55.

[7] Ibid., p. 243.

[8] Ibid., p. 243.

The conclusion reached from the above findings was not, however, one that advocated incarceration. Instead Martinson concluded:

> Our data indicate that a juvenile will do better on standard probation than if he or she is given treatment in prison; so these patterns do not suggest that juveniles should be confined *for the purpose of giving them treatment.* What they do suggest is that *if* a juvenile must be confined, then he or she should be confined in a facility which provides treatment of the proper kind. It may be that most treatments have the capacity to somehow *reduce the damage* caused by standard youth confinement. When given in the community, these same treatments may be interpreted by the juvenile as a mitigation of punishment.[9]

Martinson criticizes again what he calls the "mindless faddism which plagues criminal justice." He says that his later study shows that, "if anything, there is more of it today."[10]

As I indicated earlier, one can find programs and projects which have proven successful in preventing juvenile delinquency. Those that are described here are intended to be illustrative; the descriptions are neither comprehensive nor all-encompassing. For example, juvenile rehabilitation programs conducted in correctional institutions are not included. My goal is to identify those features that seem to characterize the successful programs. Of particular interest to us should be those common features which the successes share.

Juvenile Diversion Programs

The California Youth Authority commenced a three-year evaluation of juvenile diversion programs in that state in 1973.[11] Diversion was defined as "the avoidance or reduction of justice system processing either through outright release or through placement in alternate programs."[12] The California programs and their clients are considered to be similar to diversion programs and clients throughout the United States. Of seventy-four programs surveyed, fifteen representative ones were chosen by the California researchers for detailed follow-up. From among these fifteen, three were identified as "successful" projects, that is, they had significantly lower recidivism (rearrest) rates than their com-

---

[9] Ibid., p. 257.

[10] Ibid., p. 252.

[11] Ted B. Palmer and Roy V. Lewis, "A Differentiated Approach to Juvenile Diversion," *Journal of Research in Crime and Delinquency,* 17 (July 1980), 209–29.

[12] Ibid., p. 211.

parisons. The reduction of recidivism ranged from 33 to 56 percent over twelve and eighteen months.[13]

The evaluators, Ted Palmer and Roy Lewis, report that each of the three successful projects had a different program focus—one emphasized individual counseling, one family counseling, and one group work and recreation. Surprisingly, two of these three projects served mainly higher (poor) risk youths. The approaches used in the three projects which, according to project workers, accounted for their success were:

> . . . informality (e.g., worker minimizes the social or personal distance between himself and the youth), personal concern for and acceptance of the youth (e.g., worker helps the youth feel that his concern for the youth is more than a formal, 'it's my job,' concern), and frequency of contact (e.g., worker makes sure that he and the youth meet often).[14]

In general, more service led to better outcome performance. When the nature of this more intensive service was focused on fostering self-understanding and expression of feelings, on the relationship between the worker and the youth, on personal interaction, and was non-coercive—the projects were more likely to be successful. Palmer and Lewis offer the following caution in their conclusions:

> . . . to maximize benefits and minimize harm, diversion would be used in a differentiated way: No single approach would be recommended for all groups of youths. Yet, however differentiated it might be, juvenile diversion would not be offered as a *panacea* [italics mine] relative to . . . objectives, or as a solution for various shortcomings of the traditional system. Nor would it automatically be preferred to traditional processing for every type of youth.[15]

Other researchers have also found successful juvenile diversion. Edward Seidman and two colleagues describe a project aimed at diverting alleged offenders from the juvenile justice system.[16] Serving two small midwestern American cities, the project was part of a larger effort to examine "the systematic use of college student nonprofessionals

---

[13] Ibid., p. 214.

[14] Ibid., p. 220.

[15] Ibid., p. 225.

[16] Edward Seidman, Julian Rappaport, and William S. Davidson, "Adolescents in Legal Jeopardy: Initial Success and Replication of an Alternative to the Criminal Justice System," in *Effective Correctional Treatment* by Robert R. Ross and Paul Gendreau (Toronto, Canada: Butterworths, 1980), pp. 103–23.

as human service deliverers in several social systems."[17] The social system in this particular case was the juvenile justice system.

The project was premised on and governed by several principles: early intervention to thwart detrimental efforts at "rehabilitation;" avoiding pushout or isolation; avoiding "blaming the victim;" avoiding placing the juvenile in a client or patient role; and, improving the capacity of the juvenile justice system.[18]

The project operated through the college students who were assigned to each youth on a one-to-one basis. Students and youth were matched on the basis of mutual interests, race, and sex. "Treatment" modes or strategies included "relationship skills, behavioral contracting and child advocacy."[19] The contracting consisted of written interpersonal agreements between the youth and significant others, for example, parents, teachers, etc., which were monitored and mediated by the student counselors. The college students worked with the juveniles for six to eight hours per week for an average of four and one-half months.

Two separate evaluative studies of the project were made—one of the first year of operation and another of the second. A total of thirty-seven boys and girls were referred by juvenile officers in the two metropolitan police departments during the first year. The thirty-seven were randomly assigned to the experimental program or to a control group (twenty-five experimentals and twelve controls). The recidivism results showed ". . . all of the differences during the intervention, first year and second year follow-up intervals favor the experimental group, in that they have fewer contacts of lesser severity and fewer petitions filed than the control subjects."[20]

The second year saw thirty-six referrals—twenty-four experimentals and twelve controls. The results were a repeat of the first year's success. Seidman and his associates concluded that: "Our alternative to the traditional juvenile justice system has demonstrated efficacy in reducing the rates and severity of official delinquency in two successive years with two independent groups of youngsters."[21]

The researchers indicated that at least at that point (1976), the question, "Why does it work?" was an unanswered question. However, in a later commentary on this project, which continued after the original experiment, at least a partial answer may be discerned.[22] Robert Ross

[17] Ibid., p. 103.
[18] Ibid., p. 104.
[19] Ibid., p. 107.
[20] Ibid., p. 108.
[21] Ibid., pp. 120–21.
[22] Ibid., p. 121.

and Paul Gendreau point out that three years later the program had been allowed to deviate from the original in terms of its ideology. Instead of limiting intake to only those youth against whom the police were about to file a petition, many other children were being referred and accepted. So-called "problem children," "predelinquent children," "mental health-adjustment problem children" and "school problem children" were referred. Ross and Gendreau characterize these referrals as, "children for whom the program was never designed; children who may not be helped and, in fact, may be harmed by their involvement in the juvenile justice system."[23] This seems to be a near perfect illustration of the cure-all/panacea problem. It reinforces the point that I have repeatedly stressed, that delinquency prevention, if it is to be given a chance of being successful, must be focused upon clearly defined and appropriate target groups.

Yet another successful diversion program is described by Herbert Quay and Craig Love.[24] This successful program is the Juvenile Services Program (JSP) operated in Pinellas County, Florida. JSP accepted three different but clearly defined types of referrals. These were: adjudicated delinquents aged twelve to sixteen, children in need of supervision (CINS) or status offenders, and informal referrals from the police, schools, and other community agencies. There were established criteria to determine eligibility, according to the authors, but unfortunately these are not spelled out in their discussion of the program.

The JSP offered vocational counseling, training and job placement, academic education (tutorial and small group), and personal and social counseling (individual and group). The program made extensive use of volunteers.

Quay and Love studied 436 program participants (experimentals) and 132 controls (who came from program overflow). In-program exposure averaged eighty-nine days. Both groups were then followed for more than a year. The researchers found that the rearrest rate for participants and controls differed significantly during the postprogram period. Only 32 percent of the participants were rearrested, as compared with 45 percent of the controls. Quay and Love report that ". . . it is reasonable to conclude that the total efforts of the JSP had a significant effect on the postprogram rearrest experience of its clients."[25]

[23] Robert R. Ross and Paul Gendreau, *Effective Correctional Treatment* (Toronto, Canada: Butterworths, 1980), p. 101.

[24] Herbert C. Quay and Craig T. Love, "The Effect of a Juvenile Diversion Program on Rearrests," in *Effective Correctional Treatment*, by Robert R. Ross and Paul Gendreau (Toronto, Canada: Butterworths, 1980), pp. 75–90.

[25] Ibid., p. 89.

Interestingly, the program was most successful with the informal referrals. According to Quay and Love, this suggests the importance of early intervention, and it clearly represents successful delinquency prevention. The program failures tended to be slightly younger; showed a high incidence of prior status and property offenses; were rated as being more aggressive; saw themselves as being more aggressive and neurotic; were somewhat less bright in terms of IQ; and, had lower academic achievement.[26]

A Community-based Counseling Program: CREST

Project CREST (Clinical Regional Support Teams) began in Gainesville, Florida in 1972.[27] The theoretical foundation for CREST was that effective rehabilitation "must include structure and nurture."[28] The structure comes from consistent limits on behavior; the nurture from attention to individual growth. CREST operationalized this approach with young "hard core" probationers by using teams of university students to provide nonauthoritarian outreach services, and regular probation officers to maintain acceptable behavior by imposing the usual controls and sanctions. "The mutual goal of this dual approach is that the child develop self-control plus positive self-motivation."[29]

The graduate student counselors provided individual counseling—which was the basic mode—and sometimes group and family counseling. Tutoring and "big buddy" services were also provided. The juvenile clients had to be adjudicated delinquents, show signs of conflict or stress, be cooperative, and be part of a stable family or home.

CREST was evaluated over four years (actually four separate studies—only the last of which was an experimental study). Youths who received the CREST treatment in addition to probation were compared with youths who received probation services alone. The conclusion? ". . . the overwhelming result has been that regardless of differences in counselors, subjects, and mode of measurement, the CREST-treated

---

[26] Ibid., p. 89.

[27] Robert Lee and Nancy McGinnis Haynes, "Project CREST and the Dual-Treatment Approach to Delinquency: Methods and Research Summarized," in *Effective Correctional Treatment* by Robert R. Ross and Paul Gendreau (Toronto, Canada: Butterworths, 1980), pp. 171–84.

[28] Ibid., p. 171.

[29] Ibid., p. 172.

groups committed at least 50 percent fewer criminal acts than did the controls."[30] The recidivism rate for CREST was 30 percent; for controls it was 52 percent. "Our research findings," say the evaluators, "indicate that the effectiveness of CREST is genuine—that the dual treatment model has impact on juvenile crime."[31]

Project CREST was chosen as an exemplary project (one of only thirty-two ever so chosen) by the National Institute of Justice of the U.S. Department of Justice. What features characterize CREST? According to those who have studied it, it is the level of training given to the college student volunteers; the continuous and structured supervision that the volunteers receive; the support of the community's juvenile authorities and of the community in general; and, the strong leadership that CREST has received.

Physical Challenge as Treatment: Outward Bound

Another program that I personally find to be most interesting and intriguing is one referred to earlier by Martinson. Outward Bound was first established in 1941 in Aberdovey, Wales to train merchant seamen for survival during the World War II battle of the Atlantic.[32] Its underlying assumption is, "that rather than merely telling a young man he is capable of more than he thinks he can do, one must devise a set of circumstances whereby the youth can demonstrate this competence to himself."[33] "Outward Bound exposes adolescents to severe physical challenge and pushes individuals to their physical limit."[34]

In 1971, two Boston College psychologists named Francis Kelly and Daniel Baer reported on their earlier study of three Outward Bound schools in the United States—one in Colorado, one in Minnesota, and one on Hurricane Island, Maine. Each school had a twenty-six-day program stressing physical conditioning, technical training, safety training, and team training.

Kelly and Baer conducted a demonstration project for the Massachusetts Division of Youth Service involving 120 adolescent delin-

[30] Ibid., p. 174.

[31] Ibid., p. 182.

[32] Francis J. Kelly and Daniel J. Baer, "Physical Challenge as a Treatment for Delinquency," *Crime and Delinquency* (1971), p. 437.

[33] Ibid., pp. 437–438.

[34] Ibid., p. 438.

quent boys. The sample was divided into two matched groups of 60 boys each; one group attended Outward Bound and the other was handled routinely by Massachusetts juvenile correctional authorities. All the boys "were between fifteen and one-half and seventeen years of age, in good health and without any severe physical disability or severe psychopathology . . ."[35] The boys had minimum IQs of 75, no history of violent assaultive or sexual offenses, and were willing to participate.

One year after parole, Kelly and Baer found that only 20 percent of the Outward Bound group had been committed to a juvenile or adult correctional institution, whereas 42 percent of the control group had been committed. Their explanation for this success was that:

> Outward Bound encourages change in the adolescent delinquent. The opportunities for concrete impressive accomplishment, as well as for excitement and challenge, promote personal growth. The need to pace oneself challenges the delinquent's impulsivity, while the requirement of persistence challenges his endurance. The necessity of obeying safety laws and camp regulations causes him to question his concept that laws and regulations are to be ignored, and his dependence upon his patrol leader for success and well-being causes him to re-examine his attitude toward authority figures.[36]

Kelly and Baer found that four background variables tended to be associated with success. Juveniles who became involved in the juvenile justice system somewhat later in adolescence were more successful. Outward Bound also worked better with those youth who had at least one prior commitment, with those whose delinquency represented acting out in the community (as opposed to incorrigible-types and runaways), and with those from intact homes. In general, said the authors, "it appears that those delinquents who are responding to an adolescent crisis rather than to a character defect would profit most from such a program."[37] While pointing out that action-oriented youths may respond to action programs (such as Outward Bound) more so than to cognitive, counseling programs, Kelly and Baer stress that this approach should not be expected to be "effective with all delinquents."[38]

In a more recent (1978) discussion of Outward Bound, Paul A. Strasburg suggests that the earlier first year successful results seem to

[35] Ibid., p. 439.
[36] Ibid., p. 440.
[37] Ibid., p. 437.
[38] Ibid., p. 445.

wash out after five years.[39] He says that Kelly found a 38 percent rearrest rate in the original experimental group, and 53 percent among the controls. Although this difference may not be statistically significant, as Strasburg points out, it is still strongly in the desired direction, and perhaps even somewhat remarkable after five years of exposure to the risk of rearrest. The Outward Bound group did have fewer and less serious subsequent offenses, and spent less subsequent time in detention.[40]

Strasburg emphasizes that, "Outward Bound is not a panacea."[41] He says it works only if the youth wants the experience—forced participation actually being counterproductive. Further, it is not for those with any emotional pathology. Unfortunately, says Strasburg, Outward Bound has only a limited capacity in terms of the numbers that can be served. Also, there is need for follow-up, reinforcement experiences. Within the bounds of its acknowledged limitations, Outward Bound is a promising program model for preventing juvenile delinquency.

CHARACTERISTICS OF SUCCESSFUL PROGRAMS

The two Canadians mentioned earlier, Paul Gendreau and Bob Ross, recently analyzed ninety-five correctional treatment program evaluations publicized between late 1973 and early 1978. In their research report, they draw certain implications about why treatment programs have not been successful, or conversely, why some have been successful.

The more successful approaches, they say, were characterized by use of "a combination of several tools to treat criminal and delinquent behavior. The studies reviewed that relied on a single treatment method had notably less positive results."[42] Each of these projects that I described used some combination of methods: counseling (individual and group), behavioral contracting, advocacy, training, education, etc.

Gendreau and Ross also point out a related program characteristic—that individual differences among the juvenile subjects must

[39] Paul A. Strasburg, *Violent Delinquents: A Report to the Ford Foundation from the Vera Institute of Justice* (New York: Monarch Books, 1978), p. 253.

[40] Ibid., p. 252.

[41] Ibid., p. 253.

[42] Paul Gendreau and Bob Ross, "Effective Correctional Treatment: Bibliotherapy for Cynics," *Crime and Delinquency* (October 1979), p. 485.

be recognized. "Delinquent samples," they say, "have provided ample proof that individual differences are strikingly related to treatment outcome."[43] This of course is part of the risk of failure that comes from relying on a single method—any single method.

The successful programs, as I observed earlier with the California diversion projects, generally provide more treatment and certainly more adequate treatment. Gendreau and Ross say that the programs that seemed to be succeeding "used a greater diversity of techniques and provided more intensified services."[44]

The successful delinquency prevention programs are those that have made explicit their fundamental assumptions about the causes of delinquency, and are directly linking what they are doing to these basic assumptions. They are also those that have clear and consistent identification and classification criteria for their subjects—whether these be nondelinquents, predelinquents, or delinquents. Such an intervention or treatment—relevant classification scheme must also be derived from the causal assumptions. Inappropriate or absent selection criteria tend to be associated with failure—not success.

WHAT DOES THIS ALL MEAN?

It means that some approaches or methods work to prevent delinquency with some juveniles under some conditions—so we should not conclude that nothing works. Instead, we should ask what kinds of programs, under what kinds of conditions are effective with which juveniles, and with respect to what kinds of outcomes. This is true of not only juvenile awareness and aversion programs, but also of other approaches as well.

We should lower our expectations to take account of the realities of the failure of most past attempts at delinquency prevention, and of the complex nature of juvenile delinquency itself. In the case of some existing programs, a rethinking of their goals and expectations might be in order. We need to avoid raising unrealistic goals and expectations that cannot be achieved.

We must recognize that a potential for either social or emotional injury to juvenile subjects exists. This is particularly true where aversive methods are used. In general, nondelinquents should be left alone. We certainly do not need projects that contribute to or increase the probability of delinquency.

[43] Ibid., p. 486.
[44] Ibid., p. 487.

We should try to broaden our understanding of the causes of juvenile delinquency by testing a variety of causal assumptions. These tests should be carefully controlled and thoroughly evaluated, using experimental designs whenever possible.

Above all, we should stop our foolish and futile search for what will be the ever elusive cure-all. That highway of punctured panaceas seems destined to lead only to further failure and frustration.

Post Script

In concluding the discussion of the derivation of the panacea phenomenon in the first chapter, I reported California researcher Ted Palmer's admonition that, "the search for rapid or glamourous solutions . . . is sure to die very hard, if at all. . . ." A cluster of events coming a year and a half after my research became public seemed to bear out this conclusion.

First was a brief article in the October, 1980 issue of *Psychology Today* entitled "The Erratic Life of 'Scared Straight!' "[1] The article reported that the Rahway program had been cut back after my research, but that, "a new study . . . by Sidney Langer . . . has shown favorable results and is helping to keep the issue open." It also indicated that, "The Justice Department is awaiting the results of on-going evaluation research before adopting an official policy on the program."

Newsweek magazine followed on November 3, 1980 with an article called "Prison Program Gets a New Boost."[2] It too concluded that, "A second study [Langer's] has now given the flagging program another

[1] Berkeley Rice, "The Erratic Life of 'Scared Straight,' " *Psychology Today* (October 1980), p. 29.

[2] Eileen Keerdoja et al., "Prison Program Gets a New Boost," *Newsweek* (November 3, 1980), p. 16.

boost." The article quoted Lifer John Artis (a codefendant convicted with ex-boxer Rubin "Hurricane" Carter) saying: "Many of the inmates were disheartened after the first study came out." "The new findings renewed our determination to make the program a success."

Finally and perhaps most important, film maker Arnold Shapiro and company were back on national television. On Thursday, November 6, CBS-TV showed Shapiro's "Scared Straight! Another Story." The so-called docu-drama (meaning it was fictionalized) was filmed expressly for television in the Arizona State Prison. Its focal point is a group of delinquents going through a juvenile awareness program inside the prison.

One TV reviewer's comments should give a sense of the possible impact of the film and of the potential for reinforcement of this particular approach to combating juvenile delinquency.[3] Jerry Krupnick (*The Newark Star-Ledger*) said of the Rahway Juvenile Awareness Project itself: "It is a remarkable program, this confrontation put on by the Lifers, one that not only scares the potential for crime out of most kids who go through it, but does the same for anyone else squirming through the film." "If," said the reviewer, "just one kid going through that routine is kept out of prison, it's a super accomplishment. If the rate is 90 percent, or 50 percent, or 10 percent—my God, what other juvenile program do we have that could ever produce such results?"

Krupnick lauds the docu-drama which, he indicates, works as well or even better than the original. He says:

"Scared Straight! Another Story" is not a rerun, not a repeat. It is a new and stark and moving drama which doesn't suffer by comparison with its documentary predecessor. . . .

The point is still strong and valid and 'Scared Straight' will do just that to most people who watch . . .

The language is rough, some of the scenes are violent, but it doesn't matter. The message is there and never mind that this time it's all a fiction.

Some lessons are hard to learn it seems, and some are perhaps never learned at all.

---

[3] Jerry Krupnick " 'Scared Straight! Another Story' is Superb," *The Star-Ledger* (November 6, 1980), p. 58.

Appendix A

NAME: _____
ADDRESS: _____
_____
_____

AGE: (Circle One)

         12   13   14   15   16   17

SEX: (Circle One)

         Male   Female

RACE: (Circle One)

         Black   Hispanic   White   Other

I. ATTITUDE TOWARD PUNISHMENT OF CRIMINALS

This is a study of attitudes toward punishment of criminals. Following are a number of statements expressing different attitudes toward punishment of criminals.

Put a check mark if you AGREE with the statement.

Put a cross if you DISAGREE with the statement.

Try to indicate either agreement or disagreement for each statement. If you simply cannot decide about a statement you may mark it with a question mark.

This is not an examination. There are no right or wrong answers to these statements. This is simply a study of people's attitudes toward the punishment of criminals. Please indicate your own convictions by a check mark (√) when you AGREE and by a cross (X) when you DISAGREE.

_____ 1. A person should be put in prison only for very bad crimes.

_____ 2. It is wrong for the government to make any people suffer in prison.

_____ 3. Hard prison life will keep men from committing crime.

_____ 4. Punishment does not make some criminals any better.

_____ 5. In prison many men learn to be worse criminals.

_____ 6. We should not bother about the comfort of a prisoner.

_____ 7. A criminal will go straight only when he finds that prison life is hard.

_____ 8. There isn't any punishment that will keep men from committing crime.

_____ 9. Prisons make men worse than they were.

_____ 10. Only men who have committed several crimes should be punished.

_____ 11. We should use physical punishment in dealing with all criminals.

_____ 12. I don't know anything about the treatment of crime.

_____ 13. We should be ashamed to punish criminals.

_____ 14. Putting a criminal in a cell by himself will make him sorry.

_____ 15. It is better for us to be easy on certain criminals.

_____ 16. Only kind treatment can cure criminals.

_____ 17. Cruel prison treatment makes criminals want to get even.

_____ 18. No kindness should be shown to prisoners.

_____ 19. Many men who aren't very bad become dangerous criminals after a prison term.

_____ 20. If we do not punish criminals, we will have more crime.

_____ 21. Only by very cruel punishment can we cure the criminal.

_____ 22. Severe punishment makes men worse criminals.

_____ 23. A criminal should be punished first and then reformed.

_____ 24. One way to keep men from crime is to make them suffer.

_____ 25. We cannot make a good citizen of a criminal if we punish him.

_____ 26. Having to live on bread and water in prison will cure the criminal.

_____ 27. Cruel treatment of a criminal makes him more dangerous.

_____ 28. A jail sentence will cure many criminals.

_____ 29. Prisoners should be chained.

_____ 30. In order to decide how to treat a criminal we should know what kind of person he is.

_____ 31. Even the very worst criminal should not be mistreated.

_____ 32. It is fair for the government to punish men who break the laws.

_____ 33. Kind treatment makes the criminal want to be good.

_____ 34. We have to use some punishment in dealing with criminals.

II. SEMANTIC DIFFERENTIAL

The purpose of this study is to find out what certain words mean to different people. In filling out this form, please judge the words based on what they mean to YOU. Each page presents a concept (such as AUTOMOBILE), and a number of scales (such as good—bad, dirty—clean, and so on). You are to rate the concept on the 7-point scales which follow it.

If you feel that the concept is VERY CLOSELY RELATED to one end of the scale, you might place your cross mark (X) as follows:

AUTOMOBILE

good X : : : : : : bad

If you feel that the concept is QUITE CLOSELY RELATED to one side of the scale, you might mark it as follows:

GIRL

beautiful : X : : : : ugly

If the concept seems ONLY SLIGHTLY RELATED to one side as opposed to the other, you might mark as follows:

AUTHORITY

clean : : X : : : dirty

If you consider the scale COMPLETELY UNRELATED, or BOTH SIDES EQUALLY RELATED, you would mark the middle space on the scale:

APPLE

kind : : : X : : cruel

This is NOT a test. There are no right or wrong answers. We want your first impressions. We want your honest impressions. Work rapidly. DO NOT GO BACK.

CRIME

good	: : : : : :	bad
beautiful	: : : : : :	ugly
clean	: : : : : :	dirty
cruel	: : : : : :	kind
unpleasant	: : : : : :	pleasant
happy	: : : : : :	sad
nice	: : : : : :	awful
honest	: : : : : :	dishonest
unfair	: : : : : :	fair
valuable	: : : : : :	worthless

LAW

| good | : : : : : : | bad |

worthless   : : : : : :   valuable

beautiful   : : : : : :   ugly

unfair   : : : : : :   fair

clean   : : : : : :   dirty

dishonest   : : : : : :   honest

kind   : : : : : :   cruel

awful   : : : : : :   nice

pleasant   : : : : : :   unpleasant

sad   : : : : : :   happy

JUSTICE

worthless   : : : : : :   valuable

fair   : : : : : :   unfair

dishonest   : : : : : :   honest

awful	: : : : : : : : : : : :	nice
sad	: : : : : : : : : : : :	happy
pleasant	: : : : : : : : : : : :	unpleasant
cruel	: : : : : : : : : : : :	kind
dirty	: : : : : : : : : : : :	clean
ugly	: : : : : : : : : : : :	beautiful
bad	: : : : : : : : : : : :	good

I (MYSELF)

happy	: : : : : : : : : : : :	sad
nice	: : : : : : : : : : : :	awful
honest	: : : : : : : : : : : :	dishonest
fair	: : : : : : : : : : : :	unfair
valuable	: : : : : : : : : : : :	worthless

bad : : : : : : good

ugly : : : : : : beautiful

dirty : : : : : : clean

cruel : : : : : : kind

unpleasant : : : : : : pleasant

PRISON

awful : : : : : : nice

bad : : : : : : good

beautiful : : : : : : ugly

clean : : : : : : dirty

cruel : : : : : : kind

dishonest : : : : : : honest

fair : : : : : : unfair

happy : : : : : : sad

pleasant : : : : : : unpleasant

valuable : : : : : : worthless

POLICEMAN

valuable : : : : : : worthless

fair : : : : : : unfair

bad : : : : : : good

ugly : : : : : : beautiful

honest : : : : : : dishonest

nice : : : : : : awful

dirty : : : : : : clean

cruel : : : : : : kind

happy : : : : : : sad

pleasant : : : : : : unpleasant

PUNISHMENT

pleasant : : : : : : unpleasant

cruel : : : : : : kind

clean : : : : : : dirty

ugly : : : : : : beautiful

good : : : : : : bad

happy : : : : : : sad

awful : : : : : : nice

honest : : : : : : dishonest

worthless : : : : : : valuable

fair : : : : : : unfair

III. ATTITUDES TOWARD OBEYING THE LAW

For each of the following statements indicate whether you agree or disagree by placing a cross mark (X) in the appropriate box.

1. It's all right to take things which are covered by insurance.

Strongly Agree	Agree	Disagree	Strongly Disagree
☐	☐	☐	☐

2. It's all right to keep things you find if they are covered by insurance.

Strongly Agree	Agree	Disagree	Strongly Disagree
☐	☐	☐	☐

3. It's all right for a person to break the law; it is getting caught that is bad.

Strongly Agree	Agree	Disagree	Strongly Disagree
☐	☐	☐	☐

4. A person should obey the law no matter how much it gets in their way.

Strongly Agree	Agree	Disagree	Strongly Disagree
☐	☐	☐	☐

IV. GLUECK SOCIAL PREDICTION TABLE

Five statements are given in the following section. For each one, mark (X) the idea that seems the best way to describe most of YOUR LIFE AT HOME.

1. The discipline given to me by my father (or person acting for my father) was:
   ( ) Very strict.
   ( ) Strict, but usually fair.
   ( ) Sometimes strict, sometimes easy.
   ( ) Usually easy.
   ( ) Very easy.

2. My mother (or person acting for my mother) gave me supervision that was:
   ( ) Very helpful, with close watch over me.
   ( ) Usually helpful, although sometimes she failed.
   ( ) Helpful only when I asked for help or advice.
   ( ) Most likely to let me do anything I pleased.
   ( ) Completely useless, because she did not care what I did.

3. My father (or person acting for my father) usually showed that he:
   ( ) Liked me a great deal.
   ( ) Liked me about the same as he liked his friends.
   ( ) Neither liked me nor disliked me.
   ( ) Disliked me most of the time.
   ( ) Did not want me around.

4. My mother (or person acting for my mother) usually showed that she:
   ( ) Liked me a great deal.
   ( ) Liked me about the same as she liked her friends.
   ( ) Neither liked me nor disliked me.
   ( ) Disliked me most of the time.
   ( ) Did not want me around.

5. My family (parents, brothers, sisters) has made me think that we:
   ( ) Stick pretty close together in everything.
   ( ) Would help each other more than we would help friends.
   ( ) Can be equally happy at home or away from home.
   ( ) Would rather be with friends than with relatives.
   ( ) Have almost nothing that we like to do together.

Appendix B

Code Number

County of Residence

I. INTERVIEW SCHEDULE

1. Sex
☐ Male   ☐ Female
2. Race
☐ White   ☐ Black   ☐ Hispanic   ☐ Other
3. How old are you? _____
   When were you born? _____
4. Do you go to school?
☐ Yes   ☐ No
4a. (IF YES) What grade are you in?_____
4b. (IF NO) What do you do with yourself?
☐ Full-time job   ☐ Part-time job
☐ Other   (WRITE IN) _____
☐ Nothing
5. With whom do you live?
☐ Both parents   ☐ One Parent (WRITE IN)
☐ Other   (WRITE IN) _____

248

☐ No one
6. What does your (father/mother/guardian) do for a living?
☐ White-collar job ☐ Blue-collar job
☐ Other (WRITE IN) _____
☐ Don't know/no answer

THE FOLLOWING QUESTIONS ARE TO BE ASKED ONLY OF THE JUVENILE AWARENESS PROJECT ATTENDEES

1. Who decided that you should visit the Lifers' project at Rahway Prison?
2. Why do you think that they decided that? (PROBE)
3. Did you want to go? Why or why not? (PROBE)
4. What did you think of your visit to the project at Rahway? (PROBE)
5. Do you think that the visit was helpful to you? Why or why not? (PROBE)
6. Do you think that these visits are helpful to other kids? Why or why not? (PROBE)

II. FOR JUVENILE AWARENESS PROJECT ATTENDEES

Assure Confidentiality of Information.
Emphasize Importance of Answering Fully and Accurately.
Assure that *Information Will not Be Given to Anyone.*

Think back! Think carefully! *Since you went on the visit to Rahway Prison,* have you done any of the following things:

1. Did things your parents/guardian told you not to do?

If yes, about how many times? Once, twice, three or four times, or five or more times?

☐ Once   ☐ Twice   ☐ Three or four   ☐ Five or more

2. Did things other adults such as a teacher, the school principal, a policeman, etc.—told you not to do?

If yes, about how many times? Once, twice, three or four times, or five or more times?

☐ Once   ☐ Twice   ☐ Three or four   ☐ Five or more

3. Driven without a license?

If yes, about how many times? Once, twice, three or four times, or five or more times?

☐ Once   ☐ Twice   ☐ Three or four   ☐ Five or more

4. Committed any other traffic violations—such as drunken driving, causing an accident, careless or reckless driving, etc.?

If yes, about how many times? Once, twice, three or four times, or five or more times?

☐ Once   ☐ Twice   ☐ Three or four   ☐ Five or more

5. Ran away from home?

If yes, about how many times? Once, twice, three or four times, or five or more times?

☐ Once   ☐ Twice   ☐ Three or four   ☐ Five or more

6. Skipped school without permission?

If yes, about how many times? Once, twice, three or four times, or five or more times?

☐ Once   ☐ Twice   ☐ Three or four   ☐ Five or more

7. Bought beer, wine or liquor? Or, had someone buy it for you?

If yes, about how many times? Once, twice, three or four times, or five or more times?

☐ Once   ☐ Twice   ☐ Three or four   ☐ Five or more

8. Drank beer, wine or liquor without your parents permission?

If yes, about how many times? Once, twice, three or four times, or five or more times?

☐ Once   ☐ Twice   ☐ Three or four   ☐ Five or more

9. Taken anything of minor value—say under $2.00, such as cigarettes, candy, comic books, money, etc.?

If yes, about how many times? Once, twice, three or four times, or five or more times?

☐ Once   ☐ Twice   ☐ Three or four   ☐ Five or more

10. Taken anything of medium value—say worth between $2.00 and $50.00—such as clothing, auto parts, liquor, radios, money, etc.?

If yes, about how many times? Once, twice, three or four times, or five or more times?

☐ Once   ☐ Twice   ☐ Three or four   ☐ Five or more

11. Taken anything of major value—say worth more than $50.00?

If yes, about how many times? Once, twice, three or four times, or five or more times?

☐ Once   ☐ Twice   ☐ Three or four   ☐ Five or more

12. Destroyed property such as by throwing rocks or sticks in order to break windows, or street lights or things like that?

If yes, about how many times? Once, twice, three or four times, or five or more times?

☐ Once   ☐ Twice   ☐ Three or four   ☐ Five or more

13. Destroyed property by breaking up or helping to break up the furniture in a school, church or other public building?

If yes, about how many times? Once, twice, three or four times, or five or more times?

☐ Once   ☐ Twice   ☐ Three or four   ☐ Five or more

14. Stolen a car?

If yes, about how many times? Once, twice, three or four times, or five or more times?

☐ Once ☐ Twice ☐ Three or four ☐ Five or more

15. Broken into another person's house, garage, shed or other building to try to steal something?

If yes, about how many times? Once, twice, three or four times, or five or more times?

☐ Once ☐ Twice ☐ Three or four ☐ Five or more

16. Smoked marijuana or used some other sort of dope or narcotics?

If yes, about how many times? Once, twice, three or four times, or five or more times?

☐ Once ☐ Twice ☐ Three or four ☐ Five or more

17. Sold marijuana or some other dope?

If yes, about how many times? Once, twice, three or four times, or five or more times?

☐ Once ☐ Twice ☐ Three or four ☐ Five or more

18. Started a fist fight?

If yes, about how many times? Once, twice, three or four times, or five or more times?

☐ Once ☐ Twice ☐ Three or four ☐ Five or more

19. Beat up on someone who hadn't done anything to you?

If yes, about how many times? Once, twice, three or four times, or five or more times?

☐ Once ☐ Twice ☐ Three or four ☐ Five or more

20. Robbed someone by threatening them with a knife, or a razor or a gun?

If yes, about how many times? Once, twice, three or four times, or five or more times?

☐ Once ☐ Twice ☐ Three or four ☐ Five or more

Index

Administrative Office of the Courts (AOC),
114-15, 167
Age, delinquent behavior as function of,
199-200
American Correctional Association, 190
American Institute of Research (AIR), 24-25
American Justice Institute, reports of, 208-9
Amosian therapy, 42
Andrews, Ike, xxi, 185-89
Attitude change(s):
crime and, 162
deterrence theory and, 157
justice and, 163
Juvenile Awareness Project and, 156-69
law and, 162-63, 164-65
policeman and, 163
prison and, 163-64
punishment and, 164
self and, 163
tests to measure, 159-61
Attitudes Toward Any Institution Scale, 117
Attitude Toward Punishment of Criminals
Test, 117, 159-60, 237-38
Attitude Toward Obeying the Law Scale,
161, 246
results of, 164-66

Attitude Toward Punishment of Criminals
Scale, results of, 161-64
August, Alan, 81, 98, 112, 124-25
Aversive techniques:
behavior modification and, 37-43
described, 40-41
shock-confrontation, 70
types of, 41

Behavior:
delinquent, and age, 199-200
human, and deterrence theory, 184
methods of assessing, 133-34
Behavior modification:
Amosian theory of, 42
attitudinal change and, 158
aversive techniques of, 37-43
described, 40
evaluation of, 43-44
Finckenauer study assessment of, 132-55
"haircut" or verbal reprimand theory of,
42
Quay typology and, 42
techniques, types of, 41-42
Bindhammer, Frank, 71-76, 77-79, 92-93,
104-7, 220-21